T3-BNK-612

CONSERVATION TRUSTS

IN HONOR OF

BRUCE WATKINS

By

Wilmington West Rotory Club

DEVELOPMENT OF WESTERN RESOURCES

The Development of Western Resources is an interdisciplinary series focusing on the use and misuse of resources in the American West. Written for a broad readership of humanists, social scientists, and resource specialists, the books in this series emphasize both historical and contemporary perspectives as they explore the interplay between resource exploitation and economic, social, and political experiences.

John G. Clark, University of Kansas, Founding Editor
Hal K. Rothman, University of Nevada, Las Vegas, Series Editor

CONSERVATION TRUSTS

Sally K. Fairfax and
Darla Guenzler

NEW HANOVER COUNTY
PUBLIC LIBRARY
201 CHESTNUT STREET
WILMINGTON, NC 28401

 University Press of Kansas

© 2001 by the University Press of Kansas
All rights reserved

Published by the University Press of Kansas (Lawrence, Kansas 66049), which was organized by the Kansas Board of Regents and is operated and funded by Emporia State University, Fort Hays State University, Kansas State University, Pittsburg State University, the University of Kansas, and Wichita State University.

Library of Congress Cataloging-in-Publication Data
Fairfax, Sally K.
    Conservation trusts / Sally K. Fairfax and Darla Guenzler.
        p.   cm. — (Development of western resources)
    Includes index.
    ISBN 0-7006-1078-2 (cloth : alk. paper) — ISBN 0-7006-1079-0 (pbk. : alk. paper)
    1. Land trusts—United States.   2. Conservation of natural resources—Law and legislation—United States.   I. Guenzler, Darla.   II. Title.   III. Series.
KF736.L3 F35   2001
346.73'068—dc21   00-049958

British Library Cataloguing in Publication Data is available.

Printed in the United States of America

10 9 8 7 6 5 4 3 2 1

The paper used in this publication meets the minimum requirements of the American National Standard for Permanence of Paper for Printed Library Materials Z39.48-1984.

This book is dedicated to
Doris Howes Calloway
Helen Ingram
Mollie Beattie
Gently opening doors

Contents

Acknowledgments

If writing a book goes well, it can be sort of like a slumber party, with all sorts of folks making popcorn or telling ghost stories before they crawl off into their sleeping bags. One of the best parts of finishing is to go back through your notes and recall all the fun you had traveling about the country, meeting new people, seeing where they live, and photocopying their files. In that sense, nobody really owns a book. Well, the University Press of Kansas owns it, and Darla and I are responsible for any errors, but the rest of it was a community process that requires not simply acknowledgment but celebration.

First, I should introduce the principal contributors to this book, two of whom are listed on the title page, and two of whom are not. All of us are connected with the University of California–Berkeley and benefited from an Agricultural Experiment Station grant that supported our work. Darla Guenzler, a Ph.D. candidate in City and Regional Planning (CRP), prepared chapter 3 as her master's thesis. We began the book together, sharing the excitement of defining the project and finding the trusts. Darla did the initial field research and drafting of chapters 4, 7, 8, and 9 before gradually turning her attention toward other professional commitments. Stacey Dinstell joined us to work on the Hawaii chapter. She has master's degrees from both CRP and the College of Natural Resources (CNR), and chapter 6 provided the basis for both of her master's theses. Stacey also played an important role as fact checker, cite finder, and general backgrounder on all the diverse material needed when you compile a book with as many different subjects as this one. Jennifer Sokolove helped refine the book after the first round of reviews. In addition, she drafted chapter 11 as part of the preparation for her doctoral dissertation. I was happy to focus on private conservation activities after twenty-five years of pondering federal and state resource management.

If you plan well, your research will take you to wonderful places to meet wonderful people. That was the case with this book, although it must be a sign of my aging that Stacey was forced into going to Hawaii and Jen was obliged to make numerous trips to Napa Valley. And it was Darla, not me, who got to take pictures of turtles hatching and crawling into the sea. I did get to go to Alaska several times, which ain't half bad, although December may not be the best time to visit.

Somebody once wrote that scholarship consists of digging up old bones in one graveyard and burying them in different piles somewhere else. We have done much better than that. We believe that those who look for important resources primarily in the national parks or other federal holdings are missing not only important ecosystems but also major innovations in governance and institutional design. This book elaborates on those important scholarly points.

Here is our chance to say how much we appreciate the help given to us by the many people we imposed on in the diverse and beautiful places we studied. The list is long, which we hope will impress readers that we talked to enough people to get the story straight. Perhaps it will also encourage the next generation to make the leap into graduate school by illustrating how much fun it is to do research. Most of all, we hope that those who helped us will take some small pleasure in finding their names herein and that they will recognize both our gratitude and their own contribution to educating us and those who read this volume. They will have to look here, in this acknowledgments section, however. Darla and I decided early on to minimize direct references to specific interviewees. Some of our sources requested anonymity, and in most other cases, it is the role of the speaker or his or her relationship to the trust that matters. We therefore identified most of our informants indirectly rather than by name. The fact that we mention few specific individuals in the pages that follow does not lessen our gratitude to all who helped us.

Anne Fitzgerald provided a wonderful tutorial in philanthropies and nonprofits that is reflected in chapters 1 and 2. For chapter 4 on Dade County, Florida, we relied heavily on Frank Bernardino, Mike Norland, and Mike Spinelli. For chapter 6, Stacey relied on Melodie MacKenzie, Ed Case, Paula Durbin, Ernest Kimoto, Ryan Mielke, Tony and John Sang, Haunani-Kay Trask, Darrell Yagodich, Kenneth Toguchi, Dierdre Mamiya, Dean Uchida, Aulani Ahmad, Luana Beck, Ekela and Alfred Andrade, Larry Kaawaloa-schha, Lori Watland, Randy Manewa, Olivia Aquino, Carl Christensen, Charles Rose, Joanne Sanchez, Sherry Broder, Scotty Bowman, Time Lowe, Dorothy Sellers, and Daniel Onallis. Getting all those appointments took Stacey a long time, as you might imagine, which is why we all envied her trip to Hawaii.

In Alaska, we spoke with Pam Brodie, Charles Cole, Pam Colorado, Traci Cramer, Chip Dinnerline, Walter Elusaas, Michele Gorham, Gus Gustavson, Bob Henrichs, Don Kompkoff, Joe Hunt, Molly McCammon, Walter Meganack, Jr., Don Mitchell, Pat Norman, Steve Planchon, Monica Reidel, Lydia Robart, Arliss Sturgelewski, Craig Tillery, Ron Totemoff, Martha Vlasoff, and Nancy Yeaton.

For their help with the Great Lakes chapter, we are grateful to Jack Bails, Tim Eder, Sharon Hanshue, Stanley F. Pruss, James E. Riley, Kelly Stewart, and Sam Washington. For the North Dakota chapter, Dan Beard, K. L. Cool, Russ Dushinske, Pam Dryer, Mike Dwyer, Alan Hausauer, Dean

Hildebrand, Clif Issendorf, Lloyd Jones, Brian Kramer, Mike McEnroe, Doug Prchal, Barbara Rusmore, Joe Satrom, Keith Treagle, and John VanDerwalker were extremely helpful.

John Hoffnagle, Ann Taylor Schwing, and Adena Merenlender were most helpful on the Napa County Land Trust chapter. And proving once again that no good deed goes unpunished, after providing us with all the information we requested, they dug back through the files to find the few other little facts we forgot the first and second times around. John has now agreed to be a guest lecturer in my freshman class.

While working on her master's thesis on the Platte River, Darla worked with David Carlson, John Cavanaugh, Paul Currier, Bill Dunn, Bob Dwyer, David Bowman, Thomas Emerton, Governor Exxon, Chuck Frith, Beth Goldowitz, James Grahl, L. Steven Grasz, William Guy, Nelson Helms, Thomas Kimball, Ron Klatske, Brent Lathrop, Gary Lingle, Jack Maddux, Claire Olson, Pat Parenteau, Vince Shay, Paul Snyder, Richard Spelts, Paul Tebbel, John VanDerwalker, Bud Wolbach, and Ken Ziegler.

Our work on the Society for the Protection of New Hampshire Forests gave us a chance to spend time with Andy (Alex M.) Burgess, Jr., Edgar Brodeur, Rosemary Conroy, Jane Difley, Paul Doscher, Rose Freeman, Chris Kane, Richard Ober, Charles Niebling, Leslie Ward, Susanne Kibler-Hacker, and Dan Sundquist. Those helping on the Rangeley Lakes–Phillips trust analysis included Ted Beauvais, Arthur H. Emery, Tim Ingraham, Nancy Perlson, Alison Rieser, Karen Marchetti, and Dick Spenser.

The graphics in this volume put a new and particularly challenging twist on a lifetime of publish or perish. I have always envied colleagues whose publishers allowed them to have illustrations, and I aspired to a topic that would require some of my own photographs as well. This has not yet happened, and I am sadder but wiser now. Graphics are quite a challenge, and I no longer envy my friends in the Geography Department who frequently have more pictures than text.

We are grateful to those who helped us gather the illustrations for this book, which we assembled electronically. Even as I write these lines, I still do not believe that they are moving about in space toward the printed page. Nevertheless, Ye Qi worked valiantly to find maps and photos on the web. He spent hours helping, and we are deeply appreciative.

We took the picture of the alewife off the University of Wisconsin Sea Grant Web site, courtesy of the Shedd Aquarium in Chicago. Darla did the inking for the North Dakota and Platte River maps; Mike Spinelli spent hours playing phone tag helping Victoria Zaluda and me assemble the bits we needed for the Dade County map. Joe Hunt, Molly McCammon, and Martha Graham helped us with the pictures for chapter 5. Special thanks are due to Penny Rennick and Kathy Doogan from *Alaska Geographic*, who conspired with the folks in Kansas to produce a map of the Gulf of Alaska without any interference from me. Craig Bihrle sent the pothole pictures for the North Dakota chapter. Dick Ober and Rosemary Conroy helped us with the Mount Kearsarge photo, and Rose Freeman kindly trusted us with a snapshot from her family Bois de Brodeur album.

Our request for help on the map in chapter 9 involved us in just the kind of collaboration that this book is about. We wanted a map showing the Phillips trust lands in the context of all the surrounding protected lands. The Maine Audubon Society had a base map that had recently been converted into a canoeing map with funds from the Rivers, Trails, and Conservation Assistance Program of the North East Region of the National Park Service (NPS). That led us to Julie Isbill, who is in charge of the NPS program (and who was in one of my classes many years ago, which suggests yet another reason why teaching is a fun way to spend one's life). The original map effort involved the Appalachian Mountain Club of Boston, Massachusetts; Native Trails of Waldboro, Maine; and the Rangeley Lakes Heritage Trust. Julie put us in touch with cartographer Matt Kania in Wisconsin, who somehow put the whole thing together and adjusted it for use in this book.

John Hoffnagle of the Napa trust provided the picture of the Archer Taylor Preserve and helped us find Brian Cohan, who made the Napa County Land Trust map, working with the Green Info Nework. We are grateful to all for their help.

We are also grateful to those who read this volume to ensure that it made sense. Frequently, we inflicted ourselves on those who had provided us with the information to begin with. Frank Bernardino and Mike Spinelli read chapter 4; Molly McCammon backstopped chapter 5; and Darrell Yagodich, Kenneth Toguchi, and Ekela Andrade checked and rechecked successive drafts of chapter 6. Pam Dryer reviewed chapter 7, Jack Bails gave chapter 8 a final review, and Nancy Perlson did the same for chapter 9. Paul Doscher and Jane Difley checked chapter 10, and Adena Merenlender, Ann Taylor Schwing, and John Hoffnagle reread chapter 11 several times before we were done with it. Helen Ingram took several passes through the introduction and conclusion as they were developing, and Monica Moore and Ann Schwing reread the whole book one last time before it went out the door. One anonymous reviewer for the Press and one ultimately less so made major improvements in the structure and text. If we were not properly appreciative of their critical remarks when we first heard them, we are now. To all who helped us, we give thanks. It would not have been possible, or any fun, without them, and we are grateful for their help and the joy of knowing them.

Sally K. Fairfax

PART I: INTRODUCTION

CHAPTER ONE

A New Era in Land and Resource Conservation

This book is about trusts and how they have been used to shape land and resource conservation organizations. Our effort to understand *conservation trusts*, as we call them in this volume, reflects the assumption that the next several decades will be characterized by proliferation and diversification of resource management institutions. It does not take a crystal ball to make this prediction. The variety of new and sometimes peculiar organizations working in this field is readily apparent to even the most casual observer of conservation policy. Trusts and trust principles have an important role both in designing these new institutions and in analyzing them.

Conservation trust is not a standard term. In fact, we made it up to describe conservation organizations built on or close to trust principles. The principles themselves are widely familiar. As a lawyer could tell you, a trust involves a fiduciary relationship in which one person or organization holds or manages property for the exclusive benefit of another. For example, a grandmother creates a trust by directing a banker to manage funds set aside to ensure that her grandchild will have money to attend college. Or she might contribute to a charitable trust, one with a public purpose, to support the protection of habitat or farmland in her area. This fiduciary relationship has been described in centuries of law and policy; it is summarized with merciful brevity in the next chapter and is fleshed out in a discussion of what we call a classic trust in chapter 3.

To understand a trust as a set of institutional options for land and resource conservation, we look in considerable detail at a spectrum of organizations—some that are wholly governmental creations, some that are wholly private, and several blends of public and private efforts—in which people have established trusts to achieve their mutual aspirations. In Part II we look at three government trusts, wherein government agencies have used trust principles to blend federal, state, or local agencies into a single entity or to create a governmental organization whose funding and purposes are defined outside of the normal legislative and executive arena. In Part III we examine instances in which government and private groups working together have used trusts to structure institutions that share responsibility for jointly held and managed resources. Part IV explores a

3

variety of formats in which families use trusts to facilitate decision making for resources owned by several generations of proliferating siblings and cousins, focusing on the intersection between family trusts and land trusts. Private organizations' use of trust principles to manage funds dedicated to specified organizational goals, to solicit contributions in the form of planned giving, and to hold land for the benefit of future generations is also discussed in Part IV.

GOALS OF THIS BOOK

Our main goal in writing this book was to add trust elements to the set of options that analysts and practitioners draw on when thinking about institutional arrangements for managing and conserving resources.[1] We do that by telling stories shaped to raise questions about institutional choices: Why would a collection of siblings choose a trust to protect a farm or woodlot that they want to remain in their family for generations? What are the potential pitfalls of that choice? What happened after the press retreated from Prince William Sound and left village residents and government officials to respond to the damage of the *Exxon Valdez* oil spill? These are wonderful tales of struggles, victories, and, if we analyze them properly, quite instructive errors.

We underscore strengths and weaknesses of the trust concept. Although it is quite easy to establish one, a trust is a peculiar institution with very specific characteristics that may not be appropriate to every situation. Where and under what circumstances is it a promising vehicle for resolving a dispute or solving a problem? How do structural choices play out over time, and what pitfalls should trust framers and analysts be on the lookout for? We also suggest situations in which a trust is not a good candidate for consideration, and even situations in which forming any organization at all is a questionable undertaking. Finally, by exploring a trust as the basis for a conservation organization, we raise issues that are important for all institutional designers, even those *not* considering trust concepts for conservation.

Each of the cases that follow addresses a number of common themes: How was the trust set up, and why? How was the trust structured, and what is the relationship between the structure and the achievement of the organization's purposes? What is the fit between the trust purpose and the beneficiary? Is it possible to bind trustees to the purposes for which the organization was established without tying their hands so tightly that the organization loses effectiveness? Under what circumstances is it prudent for trustees to hire a trust staff, and when can the trust prudently rely on either volunteer labor or government agency largesse?

Finally, and most important, to whom should the trust be accountable? What is the relationship between the trust and the public—when should public input or participation in a trust be allowed or required, and how should it be achieved? The question of organizational accountability is especially important, because many of the organizations we examined were established specifically to sidestep government oversight mechanisms. In this era of intense cynicism about public bureaucracies and Congress, there is enormous appeal in avoiding the whole political "mess" by setting up new and independent institutions to accomplish clear and important objectives. This aspiration appears to underlie many of the trusts, particularly those described in Parts II and III of this volume.

We cannot, of course, avoid politics—politics is life. And the quest for new institutions creates problems of its own. Even when they are private organizations—such as land trusts or family trusts—the conservation trusts that we studied are clearly "invested with the public interest," as the Supreme Court used to say. Public accountability is therefore an important issue for all the organizations included in this volume. They have defined the problem in very different ways and used an array of approaches—some resembling federal agencies' public involvement programs, some improving dramatically on that familiar format, and others taking off in new and quite different paths toward public accountability.

We emphasize three elements of the accountability issue. First, it is important to ask how much investment in institution building is appropriate. Is a proliferation of organizations an efficient way to proceed in terms of project development, fund-raising, and volunteer effort? Are there enough capable people out there who are willing to serve as trustees and supporters of these organizations? Particularly when we turn to the issue of land trusts, the fastest-growing element of the conservation community, the question is critical: is it prudent to create so many organizations with limited human and financial resources?

Second, monitoring conservation trust activities could become a serious problem. It is hard enough to keep tabs on government agencies that have a clear hierarchical structure and reins of accountability. But a concerned citizen who has problems with a public agency can write to a congressperson or call an official clearly identified in almost any phone book in the country. The frequently small, little-known organizations that dominate our cases have public or quasi-public purposes, but they exist outside the normal reach of electoral mechanisms of public accountability. Even the large ones can be a challenge for those interested in and affected by their programs. How are citizens even to know of the existence, not to mention the names and activities, of the organizations we discuss in this book? This problem of accountability must be addressed as a central element in this era of institutional innovation.

Third, how are responsible or concerned organizations and citizens to monitor and assess the *combined* efforts of diverse groups acting in the same general region to achieve the same general goal? One way to grasp the importance of this problem is to think in terms of obtaining maps of different conservation landholdings. It is presently almost impossible to obtain maps, for example, that depict all the holdings, even if you are looking only for land belonging to the relevant federal agencies.[2] When you add to that picture full and partial titles held by federal, state, and a plethora of regional and local organizations, including conservation trusts, it becomes difficult even for those working in the area to identify what is "protected," what protection needs remain, and whether habitat, recreation, wetlands, and similar holdings are appropriately located to meet program goals. Moreover, if separate and distinct organizations have different purposes and priorities, it is not clear that integrated management of landscapes will be the result, even if all the protected pieces fit together. This suggests a need to assess the new organizations in terms of their contribution to fragmenting the landscape by multiplying uncoordinated organizational structures.

CHANGING COURSE

Exploring these themes in the context of conservation trusts is useful for two reasons. First, conservation trusts are important themselves and should be understood for what they are and what they do and fail to do. Second, they provide a useful lens into the rapidly changing mix of institutions operating in the conservation field. All the organizations discussed in this book reflect changes in the institutional setting in which land and resources are managed in the United States. Conservation trusts are one part of a major challenge to the well-established terrain of Progressive Era land management ideology and agencies. Over the last century, Americans became comfortable with the pattern of establishing government agencies—typically at the federal level—to achieve conservation goals and national interest groups to monitor them.

We are now changing course. Americans are reconsidering long-established assumptions, first about government and second about land.[3] Familiar land and resource conservation organizations are being supplemented, if not supplanted, by the kind of organizations to which trust principles seem so well adapted: local cooperatives, government-private partnerships, corporate-private projects, local consensus groups, watershed associations, and land trusts of all stripes and configurations. These new conservation organizations are working in partnership with, or in place of, government agencies, and they are actively managing public as well as private resources. Many of them proceed with a new approach to land as well, viewing it less as a patchwork of publicly or privately owned parcels and more as an integrated mosaic of ecological processes. An understanding of this changing context suggests both why trusts might be formed and the accountability problems that can result.

Dismay with Government and Politics

Recent reconsideration of ideas about government has contributed to a major reshaping of public institutions. Political scientists talk about the "contracting out" or "hollowing out" of government. What they mean is that Americans are losing confidence in the received wisdom that has long underwritten government activity: our basic idea has been that nonpartisan, technically competent civil servants are employed, preferably but not always at the federal level, to implement policies designed by Congress to achieve the public interest. In this model, civil servants are held accountable by three forces: citizens involved in government planning and participation programs, elected executives and representatives through legislation and appropriations, and the courts through judicial review of agency action.

This model of action and accountability underwrote the reforms of the late-nineteenth-century Progressive Era and opened the way for the vast resource planning and social engineering programs of the New Deal. It held together fairly well into the first generation of the modern environmental movement, which emphasized a regulatory or "command and control" approach to a growing agenda of air, water, toxic, and pesticide pollution issues. It was strenuously challenged after World War II by economists—notably in the conservation field by those associated with an organization called Resources for the Future. Nevertheless, it seemed to have worked well as a first approach to some problems, such as the building of water treatment plants and the installation of smokestack scrubbers.[4] However, concern about government inefficiency and incompetence has gradually gained a wide audience.

Reassessment of the regulatory approach became a major partisan issue in the 1990s. The long-standing Republican commitment to reducing the size of the federal government was matched by the Democratic administration's effort to "reinvent" it. Partisan posturing played out in the context of a crisis created by the rapid expansion of the federal debt during the Reagan-Bush era. Efforts to reduce government spending and the federal deficit significantly contracted agency budgets, especially in the noncontractual, "discretionary" elements of government spending, of which conservation programs in the Departments of Agriculture and the Interior constitute a substantial percentage.

These shifts in attitude reflect as well a growing cynicism about politics in general. The government appears to have attempted too much, failed too frequently, and lied too often. In place of politics, we see a growing faith in markets as an impartial mechanism for allocating resources.

Devolution and Dispersion

One result of these changing ideas about government is that the authority for implementing what we think of as public programs is both devolving and dispersing.[5] The most obvious element of this change, particularly apparent in the resources field, is an emphasis on devolution of government authority—making fewer decisions in Washington, D.C., and more at state and local levels of government. This is not, of course, a new idea, either in government generally or in the resources field in particular. For decades, a major narrative in the resources field has been the Sagebrush Rebellion, a recurring drama in which western governors and legislators, frustrated by the federal control that accompanies large federal landholdings within the states, demand that the federal government "return" the land to them. More recently, citizens have similarly demanded that the communities affected by federal resource management agencies have a larger voice in decision making. The apparent outcome of these periodic dustups—that the federal land is not turned over to the states—has masked the degree to which responsibility for managing such land has been transferred.[6]

The other element of this changing view of government can be called dispersion. Not gone, not forgotten, but certainly waning in importance are "command and control" and civil servants on the government payroll to achieve it. Implementation of government programs relies heavily on contracting with third parties and on creating incentives, through tax policy and other mechanisms, to direct private and corporate behavior. "This is not," as political scientist Lester Salamon points out, "merely the contracting out of well-defined functions or the purchase of specified goods and services from outside suppliers." Nor is it the capture story so familiar to students of the Bureau of Land Management, in which the regulated gain decisive influence over the putative regulator and bend its programs to their own advantage. Salamon continues that the "characteristic feature of many of these new . . . tools of action is that they involve the sharing of . . . the exercise of discretion over the spending of federal funds and the use of federal authority." For example, Salamon notes that the Department of Labor does not spend the $6 billion to $8 billion that Congress routinely appropriates for employment and training assistance programs. The money goes automatically to about 450 local "prime sponsors," private organizations that run programs over which the Department of Labor has limited control but for which it has major responsibility.[7]

Again, this devolution and dispersion have perhaps been masked in the resources context by the Sagebrush Rebellion saga. Those not advocating a return of the land to the states have long sought, at least symbolically, to force the sale of such land to those with a financial interest in it—primarily but not exclusively the holders of grazing permits. The repeated heated discussions and subsequent apparent defeat of these episodic moves to "privatize" federal lands have concealed the extent to which management of government conservation programs has been dispersed to private corporations and concerns.

The Land and Water Conservation Fund—
Devolution and Dispersion in Action

In a book fundamentally concerned with institutional reform and design, it is important to note that the devolution and dispersion of government authority are not simply reflections of cynicism about government or forces beyond our control. They are in part the fruit of a previous explicit reform effort. At the close of World War II, state and local governments were in abysmal shape. Political scientists lamented diverse manifestations of state and local inefficiency, and the public was dismayed at incompetence and corruption. During the 1950s and early 1960s it frequently appeared that the states' primary contribution to the body politic was a cover for racial segregation.[8]

The situation has changed, and the improving status of state and local governments has inevitably contributed to the devolution and dispersion of authority. States undertook significant, frequently painful, internal restructuring, and Congress designed federal programs specifically to build local and state infrastructure. In this context, the 1964 Land and Water Conservation Fund (LWCF) can be viewed as a period piece. Although we currently think of the LWCF in terms of funding for federal land acquisition or, more precisely, the failure of Congress to fund the LWCF adequately, its major impact is probably as a vector of both devolution and dispersion. The program contributed significantly to the capacity of state and local park departments and to the formation of private organizations oriented toward land acquisition.

The enactment of the LWCF was preceded by a national review of what was then viewed as a national crisis in outdoor recreation. The analysis was undertaken by the Outdoor Recreation Resources Review Commission (ORRRC), established for that purpose by Congress. Its 1959 conclusions and recommendations looked beyond federal parks and forests and envisioned enhanced state and local governments providing recreation opportunities where the people are were—in large cities. In so doing, the ORRRC gave legitimacy to a broad spectrum of private groups sharing that priority. One of the commission's major recommendations was a federal grant program to provide matching funds for state and local recreational land acquisition and facilities development. Although the federal agencies received a major slice of the LWCF pie, Congress's goal of devolving responsibility for recreation to states and localities was explicit.

Significantly, the way for a state to qualify for LWCF matching funds was to develop a state comprehensive outdoor recreation plan (SCORP). That process, in turn, gave impetus for local planning efforts. As intended, the fund application requirements precipitated both the development of professional expertise in recreation planning, which had not been discernible in many state and local jurisdictions prior to the legislation, and the elaboration of newly empowered state and local recreation organizations.[9] These institutions have been an important element of the devolution of responsibility for recreation to states and localities.

Less clearly intended but of special relevance in the late 1990s was the LWCF's equally important role in the dispersion of governmental authority and programs. The portion of the LWCF intended to assist federal land acquisitions soon gave rise to private groups designed specifically to procure LWCF funds to support their own acquisition priorities and to assist unimaginative federal real estate specialists in actually making the transactions.[10] The Nature Conservancy and the Trust for Public Land are among the largest and most elaborate. Although the LWCF was clearly intended to enhance state and local capacity for participating in public recreation programs, its role in the development of private nonprofit organizations has been significant as well.

Another policy change, less noticed and discussed than the LWCF grants, potentiated the institutional dispersion wrought by the LWCF. In 1964, the same year that the LWCF was created, the Internal Revenue Service (IRS) promulgated regulations allowing a landowner to take an income tax deduction for a charitable donation of a conservation easement on land she owned.[11] In the process, the regulations defined, subject to continuing modification, a conservation easement, who could receive one, and for what purposes. The IRS did not invent conservation easements, which had previously played an important role in major conservation programs. For example, the Blue Ridge Parkway in Virginia is in part a small strip of federally owned highway right-of-way surrounded by private property on which the National Park Service holds conservation easements, some of which date from the 1930s. However, the idea of a private *donation* of easements took flight after the 1964 tax code revisions.

Salamon has noted that because tax deductions or exemptions do not "show up as outlays" in the federal budget, they have "become immensely popular as a form of government action."[12] They are also a significant dispersion of federal authority—having waived a portion of the tax money it would have received in order to encourage donations, the federal government has nothing more to do with managing the resulting program. As long as the donor and the receiving organization comply with the broad requirements of the tax code, they effectively implement the federal program completely on their own. We will have more to say about the donation of conservation easements and the hundreds of organizations that have sprouted up to receive them in the next chapter and in Part IV, devoted to family and land trusts.

The pattern of choices inherent in the IRS regulations and the LWCF has clearly contributed to the devolution and dispersion of government authority, creating space for organizational innovations such as conservation trusts.

On the Right Path?

Some observers have viewed this changed course as a step in the right direction. A school of thought known as new resource economics evolved in the backwash of the Reagan-Bush era to observe that the government usually messes up what it touches. The more that private enterprise participated in government policy, and the more businesslike incentives for efficiency there were permeating public agencies, the better. The number of problems that government could solve efficiently was small, they argued, limited to a small range of nonexcludable public goods. For the rest of it, let the market prevail.

Others have been concerned about the dilution of government authority. Ted Lowi has been pointing with dismay for more than thirty years to the crisis in democratic governance created by sharing government authority with private organizations.[13] Writing in the late 1960s, Lowi lamented that powerful private groups had come to negotiate public policy and participate in the exercise of public authority. He described this growing participation of interest groups in policy implementation as "the end of liberalism" and regarded it as a crisis in democratic governance. To address the problem, he proposed tighter drafting of authorizing legislation and closer judicial oversight of policy implementation as an antidote to the private exercise of public power. One might argue that the vastly magnified role played by the courts in resource and environmental policy in the 1970s and 1980s was a response to his call for reform. Others would argue, however, that litigation became just another way for interest groups to participate in the exercise of government authority, another step in its devolution.

Trusts and trust notions occupy a particularly interesting perch in this era of devolution and dispersion. For the market enthusiasts, the trust offers a businesslike approach to program analysis and, if not an embrace of efficiency precisely, at least a reliance on prudence as the basic standard of performance. For Lowi and his descendants, the trust offers both clarity of purpose and an explicit reliance on the courts for enforcement. With a foot in both camps, it is little wonder that trusts and the fiduciary relationship are enjoying a moment in the sun. Their role in a period of devolution and dispersion of government authority is particularly interesting in the environmental field, because these political changes are closely related to simultaneous evolution in how Americans view the land and resources.

Changing Thinking About Land and Land Management

Much of our contemporary thinking about land can be summarized in terms of tension between a view of land as landscapes and a view of land as separately owned parcels. The landscape view rejects the notion that blocs of land belonging to separate owners—no matter how large—can be managed separately. It focuses instead on the notion of ecological interconnection among parcels and calls for cooperative management to protect natural systems and processes. The landscape view has long been the preferred analytical and managerial unit in air and water pollution regulation. This focus on the interconnectedness of natural systems has been carried into the politics of land management in large part by public concern about species habitat and biodiversity.[14]

The landscape focus has clear institutional ramifications. It has contributed to devolution and dispersion of authority by further eroding the status of federal ownership and agencies. The federal agencies continue to control a large part of many landscapes, but they are no longer viewed as the only important landholder in a landscape. Nor is the federal government regarded as necessarily the most appropriate owner of valuable conservation lands.[15] We have learned that attention to a particular federal park or forest is not an adequate habitat protection method. Irrespective of who owns a particular parcel, it must be seen as connected to other ownerships that make up a landscape. And we have learned to use new analytical tools such as gap analysis and corridor management for wildlife in thinking about landscape management.

Thinking about landscapes instead of parcels also has enormous impacts for private landownership, encouraging efforts to bring owners of private parcels into line with newly described notions of ecological responsibility. The basic idea is that we cannot hope to buy enough parcels but instead must find ways to work with private landholders to ensure habitat protection. Accordingly, the landscape view is sharply contested by a well-organized property rights movement working to solidify the rights of private ownership and the importance of individual parcels by minimizing the social context and responsibilities of ownership.[16]

Nevertheless, landscape-level thinking has opened the way for watershed-based or similar organizations to view the landscape as a partnership between and among diverse owners. Thus, this changing view of land has been an important factor in the devolution and dispersion of federal authority in conservation programs and in the attendant opening of opportunities for other government levels and sectors to play a major role in exercising government authority. Many federal programs now proceed in partnership with diverse private, state, and corporate entities and occasionally, as in the case of the Quincy Library Group, are dominated by well-organized local forces.

We readily grant the continued existence of the supremacy and commerce clauses of the Constitution, national media, and all the other artifacts of the American political and social scene that have enabled the federal government to emerge as the dominant influence in American political life. The federal government and national groups have not withdrawn from the conservation scene and are not likely to do so. However, we believe that sharing of decision-making authority will continue. Nonfederal and nongovernment agencies, and especially mixed organizations—public-private partnerships, cooperatives, and consensus groups—will play an increasing role in managing multiownership landscapes and watersheds. Institutional design will, we conclude, emerge as an increasingly important conservation challenge.

In that context, it is useful to understand and explore conservation trusts. While not exactly popping up everywhere, they are sufficiently widespread to merit significant attention from scholars, practitioners, and advocates. More important, the trusts that have been developed in the last two decades provide important tools and lessons that are relevant to the emerging institutional needs of land and resource conservation. All kinds of entities—conservation advocates, citizens, land managers, government employees, corporations large and small—are going to find themselves debating how to organize to achieve the goals of some newly forming group. Thus, we believe that a study of conservation trusts has much to teach us.

FAMILIAR INSTITUTIONAL
DESIGN ALTERNATIVES

In order to fully explore the pros and cons of trust principles as an organizing theme for conservation organizations and their relationship to other emerging structures, we should make comparisons among relevant organizational forms. To do so comprehensively is beyond the scope of this volume. However, because conservation trusts blend or merge at the margins with a number of familiar institutions, this section looks briefly at five additional forms of organization to help readers distinguish among them.

Government Agencies

This most familiar form of conservation organization is the model discussed earlier: interested advocates lobby for the formation of a government agency, such as the National Park Service or the U.S. Forest Service. These agencies are typically created by legislative action. However, on occasion they are established by an executive reorganization. Both the Park Service and the Forest Service, for example, make much of their "organic acts," and the received wisdom about the conservation movement of the early twentieth century is dominated by their founding myths. It is important to note, however, the Environmental Protection Agency (EPA) was created without statute by a presidential executive order, and the Bureau of Land Management (BLM) existed between 1948 and 1976 as a result of a secretarial reorganization in the Department of the Interior.

The basic fact remains, however, that no executive agent or agency of the government can take action that is not authorized by the legislature. Reorganizations at the federal level, for example, whether by a president or an interior secretary, technically just redelegate authority previously granted by Congress. The government agency does, within the limits of bureaucratic imagination, what it was authorized to do by Congress and no more. It is dependent on Congress for operating funds and, in general, returns any fees or receipts for programs to the general fund for appropriation as directed by Congress. Personnel are selected and promoted following federal civil service rules, with the exception of high officers in an agency or department, who are appointed by the president and typically subject to confirmation by the Senate. These political appointees normally are replaced when the White House changes hands.

Government Corporations

Government corporations are similar to agencies but enjoy a greater degree of autonomy and freedom from congressional and administrative controls, such as budgetary oversight and personnel regulations, than does a regular government agency. This freedom is typically justified by the mission of the corporation, which often involves fee-for-service activities and close interaction with private business.[17] Government corporations are intended, not always successfully, to be self-sustaining. The most obvious example is the U.S. Postal Service. There are three types of government corporations: (1) those that are financed by appropriations and whose

assets are owned by the government and controlled by board members selected according to the applicable statute; (2) mixed public-private corporations, which include both public and private assets and are run by a board
selected jointly by the president and private stockholders; and (3) private
corporations that are established by federal statute but privately financed
and owned with no continuing government involvement.[18] Until the depression era, government corporations were rare. During the term of
Franklin Roosevelt, government corporations became common and relatively permanent. Probably the most significant government corporation
in the resource management field is the Tennessee Valley Authority (TVA).

Nonprofit Corporations

Nonprofits are one form of private corporation. A corporation is a legal
fiction—the law treats a corporation like a person, capable of entering
contracts, incurring liabilities, and paying taxes. The corporation and the
rules for establishing one are defined in state statutes and provide a vehicle by which individuals can pool resources to pursue joint activities.[19]
Basically, the corporate structure separates ownership from management
and distances the owners from the corporation's liabilities. Under normal circumstances, a shareholder's assets are not available to pay corporate debts.[20]

   A nonprofit is a corporation organized under appropriate state law
and operated "for one of the nonprofit purposes recognized under state
corporation law and federal and state tax statutes."[21] Typically, those purposes include religious, educational, and diverse charitable activities.
Nonprofits are sometimes called 501(c)(3)s after the section of the Internal
Revenue Code that discusses the most familiar kind. Some nonprofit clas-
sifications allow the organization to receive contributions that are deductible from the donor's income taxes. Among the general rules governing
nonprofits is the requirement that if the corporation is dissolved, any remaining assets are to be distributed to a similar tax-exempt, nonprofit group
and cannot be used to benefit individuals or any for-profit group.[22]

   Nonprofit does not, however, mean that the organization cannot
make a profit. "Unrelated business income" is allowed, but it is taxed. In
addition, under most circumstances, corporate directors, trustees, officers,
employees, and members are not personally liable for corporate debts.[23]
Nonprofit status gives an organization a formal and perpetual legal existence apart from the founders and people who contribute to it, and it creates opportunities for its employees to gain tax-deductible benefits not
generally available to participants in self-employed businesses.

   Like trusts, nonprofits are surrounded by a mystique of goodness. One
commentator notes that, freed from the "constant demands of profit mar-

gins and elections," nonprofits, which he calls the "independent sector," can "experiment with new strategies of social action, respond quickly to new social needs, and generally provide 'social risk capital.' . . . All the major social movements in the nation's history have started in the nonprofit sector," he asserts, citing child labor legislation, abolition, mental health care, women's suffrage, Prohibition, civil rights, consumer protection, environmentalism, the peace movement, the women's movement, and the nuclear arms control movement.[24]

This standard view of nonprofits as separate from government and inherently altruistic is currently under sharp review.[25] The fact is that the small and struggling nonprofits in our communities control very little of the funds and personnel in the nonprofit sector. Nonprofits also include major universities, hospitals, foundations, and many special-interest groups. They are the repositories of some of the greatest accumulations of private wealth in the nation, little of which was assembled altruistically. The degree to which the social agenda of the nation can be defined and manipulated by these bastions of private wealth—outside of the more readily accountable government structures and with large tax subsidies, to boot—concerns many.

More recent observers have looked at the close relationships between the government and the nonprofits that have emerged to implement, under contract, an increasing number of government programs. Some scholars have wondered about the nonprofits' independence. Others have queried the smaller ones' ability to sustain themselves in the face of government's growing tendency to form nonprofits that compete with private nonprofits for public support and attention.[26] The whole issue of the role of nonprofits in society and politics is under trenchant reconsideration in the wake of devolution, dispersion, and the contracting out of policy implementation.

For purposes of our discussion of conservation trusts, we set most of these issues aside. In this volume, we focus on the nonprofit corporation's eligibility for exemption from federal corporate income taxes and other tax benefits under the Internal Revenue Code and similar exemptions under state tax codes.

The disadvantages of a nonprofit consist largely of the time, effort, and expense necessary to become a corporation and the reporting and paperwork required to maintain one. Establishing and maintaining a nonprofit constitutes a significant investment of social capital. In addition, nonprofits are limited in their activities: they have to adhere to the statutory purposes described in their charters, or they lose their nonprofit status. This has led to some well-publicized disputes—involving organizations such as the Sierra Club and the American Association of Retired Persons—over whether institutional activities meet IRS standards. Typically, these questions become visible only when someone in Congress decides that an opposing group requires investigation. Organizations that do not make a taxable profit and do not need to attract tax-deductible donations may find the requirements unjustified.

Foundations

Foundations are a subspecies of the nonprofit corporation. They must serve a statutorily defined charitable purpose, but they do it in a specialized way: by making grants of money to other nonprofits and similar entities, including governments. A foundation may also provide services, conduct research and publish findings, and hold conferences. The foundation receives and invests tax-deductible gifts from donors—the foundation's endowment— and uses the interest and dividends earned, and sometimes other gifts as well, to make grants and operate programs to accomplish its charitable purposes. Private donors can create either private or corporate foundations. Community foundations are public charities, which are public organizations formed to benefit a community or region; they are required to have "broad public participation, diverse donors," and are subject to "less stringent regulations and more favorable" tax treatment than are most other nonprofit charitable organizations.[27]

Consensus, Watershed, and "Friends of" Groups

It is perhaps misleading to try to make a category out of the diverse organizations that have sprung into existence to facilitate community or regional discussion of resource management issues. Typically, "friends" of a river, forest, or threatened species form a group to seek consensus among protagonists confronting a development proposal or a major planning effort. The only thing consistent about these organizations is their variety—some have staff support, formal organizations with bylaws, and perhaps 501(c)(3) status; some friends include relevant government officials and may even have some formal role in an ongoing planning process; other groups exclude government bureaucrats, sometimes rather flatly, to emphasize discussion among citizens. The Quincy Library Group is perhaps the best known of the genre. It started when folks who often fought about northern California national forest issues began to meet in the local library, where they could not shout at one another. The Quincy Library Group has evolved into an elaborate political organization and has successfully shepherded through Congress legislation obliging the U.S. Forest Service to comply with the consensus plan the group devised.

Such organizations do not constitute a category with consistently defined earmarks and characteristic traits. Nevertheless, they are an important reflection of both the dismay with government and politics and the dispersion and devolution of government processes discussed earlier. We believe that familiarity with conservation trusts and trust principles may be of great utility to those involved in "friends of" organizations, however they are structured.

TRUSTS THAT ARE *NOT* THE SUBJECT OF THIS VOLUME

In the next chapter we discuss trust principles in considerable detail. Here, we distinguish conservation trusts, and trusts in general, from several potentially confusing applications of trust terminology. The word *trust* turns up in a number of contexts in the conservation field; some are quite closely related to the conservation trusts on which we focus, and others are not.

Almost all the relevant uses of the word *trust* are associated with a fiduciary relationship—that is, when one person holds and manages property or acts on behalf of another. However, most of the other trusts are ultimately quite different from the form we describe in chapter 2 and emphasize throughout this volume. To clarify the terminology, we briefly distinguish the conservation trust from the public trust, the sacred trust, the Indian trust, a few pretend trusts, and, most complex of all, a growing institutional category known as the land trust.

Public Trust

When we talk about trust principles in the chapters that follow, we are not referring to the public trust doctrine. Since Professor Joseph Sax first resurrected the idea from the relative obscurity of water law, the public trust has become a major element of environmental protection.[28] The doctrine is an element of English common law that can be traced to ancient Roman codes. The basic idea is that some resources—most typically access to submerged and tidal lands under navigable waterways and, less frequently, wildlife—are the inalienable property of the people. Such resources cannot be privately owned but are instead held by the sovereign for the common benefit of all the people. Therefore, if a private party owns a public trust resource, the private rights—or *jus privatum*—are always held subject to the exercise of superior public rights—or *jus publicum*. The sovereign—or, in the U.S. context, usually the state government—is frequently described as holding the public rights "in trust" for the people.

The concept of one party holding property for the benefit of another—that is, a fiduciary relationship—is common to both the public trust and the conservation trust. Sometimes the two look similar. However, current interpretations of the public trust are most likely to embrace environmental protection or preservation.[29] In contrast, the dominant theme of the conservation trust is to make the trust productive in order to achieve the purposes of the settlor—frequently, to make money for the beneficiary. One of the major issues of this book is whether the trust principles described in chapter 2 can operate effectively in conservation programs, given the underlying emphasis on producing revenues. For now, it is important to note both the common and distinctive elements of public and conservation trusts in order to avoid confusion.

Sacred Trust

Public office has been described as a "sacred trust," though this was more common in the past than in the present political climate. Public resource managers—those working for state or federal parks, forests, or wildlife programs, for example—frequently describe their work on behalf of the public as a public or sacred trust. The basic idea is similar to the fiduciary relationship—one individual, whether it is the mayor or the district ranger, is chosen to act on behalf of others. Therefore, the officeholder is expected to adhere to a higher standard of morality and care than she would if acting in her own behalf. Those acting under such a sacred trust must be "purer than Caesar's wife," avoiding not only wrongdoing but also the *appearance* of wrongdoing. Although in conservation matters the sacred trust sometimes runs into the edges of the conservation trust or public trust, the three are relatively easily distinguished in practice.

Indian Trust

Indian reservations are frequently described as trusts. The federal government is sometimes said to hold the reservations "in trust" for the Indians or, more broadly, to have a "special trust relationship" with Native Americans. This judicial doctrine arises from Supreme Court Justice John Marshall's efforts, in the 1840s, to define the U.S. government's relationship with the tribes. He did so by calling them "domestic dependent nations,"[30] from which the apparent trust notion arises. However, government policy toward the Indians has unevenly relied on trust principles and has rarely evinced the "undivided loyalty" that a trustee is required to demonstrate toward the beneficiary of a trust. When it is in the interest of the federal government to act as the Indians' trustee, especially when dealing with a third party doing business on a reservation, it may in fact do so, dusting off and defending trust principles with occasionally impressive vigor. When it is not in accord with federal interests to act with undivided loyalty to the Indians, the government does not do so. We are not alone in suggesting that trust nomenclature is routinely misapplied in the context of Indian policy.[31] Three of the trusts examined in the chapters that follow have a more or less direct role in responding to the status of Native Americans, native Hawaiians, and Alaskan Natives. The federal government continues, even in the more specific trust contexts we describe, to be a fickle trustee for original Americans.

Pretend Trusts

Indian policy is not the only area in which we find pretend trusts. Organizations frequently create the misimpression that a trust exists in order to give a fund or program a public-spirited ring that is not wholly justified. Congress is fond of creating pretend trusts that ostensibly contain funds dedicated to a specific purpose. In fact, the funds typically do not exist even as bookkeeping fictions. Although the Social Security Trust Fund is probably the best example of this congressional proclivity, those interested in natural resources should be aware that the Reclamation Fund is also a pretend trust. Under the Mineral Lands Leasing Act of 1920, 40 percent of the revenues from mineral leasing are to be deposited in the Reclamation Fund, as are 50 percent of the revenues from licenses issued for hydroelectric projects on public lands.

One might presume that there is a fund into which these indicated revenues are deposited and against which expenditures for reclamation are drawn. This would be an error. There is no fund, no deposits or withdrawals, no interest on funds, and, most importantly, no holding off on reclamation expenditures until there are sufficient reserves in the fund to cover anticipated costs. The only thing the Reclamation Fund accomplishes is to take 40 percent of mineral revenues away from the state of origin. The primary beneficiaries of reclamation expenditures have been California and Arizona, while the major mineral revenue–generating states are Wyoming and New Mexico.

The Land and Water Conservation Fund discussed earlier is similar. Park entrance fees, motorboat fuel taxes, and revenues from outer continental shelf oil production are supposed to make up a fund that provides matching grants to localities and funds to federal agencies to purchase land for outdoor recreation and, more recently, for habitat and wetland protection purposes. In theory, the fund is supposed to receive deposits of $900 million per year from these sources. In fact, no deposits are made, no funds accumulate, and no interest accrues.[32] Land acquisition funds are subject to congressional appropriation, just like any other federal expenditure. The pretend fund provides land acquisition advocates an opportunity to urge Congress to spend up to $900 million a year and to complain when it does not. LWCF funds are in no sense of the term "trust" funds.

The conceptual appeal of trusts has also been utilized to mislead or to allay fears. For example, the Presidio Trust was established following transfer of the Presidio area of San Francisco from the Department of the Army to the National Park Service. Originally, the trust was intended to function in partnership with the National Park Service to manage existing historical barracks, research installations, a golf course, and similar facilities to produce funds to maintain what was envisioned as a unit of the existing Golden Gate National Recreation Area. What emerged from the legislative struggle is called a trust, but it is in fact a "wholly owned government corporation to be known as the Presidio Trust."[33] The organization created has few of the features of a trust as described in chapter 2. The term may have made the proposal more appealing, but it has little to do with the operation of the facility.

Land Trust

Many organizations formed to protect land use the phrase *land trust* or *trust* somewhere in their titles, as in the Trust for Public Land or the Vermont Land Trust.[34] Yet the term *land trust* has no specific legal meaning. The mere fact that an organization describes itself as a land trust or has *land trust* in its organizational name conveys little information about how it is structured or how it operates.

Typically, land trusts are organized as nonprofits, but their size, scope, budget, and activities vary widely. Broadly, land trusts employ some or all of five basic techniques aimed toward land conservation: the purchase of land, the acceptance of donations of land, the purchase of conservation easements, the acceptance of donations of easements, and the acquisition of land or easements that are reconveyed to another public or private institution. The best way to find out whether an organization considers itself a land trust is to obtain a guide published by the umbrella interest group, the Land Trust Alliance (LTA), and see whether it is listed. Those that have paid the dues to join the organization are listed as land trusts. Those organizations that undertake land trust–like activities but are not LTA members are not listed.[35]

Because land trusts hold land or easements that are generally intended to benefit the public, critical elements of a fiduciary relationship are apparent. However, not many are structured as true trusts or even operate under any semblance of trust principles. At least one state is concerned about the potential confusion created by the use of the phrase. The Michigan Office of the Attorney General does not permit general land conservation groups to include the term *trust* in their titles, specifically to avoid any possible misunderstanding about the nature of the organization. Other words are used, such as the Little Traverse Conservancy, the Kalamazoo Nature Center, and the Grass River Natural Area.[36]

We do not consider land trusts to be trusts, because few organizations that operate as land trusts are actually organized as trusts along the lines described in chapter 2. Nevertheless, the two uses of the term do overlap, and we examine several organizations listed in the LTA guide that are organized as trusts. We also address land trust organizations that utilize formal trust principles in parts of their operations without being formally organized as trusts.

RESEARCH METHODS

As social scientists, we are aware that it is traditional to say something about research methods. Ours were simple. We set out to identify conservation trusts throughout the country in a variety of ways: through conversations with colleagues and land protection professionals, on the Web, and in legal opinions. When we found an organization that sounded as though it met our definition of a trust, we contacted the group directly and asked about it. Some preferred not to talk, and we let them be. Others sent us minutes of meetings, annual reports, and similar materials. Many organizations with the word *trust* in their titles turned out to be something else. In all the cases discussed in this volume, we visited, sometimes repeatedly, to conduct open-ended interviews with framers, trustees, lessees, opponents, or observers. We selected cases and materials to emphasize conservation trusts as an institutional design option and focused our attention on issues of accountability.

ROAD MAP TO THE BOOK

Chapters in the book are organized under four headings. The remainder of Part I includes a discussion of trust principles and our first case study, illustrating those principles in action. Although it belongs analytically in Part III, we are calling the Platte River trust a classic trust. We do this to flesh out the trust principles introduced in chapter 2. In the Platte River trust, all the parts of a trust are there and functioning well and recognizably.

Part II focuses on three trusts established in and by government agencies. The Dade County Wetlands Trust is a consortium of federal, state, and local officials responsible for funds paid by developers in Dade County, Florida, to mitigate damages caused by their activities; the *Exxon Valdez*

Oil Spill Trustee Council is made up of federal and state public agency officials administering a restoration program with civil settlement funds; the Department of Hawaiian Home Lands is a state agency organized as a trust to manage lands intended to provide homesteads for native Hawaiians injured by the arrival of Europeans and the theft of their lands. These stories provide an opportunity to view trust principles primarily in the context of blending multiple government agencies responsible for decision making or for common resources. Public accountability is a major issue in these cases. In the Hawaiian case, enforcing the trust suggests the magnitude of the problems encountered when major resources are placed in limbo, not quite in and not quite out of the normal channels of government accountability.

Mixed public-private trusts take a further step toward the dispersion and devolution of public authority. We examine two examples in Part III. (Had we not included the Platte River trust in Part I, it would also fall in this part.) These trusts manage funds paid for damages caused by the development of public resources, and they include a mixture of government agency personnel or political appointees and private interest group representatives as trustees.

In North Dakota, a challenging political environment is intensified by poorly drafted trust purposes. The Platte River trust has confronted a similarly hostile climate but has struggled less, in part because the trustees have taken better advantage of the guidance that trust notions provide. The Great Lakes trust is a major success in sharing authority among federal, state, tribal, and private entities. However, its programs are not clearly necessary to conservation in the region. By comparison, although the North Dakota story is less encouraging, the organization plays a critical conservation role. The juxtaposition raises important questions about the careful fit between trust structure and trust purposes, and also about the utility of establishing an organization at all.

Part IV treats private and family trusts together with land trusts. This is not because they are similar in terms of trust principles. The family trusts use the tools described in chapter 2 to structure their deliberations and allocate the expenses and responsibilities of holding land in common. The land trusts are not trusts but nonprofit corporations. We include them in our discussion because they blend with true trusts on the ground. The conservation easement provides family trusts a way around what is known in trust parlance as the rule against perpetuities. Further, the land trusts' enforcement role provides a context in which family conservation choices can be sustained. Finally, the land trusts make interesting use of trust principles and the fiduciary relationship in their structures.

Each case study tells a story, and they overlap on significant points to teach us about designing conservation organizations in a rapidly evolving institutional environment. As government power is devolved and dispersed, the kinds of institutional arrangements that trust principles facilitate will become an important part of the conservation agenda. Chapter 12 draws these lessons together, focusing on two general issues. The first has to do with applying trust principles: under what circumstances does it make sense to consider doing so, and what should framers look out for as they move in that direction? The second is concerned with what have we learned about accountability in a hollowed-out state where private entities exercise government authority on their own or in partnership with government agencies. Our goal is to explore the role of trusts and trust principles in that process.

Trusts and fiduciary relationships are the subject of a course typically required in law school and are the focus of an extensive and frequently tedious accumulation of case law and scholarly commentary. Our goal requires that we tread, albeit lightly, into that field. Chapter 2 briefly introduces some basic terms and concepts as they pertain to organizational design.

CHAPTER TWO

The Trust as a Framework
for Institutional Design

We have been clear about what we do not include in our term *conservation trust*. The purpose of this chapter is to provide detailed background on the particular characteristics of the trusts this book explores. Although any treatment of trusts will have a legalistic undertone, this chapter minimizes the legalisms in favor of framing the institutional questions that concern us. The first section introduces some basic terms. They are elaborated in the second section, presenting a stylized, simplified introduction to the legal format of a trust. The third section molds trust terms and principles into the design issues at the heart of the cases.

BASIC TERMS AND CONCEPTS

The trust is a particular species of the fiduciary relationship introduced in chapter 1. Although the trust appears in English common law shortly after the Norman Conquest, it came into prominence in the United States only toward the end of the nineteenth century. Since then, it has developed rapidly, and whenever a trust is established, its operation—particularly the activity of the trustee—is immediately subject to a large body of common and statutory law. Thus, the trust provides a familiar template for arranging ownership, management, and control of resources. Courts have experience in defining and applying trust principles in a variety of contexts. Although that legal framework varies slightly from jurisdiction to jurisdiction, it is possible to make a number of useful generalizations about the rules surrounding a trust and the obligations owed by the trustee to the beneficiary.

A trustee holds and manages property, under exacting rules, for the exclusive benefit of another. The key elements of a trust are the *settlor*, who establishes the trust;[1] the *trust documents*, which define the terms and purpose of the trust; the *trust property* or *corpus*, which includes the money or other resources dedicated by the settlor to the trust purposes; and the *trustee*, frequently a bank or similar professional entity or individual, who is selected by the settlor to manage the corpus, often for a fee, for the exclusive benefit of the designated *beneficiary*. The trustee owes the beneficiary a duty of undivided loyalty. Typically, the trust resources are stocks and bonds, money, or other financial assets, and the trustee must make the resources productive, in monetary terms, to achieve the trust purposes.

In chapter 1 we presented a spectrum of conservation trusts—government, public-private, family, and land trusts—that we use to organize the rest of this volume. These categories may be useful for understanding the role of trust principles in the changing array of government institutions, but they are not standard terms with specific legal meanings. The distinction between charitable and private trusts, however, is defined in statute. A private trust has a private purpose and private beneficiaries, such as the grandmother arranging for the education of her heirs. The beneficiaries are either identified persons, such as "Susan Brown," or persons capable of being identified, such as "the grandchildren of Mary Brown." Most of our discussion centers on variants of the charitable trust, which is the form established if the purpose of the trust is to convey some benefit to society.

Charitable trusts enjoy a number of advantages and privileges, such as exemption from federal and state income taxes. Permitted charitable purposes are therefore of great interest to the IRS and are described in the Internal Revenue Code. Charitable purposes change over time but typically include religious, educational, and cultural goals. Most important for our discussion, public recreation and the conservation of natural resources or scenery are charitable purposes. Even if a charitable trust is established with private resources, by granting tax exemptions, society makes significant contributions to the trust. In validating the creation of a charitable trust, the court weighs the advantages to society expected from the trust against the disadvantages, such as loss of tax revenues, to ensure that the charitable purpose is substantial.

Charitable trusts are distinct from private ones on two key points. The first is the beneficiary. In a charitable trust, no matter what the purpose of the trust is, the general public or some significant portion of it is *always* the beneficiary. For example, if the purpose of a trust is to protect migratory birds, the birds may receive benefit, but they are *not* the beneficiaries; the general public that enjoys the continued existence of the birds is the beneficiary. Unfortunately, the nature of the beneficiary complicates charitable trust enforcement. Members of the general public are generally not allowed to sue to enforce the terms of the trust, as can beneficiaries of a private trust. Because enforcement relies primarily on the state attorney general to take appropriate action, it can be difficult to enforce the terms of a charitable trust. Charitable trusts also differ from private ones in their longevity. Private trusts must terminate; charitable ones can be (but are not necessarily) perpetual.

The government trusts we discuss in Part II are an odd species of trust. The purpose of a government trust is unavoidably charitable. However, as government entities, they do not need protection from state and federal income taxes, and they do not comply with the tax code on these points. They exist in an institutional limbo that also makes the trust terms difficult to enforce. In discussing conservation trusts, we have to evaluate the wisdom of employing a tool with a specific enforcement mechanism and then basically disconnecting it.

TRUST PRINCIPLES

Establishing a trust, private or charitable, is a relatively simple matter, especially compared with the number of forms required to create a 501(c)(3) or the lobbying and drafting that precede the formation of a government agency. A trust comes into existence when three elements are present: a trust property, a beneficiary, and the intent of the owner of the trust property to create a trust. Ideally, a trustee is also identified, but the absence of one does not prevent the establishment of a trust, because the court can appoint one. The issue of whether a private trust exists emerges primarily when someone affected by the presence or absence of a trust raises the issue in court. In the absence of a trust property and beneficiary, it is not possible to have a trust. Charitable trusts differ slightly because courts must approve the creation of each one to ensure that its purpose is charitable and that the anticipated public benefits justify its social costs.

Normally, the settlor goes through requisite formalities, declaring an intent to establish a trust in a written document. However, at least in theory, the formalities can be quite informal. The courts can infer that a trust exists without any documents at all. Even in the absence of a formal statement by the settlor that she intends to start a trust, the court may conclude that one has been established if (1) the other key elements of the trust are present and (2) the behavior of the settlor confirms an intent to create a trust. The issue of the presence or absence of a trust turns on the putative settlor's intent. In current practice, properly prepared trust documents are almost always present. This is particularly true for charitable trusts, in which the courts apply much more exacting standards with regard to the settlor's intent. Some of the trusts we look at are so lightly structured that it is difficult to locate them. However, in only one case, that involving native Hawaiians as beneficiaries, has the existence of the trust been a contentious issue.

Once a trust is established, the rules for trust administration are clear, relatively easily summarized, and focused primarily on ensuring that the trustees do not enrich themselves or others with trust resources but use them exclusively to achieve the purpose of the trust. In order to start bending our discussion of trusts toward institutional design issues, we present six principles of organizational design: clarity, accountability, perpetuity, enforceability, prudence, and changing or terminating a trust.[2]

Clarity

Trust law requires that the purpose of the trust—whether express or implied—be clear and unambiguous. Clarity does not require that the trust purpose be minutely described. Generally, the purpose does not enumerate specific activities that would achieve the trust purposes. The trustees are given discretion to interpret trust purposes in the light of emerging needs and changing conditions.

The core of clarity in both private and charitable trusts is the notion of "undivided loyalty." The trustee is obligated to use and manage trust resources to achieve trust purposes for the *exclusive* benefit of the designated beneficiary. The trustee cannot enrich herself with trust resources and cannot divert trust resources to enhance any interest, no matter how meritorious, to the detriment of the beneficiary. Trustees are not allowed to permit uses of trust resources that do not produce a congruent benefit for the beneficiary.

For more than half a century, political scientists have been observing that, in government organizations, goals are unclear and ambiguous because the political and legislative processes that define them are fragmented and conflicted.[3] In the field of conservation, the trust's rather stark undivided loyalty command has particular appeal when compared with the multiple-use mandate that directs activity in the U.S. Forest Service and the Bureau of Land Management. Both these agencies are required to manage the resources under their authority "in the combination of uses that best meet the needs of the American people."[4] This ambiguous goal gives managers enough discretion to justify almost any judgment made regarding investment of public funds and utilization of public resources. The agencies have long used this flexibility to engage in "below-cost" timber sales, leasing of grazing rights, and the creation of recreation programs—basically subsidizing activities that benefit powerful constituencies and create more jobs and larger budgets for the managers. Such activities would be carefully scrutinized under the undivided loyalty standard of a trust.

While intense scrutiny against a clear standard is a great advantage in the eyes of those who criticize federal land management's "perverse incentives,"[5] trust principles are not an easy sell in the conservation community. Some of the trust's potential appeal is lost because the undivided loyalty principle is normally stated—as are trust principles generally—in terms of compensation, profit, and economic returns. Although the undivided loyalty obligation can work as an antidote to the kinds of political power that grazing lessees and timber purchasers have long enjoyed on federal lands,[6] the problems inherent in applying to ecological conservation a system that has long been viewed as a means of managing money and stocks are not easily resolved. No matter how ecological the trust purpose, productive management of a trust's financial assets is one of the trustee's chief concerns.

Accountability

Trust accountability requirements focus mainly on full disclosure of financial transactions to the beneficiary. Trust principles presume that a trustee knows more than the beneficiary about business and trust affairs. To ensure that the beneficiary has the information necessary to evaluate trustee performance, trust principles obligate the trustee to be completely open and honest in disclosing information to the beneficiary. It is not up to the beneficiary to demonstrate that the trustee has been unfair. The courts, and some state statutes, typically hold that in dealings between the trustee and the beneficiary, the trustee operates under a "rebuttable presumption of fraud or undue influence."[7]

Again, this principle does not translate perfectly from a typical monetary trust into a conservation trust, for several reasons. It is not clear, for example, what kind of information is required to evaluate conservation trustee performance. And given the diffuse nature of conservation trust beneficiaries, to whom should the trustee be disclosing fully? Trust accountability principles emphasize fund management, but the issue of accountability in conservation trusts is far broader. When trustees are spending public funds purposely set outside the normal appropriations process or acting, to a greater or lesser extent, as public entities, the issue of *public* rather than simple fiscal accountability becomes central.

The National Environmental Policy Act (NEPA) defined an approach to accountability that has become familiar in the resources field. It emphasizes public comment on proposed agency actions. How far should public expectations regarding public involvement extend into conservation trust management? In circumstances that resemble NEPA application contexts, it would be politically difficult for the trustee to achieve trust purposes without allowing NEPA-like public involvement. However, when a trust has been established to pursue goals that are not supported by the local power structure, how much public participation is appropriate? Similarly, what kind of public accountability is reasonable when the resources underwriting the trust are primarily private?

Given the rapidly evolving range of institutions implementing government programs, what constitutes public accountability, and how should it be achieved? Our cases offer no single or comprehensive answer. Framers and trustees in various circumstances have addressed this question quite differently. Generally, they have been concerned and imaginative and have built a diverse set of alternatives to the NEPA model for thinking about accountability. At a minimum, it is clear that federal agencies, whose response to the public involvement mandate has been grudging and mechanical, have much to learn from the trustees in several of our case studies.

Perpetuity

Trusts are not normally perpetual. When creating a trust for a grandchild's college fund, for example, there is little reason to extend the trust beyond the beneficiary's matriculation. Perhaps the grandmother might even choose to set a time limit on the trust, requiring the beneficiary to complete college before reaching age thirty or forfeit the financial support.

More significantly, perpetuity is generally eschewed in private trusts on the general theory that land or other real property should not, as a matter of public policy, be tied up indefinitely. The basic idea of what is sometimes discussed in terms of the "dead hand" is that decisions made by individuals or groups long past should not forever constrain choices and resource use by future generations. Early in the development of trust law, principles emerged to limit the amount of time property can be held impervious to transfer. What is known as the rule against perpetuities presents a quandary for conservationists, because the conservation field tends to embrace perpetuity as a goal. Protection has to be perpetual, some suggest, if we are to call it protection at all. Others would argue that protection that is not perpetual is not a good expenditure of public funds. Decisions to develop appear to be perpetual, so why not decisions to protect?

Trust law, as noted earlier, divides private from charitable trusts on this point. A charitable trust is easily exempted from the rule against perpetuities, while a private trust is bound by it. This result does not satisfy if the private trust is conservation oriented, nor does it resolve the basic issues raised by dead-hand questions. Perpetuating a conservationist settlor's best intentions can, as illustrated in several of our case studies, complicate efforts to manage landscapes rather than parcels.

Perpetuity also has a financial component. A perpetual purpose typically requires a perpetual source of income to support it. In response to this need, settlors and framers have with dismaying regularity attempted to conserve the liquid assets of the trust by limiting the financial instruments in which trustees can invest. Laudable though this goal is, such restrictions are frequently counterproductive. Trust assets invested in secure government bonds, and trust funds in which trustees are barred from investing in equities, have tended to lose asset value to inflation. If the trust is intended to be perpetual and a significant portion of the trust resources is monetary, it is important that the trustee's investment strategy not be so constricted that the funds wither due to inflation. This reality has been a problem for many of the conservation trusts we studied, particularly those involving the federal government.

Finally, the issue of whether a particular organization should be perpetual has concerned many of the trusts discussed here. The tendency among conservationists is clearly in favor of perpetual commitments. In some cases, this choice seems prudent. However, those who presume that forever is necessarily better should review several cases in which a perpetual trust may not be in the best interests of conservation.

Enforceability

It is fundamental that the principles we have been discussing—clarity in goals, accountability, and commitment to perpetuity—are not merely hortatory expressions of good intentions. Unlike the "whereases" at the beginning of legislation and the lofty aspirations expressed in memoranda of understanding, trustees' duties are *obligations* that are legally enforceable. The basic format is that the beneficiary is entitled to sue a trustee in order to enforce the principle of undivided loyalty or any other obligation of the trustee. Thus, a trust brings with it a long tradition of close judicial scrutiny. Indeed, the reliance on judicial enforcement is almost unalloyed. For good or ill, those aggrieved by a trustee's decisions cannot typically locate the trustee's superior in some hierarchically arranged organization. Nor is there typically an internal appeal process under which concerned outsiders can or must be given access or a hearing. Trusts are enforceable by beneficiaries in the courts.

For most of the last thirty years, environmental and conservation interests have been well served by judicial review. It is not clear, however, that they should happily anticipate similarly rewarding results of trust enforcement in the conservation organizations evolving under trust principles. First, it is important to note the important role that beneficiaries play in trust enforceability. While barring most outsiders from the enforcement process, trust principles presume that the beneficiary will be willing to review and challenge trustee decisions. An individual member of the public is rarely granted standing to sue for the enforcement of a trust. But when the general public is the beneficiary, as is the case with charitable trusts, trust enforceability becomes complicated. Almost without exception, the attorney general of the relevant state is the "law officer required to protect the people of the state and they are the beneficiaries."[8] In fact, unless provided for in the trust instrument, even the settlor is not entitled to enforce the terms of the trust.

This feature of charitable trusts twists the principle of enforceability somewhat. Instead of having a set of highly interested beneficiaries who could directly challenge the actions of a trustee, most potentially interested parties are held at arm's length. If they become aware of a trust violation, they have to convince the attorney general to challenge the trust. This is true even when the trust is embedded within state or federal agency operations. But the attorney general typically is not a close observer of such trusts. More specifically, any decision to challenge a trust includes an important political calculus.

Enforcement is thus frequently truncated in our conservation trusts. The issue is a real concern, and although several of the conservation trusts have been quite innovative, our case studies provide more cautionary tales than success stories.

Prudence

Prudence is a key element in trustee decision making. Currently applicable notions of prudence emphasize risk management. In a financial context, prudence requires diversification of trust resources and analysis of the degree of risk that is appropriate, given the goals of the trust.[9] Because so many conservation trusts are dependent on the management of trust funds to achieve trust purposes, these financially based standards are entirely relevant. Again, however, determining whether they adequately encompass all facets of conservation trust management is a major concern. When evaluating a trustee's decisions, the courts have used a standard of prudent behavior, sometimes called the prudent man or prudent investor rule.

We encounter the notion of prudence most frequently in the context of *political* prudence. Trustees must create or sustain a political environment in which they can function and carry out trust purposes. Frequently, the trust has been established because the political environment is hostile to the purposes of the trust. Particularly under those circumstances, it is not always possible to distinguish between political prudence and the bending of trust purposes to meet the priorities of powerful stakeholders. Prudence becomes a difficult concept, easiest to identify in the breach, when trustees are pursuing activities that seem imprudent. Frequently, it appears that trust principles simply add vocabulary options to standard political battles: advocates displeased with a trust activity are likely to argue that it violates the trust. The notion of prudence, however, provides a framework for identifying the risks and benefits of options and for analyzing compromises. Highly politicized boards do not take full advantage of trust principles in all instances, but they can have a stabilizing effect on the debate.

Changing a Trust

Although a trust comes into existence relatively easily, once established, it is difficult to change. The terms of the trust cannot be altered by the trustee, the settlor, *or* the beneficiary unless the trust agreement includes specific directions for doing so. The basic rule, absent such provisions in the trust document, is that only a court can modify the terms of a trust. These modifications might be made on application from the beneficiary, the trustee, or any combination of the parties, usually the trustee and the beneficiary jointly.

Changing the trust may become significant when, with the passage of time, the trust purpose becomes impossible to achieve, is no longer relevant, or has already been achieved.[10] What then happens to the trust corpus? Even when the trust instrument gives the trustee power to change elements of the organization, it does not always extend to significant alterations in trust purposes or structure. Indeed, the emphasis appears to be more in the opposite direction: the trust is used specifically as an instrument to bind future trustees to the intent of the settlor or framer. One would not likely set up a trust if one were willing to see it change fundamentally every time the trustee considered it politically prudent to do so.

There is one cumbersome and not wholly reliable way out. Under what is called the cy pres doctrine, the court has the authority to address issues similar to those discussed in the context of the rule against perpetuities. This doctrine gives the court enormous discretion to redesign a trust to satisfy the settlor's intent in light of changed circumstances. For example, if a settlor provides that a gift is to be used for a specific charitable organization that ceases to exist, the court may refuse to apply cy pres and allow the settlor's residual heirs to inherit the resources. Or it may invoke the doctrine and cause the trust resources to pass to another similarly situated organization. To illustrate, an early case involved a trust created to support activism intended to end slavery. When slavery was abolished, the court approved changing the focus of the trust from abolition activities to the education and aid of ex-slaves. This change occurred over the objections of the residual heir, who had sued to claim the assets of the trust. A similar case involved a bequest intended to establish a home for deaf children on the testator's land. Because the fund was not adequate to accomplish that goal, the court allowed the trust to be used to support a similar home already operating nearby.[11] The notion of cy pres allows the courts to move the margins slightly to adapt old purposes to new realities or to correct imperfections in the trust that prevent the achievement of the settlor's goals.

A SPECTRUM OF CONSERVATION TRUSTS

Trust principles are clear and coherent over time and across many state and local jurisdictions. Nevertheless, all trusts are not the same, largely because trust principles are used in a wide range of situations. While the basic template is well understood, settlors and framers have enormous discretion to fill in the gaps with their own priorities. This is in part the charm of trust principles as an organizing tool. They fit well into many niches in the changing mix of public and private conservation institutions. The results of their application are diverse: not every trust resembles what might be called a classic trust. The conservation trusts we examine have been founded in a number of diverse settings to achieve myriad purposes and serve very different beneficiaries. The trusts have also organized themselves along a number of different lines—some emphasizing a heavy investment in scientific and professional staff, others choosing to rely on volunteers, and some, particularly family trusts, having no staff at all.

Our stories emphasize the founding context of each trust. Trusts are formed in four different contexts. First, trust instruments are frequently used to resolve public conflict. Typically, these trusts are defined in litigation or during negotiations on legislation. One characteristic of these trusts is that opposing parties in a dispute wind up working together, with more or less success, to run the resulting organization. These trusts also tend to be responsible for public funds and therefore have significant, although not always clearly defined or addressed, responsibilities for public accountability.

Second, some trusts are philanthropic in origin. A benefactor works to protect a particular piece of property or uses a nonprofit's "planned giving" program to create support for specific organizations or programs.

Third, trusts are frequently used to manage resources available under diverse mitigation programs. As a result of either a statutory requirement that developers contribute money or set aside land or a privately negotiated agreement between developers and their opponents, land or money becomes available to mitigate the impacts of development.

Fourth, some trusts are created to help families make decisions about their land. While these are private trusts, they are generally intended to prevent the conversion of family farms or woodlots. Although occasionally a family owns and protects a major holding, more typically, family trusts are important because family lands are an important element of a landscape. Because private trusts cannot be perpetual, the families in our cases have frequently used conservation easements, which are perpetual, to achieve both continued family use and access and perpetual restrictions on subdivision.

As the diversity of founding contexts suggests, trusts are established for an impressive variety of purposes. Most of the trusts we explore have as their primary purpose the protection of biological resources—wetland, forested, and freshwater ecosystems. However, we also discuss a government trust in Hawaii intended to use trust land to "rehabilitate" native Hawaiians and the enormous trust established after the *Exxon Valdez* disaster to restore the oil-spill area. The beneficiaries of these trusts are almost always the general public, even though the injured birds, fish, and habitat define the trust purpose and are the focus of trust activities.

It is perhaps surprising that many of the trustees we studied appear to be only dimly aware, if at all, of their formal obligations as trustees. While some of the trusts have built organizational cultures around clearly articulated trust principles, others have ignored them almost entirely. Several appear to be wrestling with the meaning of their trust structures many years after their founding.

Our conservation trusts have also taken very different approaches to configuring themselves as organizations. All the trustees we encountered pursue their trustee duties as a small part of their lifework. Yet managing an organization, and the funds that support it, is a major task in the best of circumstances. The conservation trusts have generally relied on dedicated staff to develop and implement programs and manage day-to-day affairs. Voluntary trustees cannot devote the necessary time to such activities. But staff are expensive and require wages, benefits, office space, and equipment. The staff must be appropriate to the organization's tasks and to the revenue and other resources available to the trust.

Trustees have answered the staff question differently. Some have not hesitated in immediately hiring full-time staff. Others have "borrowed" public agency staff or relied on volunteers. Frequently, the trustees have taken an incremental approach, starting by depending heavily on government agencies involved in the trust, or on volunteers, and moving gradually to a more professional staff. The shift provides continuity and some distance from the organizations that serve as framers, but not always a close adherence to trust basics.

It is not our purpose to campaign for or against the establishment of conservation trusts. Nevertheless, we believe that trust principles have an important role to play in the devolution and dispersion of public authority. Their most important virtue in filling that role is the familiarity of trust principles. Something that has been around since the Norman Conquest has been adequately field-tested and is familiar to a broad variety of decision makers, courts, lawyers, citizens, landowners, and potential participants. We think that this broad familiarity and acceptability are important advantages in the unfamiliar terrain of hollowing out government.

Broad familiarity is accompanied by simplicity. Although, as we shall see, it is possible to forget or ignore trust principles, they are not complex. Working out their application requires attention and effort, but the basic ideas are easy to understand and discuss. Furthermore, it is probably easier to establish a trust than to establish any other organizational entity, and the common law of the trust also provides a default position for almost any question that the framers fail to address or address inadequately.

This suggests, correctly, that the trust is also flexible—it can be adapted to fit almost any circumstance. The stories we tell suggest that the trust model can be applied to create an organization out of a collection of bureaucrats, opposing parties in litigation, neighboring landowners, or a mixed group of cousins, bureaucrats, neighbors, and other interested public and private parties with a shared concern—though not necessarily a shared perspective—regarding a resource. Trust notions seem ideally suited to an era of third-party government.

It is also true, we believe, that the trust instrument is not wholly neutral as to management. Just as a corporation invites and requires its directors to make a profit, and a government agency suggests to its leadership that budget maintenance and agency autonomy are key goals, the trust instrument has a built-in agenda. It aims the trustees in the general direction of guardianship and conservative management of both natural and financial resources. This bias in the direction of sustainable management strikes us as a benefit when seeking an institutional frame for a conservation organization.

Trusts are not ideal in every way. There are several problems inherent in the trust concept that ought to cause potential framers at least a few sleepless nights. One recurring problem is that trusts are so easy to establish that the risk of doing it badly, without proper planning, is high. Second, trust accountability mechanisms based on the idea that the beneficiary wants money may not fit with conservation purposes. It is important to pay attention to the issues of accountability in the absence of generally accepted yardsticks that measure progress toward ecological goals. Similarly, trust enforcement presumes an attentive, aggressive beneficiary. When a trust's purpose is to protect migratory birds or fish-spawning habitat, it is important to think about a procedure for alerting the general public, or some attentive subset thereof, to act in the traditional role of an aggrieved beneficiary for trust enforcement purposes.

In the cases that follow, we identify pros and cons of establishing a conservation trust—circumstances in which it makes sense to consider establishing a trust, what framers should look out for as they move in that direction, and where trust principles seem inappropriate. We begin with what might be considered a "best-case" analysis—an organization in which a clearly articulated trust framework works well.

CHAPTER THREE

Platte River Whooping Crane Maintenance Trust: A Classic Trust

The Platte River Whooping Crane Critical Habitat Maintenance Trust (PRT) was formed during an archetypal environmental dispute of the 1970s—the Grayrocks Dam controversy. This major water development project—providing both irrigation and hydropower—was temporarily halted by standard-setting litigation. As the Grayrocks case went forward on appeal, all the parties were motivated, each by the pinch of their own particular shoe, to negotiate a settlement that permitted the construction of the project and the formation of the trust. The PRT was a key element in the first congressional amendments to the Endangered Species Act (ESA) and was the first permanent exemption granted by the resulting Endangered Species Committee, commonly known as the God Squad.

We begin our discussion of conservation trusts with the PRT for two reasons. First, despite its contentious origins, the PRT embodies in easily recognizable form most of the trust features and principles discussed in chapter 2. Second, we believe that trust principles—in particular, continuing trustee and staff efforts to develop and maintain a strong connection to the trustees' obligations—are an important element of the PRT's considerable success. Two decades after its founding, this combination of state, corporate, and private entities has become an effective organization. It is widely acknowledged to be the premier expert on Platte River ecology, and it has become one of the few effective environmental groups in the region. In addition, the trustees have carefully nurtured the corpus, while supporting a large staff and a major research program. Created in 1978 with a $7.5 million endowment, the trust's assets have more than tripled. The PRT is an uplifting point of embarkation for an exploration of the utility of trust principles in an era of devolution and dispersion of government authority.

Our discussion has two major parts. The first describes the ecological and social context and the founding of the trust. In the second, we examine the structure, history, and activities of the trust. We follow the format

Research forming the backbone of this chapter is reported in Darla Guenzler, "The Use of a Charitable Trust Instrument to Conserve Biological Diversity: The Platte River Whooping Crane Maintenance Trust" (Master's thesis, University of California–Berkeley, 1997).

established in chapter 2 fairly closely in order to indicate how the trust elements described in the abstract actually fit together on the ground. The PRT, we conclude, is an important combination of public and private organizational elements. During a period when advocates are loudly proclaiming the virtues of one over the other, the role of trust principles in shaping an organization that effectively combines both public and private is worth attention.

PRT'S FOUNDING CONTEXT

First and foremost, the Platte is a working river—70 percent of its water is diverted for agricultural and municipal uses. State-level decision makers have historically opposed actions that might affect commercial uses of the river, including nearly all programs that could be characterized as environmental protection. Local conservation organizations simply did not exist at the time of the Grayrocks dispute, and few national groups or agencies were actively involved in the area. But in addition to its economic importance, the Central Platte area is a valuable ecological resource. It is the key component of the Central Flyway, a migratory route between the breeding grounds of the Northern and Southern Hemispheres. Tens of millions of birds—more than 300 species—travel this route, including four-fifths of the world's sandhill cranes and 7 million to 9 million ducks and geese. Perhaps more important, at least to the PRT's founding, is a bird that is rarely there: the Central Platte is critical habitat for the endangered, nearly extinct, whooping crane.

In the absence of conservation advocates, water disputes in the area have typically been among rival diverters, not between environmentalists and developers. Wyoming, Colorado, and Nebraska have been fighting over water in the Platte and its tributaries for nearly a century. The U.S. Supreme Court ostensibly resolved the dispute in the 1950s "North Platte Decree," which apportioned water among the states for many years. The management scheme actually worked against Nebraska farmers. When the Platte is low, groundwater naturally drains into the river, depleting the amount available for pumped withdrawal. This means that maintaining a higher annual mean flow benefits both wildlife and Nebraska farmers.

It was generally recognized by the mid-1970s that the cumulative effect of diversions was altering the ecological character of the Platte, and two environmentally oriented organizations—one private, one federal—became active in the area. The National Audubon Society established a small sanctuary in 1973 with an initial purchase of nearly 800 acres. Further Audubon efforts were limited to parcels adjacent to or near the first property. It did not attempt a broader Platte land protection program. After listing the whooping crane as endangered, the U.S. Fish and Wildlife Ser-

The Central Flyway corridor is shaped like an hourglass. The Central Platte area occupies the waistline position and is therefore disproportionately important. (Cartographer: Darla Guenzler)

vice (FWS) also took steps to acquire land for a wildlife refuge along the Central Platte. The attempt failed and proved so politically disastrous that the FWS was almost literally run out of the area. Interviews conducted nearly thirty years later reveal continuing strong resentment and fear of the agency's regulatory and condemnation powers.[1]

As the FWS's efforts to acquire land for a Platte River refuge withered in the mid-1970s, concerned agency employees held a briefing in Washington, D.C. National Wildlife Federation (NWF) representatives left the gathering determined to do something about the Platte. The NWF soon chose the Grayrocks dam project as a place to draw the line and to focus attention on the destruction of Platte River habitat. The environmentalists' challenge was, ironically, abetted by Nebraska's concern that the proposed Grayrocks project would disrupt the state's agricultural water supply.

The Grayrocks Litigation

Grayrocks was part of the enormous Missouri Basin Power Project (MBPP) proposed by a consortium of six utilities. The project included a coal-fired power plant, a dam, and a reservoir. Although the MBPP would be built and owned by all six consumer-owned power companies, Basin Electric Power Cooperative (Basin) was the project manager and took the lead in the litigation and negotiations. In February 1972, the formal planning process started, and by mid-1974, Basin had begun the complex processes of securing forty-three state and federal permits. When the final environmental impact statement was released in May 1976, project proponents began construction, and opponents quickly lined up.

The plaintiffs were an odd collection. Grayrocks was, from the state of Nebraska's point of view, simply one more skirmish in the decades-old battle over Platte River water. Ironically, given Nebraska's water use priorities, the state used newly enacted environmental laws to attack the project. In a separate suit, later joined with the state's, the NWF took the lead representing four groups from the project area.[2] While construction proceeded, the district court deliberated. In October 1978, it held for the plaintiffs on all key points.[3] Project proponents were stupefied. Grayrocks was among the first cases to focus on cumulative effects under the National Environmental Policy Act (NEPA) and the ESA requirements for consultation with the FWS. Basin immediately appealed.

As it turned out, the legal victory put the NWF in almost as uncomfortable a position as the losers. The court's decision shut down the largest construction project in the world at the time and weighed heavily in a growing backlash against the ESA. The Grayrocks case closely followed the Tellico Dam (snail darter) controversy[4] and heightened sentiments in Congress in favor of dismantling the ESA. Having no chance to bask in its victory, the NWF encountered the wrath of environmentalists. It needed to settle the Grayrocks case, by then on appeal, before Congress found an answer that would destroy the ESA.

The Settlement

Immediately after the district court decision, a Wyoming congressman proposed legislation to amend the ESA, exempt the entire MBPP development from its provisions, and nullify the court order. Five days after it was introduced, the bill passed in the House. Legislative action was temporarily slowed in the Senate, and the parties turned with urgency to negotiating a settlement. Within two weeks, the three major parties to the Grayrocks litigation—Basin, the NWF, and Nebraska—had agreed to establish a trust to protect Platte River habitat for migratory birds.

The basics of the trust rapidly took shape, but all three parties had significant and conflicting priorities for the new organization. Although it had relied on new environmental legislation, Nebraska was concerned only about water supply for irrigation. The state focused on elements of the settlement concerning management of the reservoir and water flows. The NWF had two goals. The first was to gain greater protection of the Central Flyway area of the Platte River. Less obviously, it wanted an organization with a full-time presence on the river that could nurture popular support for the Platte. Recently burned, Basin feared creating a "litigating monster" that could derail power development throughout the United States and Canada. The power company insisted on confining the trust's activities to a narrow geographic area and limiting its ability to engage in litigation.

The parties reached a settlement before the U.S. Court of Appeals for the Eighth Circuit heard Basin's appeal. The litigants lightly embellished familiar contours of trust principles to meet their particular institutional goals. One part of the settlement obligated the MBPP to establish a trust fund of $7.5 million to protect habitat for the whooping crane and other migratory waterfowl. The court's approval of the agreement was conditioned on the project's receiving an exemption from the ESA. Congress barely had time to complete ESA amendments that would make that possible. The God Squad, which the amendments created, granted its first exemption to the Grayrocks project.[5] The court dismissed the case, and the PRT was officially established.

TRUST FRAMEWORK AND ACTIVITIES

In spite of the contentious setting in which the trust idea was introduced, negotiation of the trust document was fast and relatively amicable. In part, this speedy resolution was possible because trust principles define so much of what might have been controversial.[6] Indeed, although the provisions of the document are obviously of great significance, it is important to observe elements that fall into place without specific mention simply because of common understandings surrounding a trust. Also, because the declaration encouraged the trustees to incorporate as a 501(c)(3) organization, a typical practice for conservation trusts, a number of issues about trustee liability, trust termination, and trust activities were resolved without further ado in the document itself.

Purpose

The trust declaration clearly and concisely defines the PRT's purpose: to finance programs, activities, and acquisitions to protect and maintain the physical, hydrological, and biological integrity of the Big Bend area so that it may continue to function as a life-support system for the whooping crane and other migratory species that use it.[7] The purpose is quite broad, cast in terms of landscape ecology. But it is clear—we know what the trust is supposed to do. We also know where it is supposed to do it: PRT operations are limited geographically.[8] As noted, Basin wanted to keep the trust focused.[9]

Beneficiary

The PRT's purpose is to protect migratory birds and habitat. Although it sounds like the birds are the beneficiary, as noted in chapter 2, this is technically incorrect. Because the PRT is a charitable trust, the general public is the beneficiary. The birds are merely the intermediaries through which the benefit to the public is realized. This legal point is necessary because the trustees are required to act with undivided loyalty to the beneficiary. However, they also need decision rules that allow them to frame alternatives and make choices. Trustees and observers find it most useful to focus on the cranes when planning trust activities.

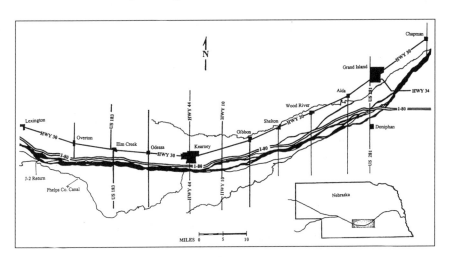

The trust declaration clearly confines the organization's activities to an eighty-mile stretch of the Big Bend area on the Platte River between Overton and Chapman, Nebraska. (Source: Platte River Whooping Crane Maintenance Trust, Inc., "The Platte River Whooping Crane Maintenance Trust, Inc.: The First Ten Years, 1979–1989" [Grand Island, Nebr., 1989], 11–12; courtesy Darla Guenzler)

Trust Property

Any trust, by definition, starts with property that the trustees manage for the benefit of others. The PRT was established with a lump-sum payment of $7.5 million from the water project cooperators. The fact that the court approved the settlement provided some leverage if the promised resources had not been forthcoming from the power consortium. This may sound obvious, but for those establishing a trust, a mechanism to ensure that the settlors will pay up is a good place to start. Not all the trusts in this volume have been so well positioned.

The trust declaration allows the trustees to pursue returns as would any reasonable and prudent investor.[10] The framers directed the trustees to achieve "as high and as steady an annual income as may prudently be obtained."[11] "High" and "steady" are not, of course, the same thing—the freedom granted in the declaration to the trustees is not license to invest speculatively. But the freedom to balance risk and return, rather than simply avoid risk, is a crucial element of the PRT's success. Although this also may seem obvious, it is more typical to burden trustees of charitable trusts with conservative investment restrictions.

Trustees

The PRT declaration is typical in that it says relatively little about the trustees. What it does say, however, is critical. Each of the three major parties to the litigation—Basin, Nebraska, and the NWF—appoints one trustee,[12] for a total of three. The original litigants thus retain a continuing role in the organization. And because the agreement defines no term of office, the trustees serve at the pleasure of the organization that appointed them and can be removed. The trustees receive no compensation from the trust (except for expenses incurred in attending biannual meetings). This suggests that the trustees provide direction, not hands-on management. This arrangement forces trustees to choose between extremely restricted activities and hiring a staff to run the programs.

Although this format for appointing trustees seemed almost natural for the PRT, creating an organization that relies almost exclusively on the goodwill of former opponents in a protracted conflict is not always a wise idea. Once the litigants choose the original trustees, it is not necessary to have them continue to select the board of trustees. In many of the organizations we explore, the board itself is responsible for recruiting new members. Authorizing elected officials—in this case, the governor of Nebraska—to appoint trustees, especially when the trustees have no specified term of office, is not a mandatory approach either. The appointing organizations' tendency to want the trustees to represent their own interests is perhaps most notable in the case of newly elected governors, who may use the appointment as a small political reward, but it is not confined to them. Returning to the protagonists for new trustees could also perpetuate conflict in the new organization, hindering the creation of a new and possibly fruitful consensus.

Although the PRT approach has potential problems, it is not antithetical to trust principles, and in practice, it has created real benefits. Having trustees responsive to diverse political interests or elected officials can be an effective means of creating trust accountability. However, especially when elected officials appoint trustees, there is a danger of compromising the trustee's undivided loyalty to the beneficiary or politicizing the trust. Preventing random removal of trustees by establishing a fixed term of office is one way to address this possibility. Apparently preferring a representation and accountability emphasis, the PRT framers did not do so.

Identifying particular trustee qualifications—such as knowledge of the issues or expertise in specified fields—is also a familiar feature of many boards. Trusts frequently find it helpful to establish formal or informal guidelines to include a lawyer or someone with financial management experience. With or without designated expertise, geographic origins, or similar qualifications, the ideal trustee should have some interest in and knowledge about an issue. Locating such persons without strong personal stakes or biases that could create a conflict of interest is a significant challenge. Here again, the PRT declaration is silent, allowing the three appointing organizations great latitude in selecting trustees.

Trustee selection has not been a problem for the PRT. Trustees have included a bank president, the general manager of Basin, the president of the NWF, an ex-governor, a former state and federal legislator, and a rancher of statewide esteem. Trustees have brought crucial knowledge to the board, such as expertise in financial management, legal knowledge, and understanding of the basin's water rights history, legislation, and policy. But each has also made a conscious effort to act as a trustee. PRT trustees have understood the nature of the fiduciary relationship and the duties that flow from it. They have been diligent regarding the duty of undivided loyalty. The trustees have made difficult decisions, such as pursuing litigation, with which they personally disagreed but which they believed were required by their obligation as trustees. One trustee with a development background reported telling himself as he drove to each of the meetings, "Now remember, you're an environmentalist. Let's be a good one." In spite of the risks surrounding the appointment process, the board has been very stable, with only eight trustees serving in the trust's twenty-year history (an average tenure of 6.75 years).

The successful functioning of the PRT trustees has not just been a fortunate happenstance dictated by their estimable personal characteristics.

Two additional factors have been important in creating the PRT's strong trust culture: acculturation efforts made by existing board and staff, and the role played by the appointing organizations in trust affairs. The trustees and staff have worked hard to familiarize new trustees and staff with trustee duties and PRT programs. Although much information is conveyed informally by the existing trustees, orientation of new trustees is specifically a responsibility of the executive director. Each new trustee receives a written description of charitable trusts and the trustee's duties and responsibilities. This was particularly important when the organization was starting out, when the first director routinely spent a day briefing each new trustee about the PRT's history, activities, and projects.

A second, easily overlooked, factor concerns the trustee's ongoing relationship with the appointing organization. Given the nature of its beneficiary, the PRT cannot rely for accountability on the aggressive involvement of either the birds or the general public, as is anticipated in normal trust operations. The continuing relationship with diverse founders plays an important role in trust operations. For example, it is not only the trustees that come and go. The individuals from the three organizations that appoint trustees also change. The trust needs to keep the appointing authorities informed about trust purposes and the role of the trustees. Nevertheless, the trustee is specifically not the appointer's representative, nor should the trustee "answer to" the appointing authority. The PRT reflects two models of continuing relationships. The NWF and the Nebraska governor informally communicate with the trustees they have appointed. The NWF is most interested in any trust actions that have basinwide or national significance, while the state is interested primarily in water issues. Even on these topics, communication typically occurs informally by phone calls between the trustee and a representative of the appointing organization. In contrast, the Basin-appointed trustee makes both an oral and a written report to the annual meeting of the MBPP. Interestingly, the PRT staff prepares the report, primarily a review of its activities for that year.

Balancing this delicate mix of priorities is a continuing challenge. Although the governor of Nebraska has removed trustees for explicitly political reasons and some appointments have been intensely controversial,[13] it is not clear what this has meant to PRT operations. The PRT framers established a system under which opposing parties in litigation selected a small number of trustees with no parameters to guide their selection. Emphasizing the board itself as a mechanism of accountability creates some risks. However, the trustees have worked as an effective team in a tense and polarized political arena. In this case, their success appears to depend in part on careful and constant reiteration of their basic obligations.

As noted in chapter 2, regardless of the type of trust or contents of the trust declaration, all trustees are subject to general trust principles. Like most trust instruments, the PRT document does not mention them. It does, however, include a standard list of general authorities appropriate to land and financial management responsibilities that is worth reviewing. The trustees may, for example, accept real, personal, or mixed property by gift, bequest, or devise. They can hold, sell, lease, or exchange this property in any way, so long as it does not violate the terms of the trust declaration.[14] The document focuses on duties particular to its purpose. Reflecting Basin's concerns, the trust document forbids the organization to engage in "litigation other than litigation directly related to the administration of the Trust."[15] Nevertheless, in general, the declaration gives the trustees broad discretion to carry out "projects and activities for the protection and maintenance of the Big Bend Area."[16] These activities include, but are not limited to, "management of the critical crane habitat, the acquisition of land or interests in land, the conduct of scientific studies of whooping cranes and of critical crane habitat on the Platte River, as well as the acquisition of all types of rights in or to water or water storage."[17]

In addition, the document requires the trustees to undertake three specific actions: (1) develop a written habitat monitoring plan that describes "changes in riparian, wetland, and island habitat within the Big Bend area of the Platte River and other segments of the Platte River utilized by sandhill and whooping cranes near Lewellen and Sutherland, Nebraska"; (2) achieve that goal "under the supervision of a technical steering committee comprised of qualified ecologists and water resources specialists selected by the Trustees"; and (3) "prepare habitat monitoring reports for public distribution on a regular basis."[18]

Staffing

These mandatory activities have shaped trustee decisions about staff. The trustees began by contracting with a consultant to develop the plan. As the organization progressed, however, the trustees hired an executive director and additional staff who took over development and implementation of the plan. Meeting only twice a year, the trustees depend heavily on the executive director to initiate proposals and provide substantive guidance. The executive director is presently assisted by seven full-time personnel and undertakes tasks such as conceptualizing and drafting organizational policies, crafting budgets, advancing programs, and presenting and recommending specific acquisitions. As a matter of law, all responsibility ultimately rests with the trustees; in practice, the executive director is in charge. The creation of an organization with staff and a conservation presence in the Platte region comports with the NWF's goals for the organization.

Several other factors have combined to push the PRT in the direction of building a highly trained scientific and research staff. The first is the declaration's requirement for a habitat monitoring plan. This necessitated access to scientific information and expertise. The trustees accordingly selected an executive director who believed in the persuasiveness of scientific information, confident that "if you put the numbers out there where people can see them, then they will change their behavior." He urged the hiring of a scientific staff, which in turn developed an aggressive research program. The present executive director was previously the trust's plant and wetlands ecologist. The current PRT staff includes a plant and wetlands ecologist, an avian ecologist, and an aquatic ecologist.

The scientific emphasis is also a matter of prudence: faced with the residue of a bitter and continuing conflict over water and with obligations to monitor, manage, and restore habitat, the trustees were attracted to the relatively noncontroversial nature of "doing research" and allowing research to guide their decisions. Heavy investment in science helps shield the trustees from the political fray—they can stand above politics and make decisions according to science.

Nonprofit Status

The trust document urges the trustees to incorporate as a nonprofit corporation and prohibits the trustees from undertaking activities that would threaten its tax-exempt status.[19] The trustees formed the Platte River Whooping Crane Maintenance Trust, Incorporated, which holds all PRT assets. As discussed in chapter 2, the formation of a nonprofit corporation answers a number of questions—such as what to do with the assets of the trust if it should cease to exist—and limits the liability of the trustees for trust debts. The document also defines, in a general sense, trust activities and underwrites the trustees' emphasis on science. As a 501(c)(3) organization, the trust is strictly limited in its ability to influence legislation or participate or intervene in any political campaign.

Amendments

The PRT trust declaration is rather generous in granting broad authority concerning amendments. The framers contemplated a perpetual trust, and the document allows the trustees to make an unlimited number of amendments *if* they are in unanimous agreement. However, when trustees propose to amend trust purposes or provisions about trustee appointment and duties, written approval from each of the framers is required. The trustees exercised their amendment power in 1980,[20] seeking and receiving the approval of all the framers.

Most of the new language appears to reflect a settling-in process. For example, early expectations were that the trust program would rely on proposals from the FWS and the Nebraska Game and Parks Department. When the trustees decided to develop their own staff and programs, the declaration was amended to emphasize "consultation" with appropriate organizations. Another modification altered the declaration's strictures regarding permanent invasion of the initial principal. Initially permitted to do so by unanimous vote, the trustees restricted themselves to paying back any invasion of principal and formalized that conclusion in the trust declaration.

Accountability

Accountability is a special challenge for charitable trusts. The cranes have proved uninterested in reviewing balance sheets—they frequently leave town for extended periods when the books are presented for comment. In fact, the PRT makes no routine or annual reports to any public official or to the general public.[21] Accordingly, in the PRT context, trust accountability has focused on two elements: the continuing involvement of the framers and the attorney general.

As noted in chapter 2, the settlor is usually obliged to step aside once a trust is established. Accountability then focuses on the relationship between the trustee and the beneficiary. Because the PRT framers have a continuing role in trust matters, accountability relies in part on a balance among the three original litigants. Trust principles draw the court into accountability issues as well. Again, the charitable trust differs from the basic trust model in important ways. Due to its public purposes, the state attorney general, not the beneficiary, has responsibility for enforcing the terms of charitable trusts.

In the PRT's experience, that reliance on an elected official has probably been more abused than the framers' continuing role in trustee appointments. In spite of Basin's efforts to limit the PRT's authority to litigate, the trustees successfully petitioned to file an amicus curiae in a case involving water issues that affected Central Platte habitat. The PRT also became involved in a Federal Energy Regulatory Commission relicensing process for the McConaughy Reservoir, Nebraska's primary water storage facility. The attorney general, who was up for reelection at the time, questioned whether the trustees were violating the terms of the trust declaration limiting the PRT's authority to litigate. The trustees countered that Platte water management was central to trust purposes. The district court agreed with the trustees,[22] and on appeal, so did the Eighth Circuit Court.

The PRT is notable for the extent to which it has chosen not to involve the general public in its activities. The trustees have made a perhaps surprising decision regarding the trust's relationship to its political environment: they have not sought or encouraged interaction with the public. They generally hold their meetings in executive session with only the staff and invited guests present.

Activities

Although the trust document and trust principles were pivotal in the PRT's development, a brief look at what the trust actually does underscores the importance of operational flexibility. Because the trustees meet only twice a year, day-to-day trust programs are largely designed and implemented by staff, who are not specifically mentioned in the declaration. This too is standard, but it is important to connect the trust document and principles to trust activities.

Although pursuing financial returns is not the primary purpose of the trust, it is important. The PRT depends for operating expenses on the income from the trust corpus rather than on grants, research contracts, membership drives, or bake sales.[23] A crucial element of the trustees' success has been the discretion granted by the trust declaration. It contains virtually no restrictions—beyond the trustees' fundamental obligation to proceed with prudence—on investment policy. Soon after establishing operations, the trustees developed a general investment policy to guide corpus management. Although the funds continue to be the central element of the corpus, almost twenty years later, the trust assets have expanded to include nearly 10,000 acres of land. The trust also owns several buildings that house its offices and an assortment of vehicles, tractors, and office equipment.

Most of the trustees have been successful businessmen inclined to take a businesslike approach to their responsibilities. In 1981, they adopted objectives and policies intended to translate the broad trust purposes into a guide for short- and long-term trust activities. Prudently, the trust's working policies and objectives have put major emphasis on the latter. Trust goals include maintaining agricultural and other traditional uses of the land and demonstrating that wildlife habitat is compatible with sound agricultural practices. These priorities reflect the notion of political prudence discussed in chapter 2. The trust will continue to exist in an agricultural setting and cannot protect adequate habitat without demonstrating that doing so is consistent with profitable agriculture.

Scientific activities have been the PRT's primary focus. The trustees have funded numerous staff studies of topics such as habitat requirements of waterfowl, aquatic organisms, and wet meadow invertebrates; species diversity; and water flow regimes. The research influences their management decisions and informs their habitat restoration activities, such as prescribed burns and habitat creation. Staff members have generated dozens of articles and a book entitled *Migratory Bird Habitat on the Platte and North Platte Rivers in Nebraska,* which served as the staff's first status report.[24] Trust research is respected by scientists and credible in public debate. Trust research and recommendations have been included in the Platte River Management Joint Study and cited by the Nebraska Department of Games and Parks' petition for in-stream water rights. The courts have relied on the trust's information in decisions concerning the relicensing of McConaughy Dam by the Federal Energy Regulatory Commission. Curiously, perhaps, all research funding comes from trust income; the staff does not seek funds from public agencies or private foundations. Even when the PRT is engaged in other activities, its demeanor is scientific. The organization sees itself and is perceived by others as being the expert on Platte River ecology and hydrology. The emphasis on research is unlikely to change.

The other major PRT activity is habitat acquisition. In all, the trust has purchased approximately 7,600 acres in fee simple and owns perpetual easements on another 2,000 acres. The PRT's acquisition program is guided by its research. The staff divided the eighty-mile Big Bend stretch of the Platte River into ten subunits, with the goal of building a habitat complex of at least 2,000 acres in each area. Work proceeds slowly because all sales are on a willing-seller basis and because few properties with potential habitat value are available for purchase.

The trustees completed about 90 percent of their acquisitions before 1993. They then concluded that further acquisitions were not prudent. Until the water management system on the Platte is modified, they reasoned, habitat values would continue to decline no matter who owned the land. The trustees also concluded that most of the valuable habitat likely to come on the market had already been sold, and it would be some years before another generation of sellers entered the market. The lull in the acquisition program lasted until almost the end of the 1990s. At this writing, the trustees are again pursuing land acquisitions.

The PRT is unusual in that the trustees have chosen to manage the land acquired. The trust leases portions of its property for crop production or grazing. This meets three objectives established early in trust development. First, harvested corn and hay fields are a food source for the cranes and a buffer for more sensitive areas. Second, lease earnings are an important part of the trust's annual income. Finally, the acquisitions allow the trust to demonstrate that agricultural production is compatible with the conservation of wildlife. In addition, the lands have evolved into demonstration areas for innovative restoration practices developed by the PRT: the trust reintroduced fire, actively disks the islands and sandbars to control vegetation, and has restored some agricultural fields to grasslands and wet meadows. Others have adopted some of these activities. For example, farmers now burn unwanted vegetation, and both Audubon and the Nature Conservancy disk river channels using PRT equipment and skilled staff.[25]

The trustees have joined selected litigation to fulfill the obligations created by the trust declaration. This has, as noted earlier, occasionally had serious repercussions for the trust. For example, when the trustees successfully petitioned to join a particularly controversial lawsuit, the governor removed the trustee who had served as president since the PRT's inception. Nevertheless, the PRT was involved as a party in the relicensing process of the McConaughy Dam and Reservoir. This massive project is upstream of the Big Bend stretch of the Platte River. When the process began, the trust offered assistance in calculating the necessary flows and release patterns to support the downstream habitat requirements, but it was refused. Subsequently, the trust filed suit and became deeply involved in litigation. However, when the court held that environmental impacts had to be considered in the granting of interim permits, the litigation evolved into a data war that continues to engage trust staff and resources after a decade.

Litigation presents a difficult issue for the trust. Trustees must constantly weigh controversial visibility against their knowledge that changing the water management regime is essential to protecting habitat. This balancing of the risks and benefits of litigation must also weigh the impact of litigation on staff time and trust resources. During the 1990s, litigation absorbed a major portion of the PRT's attention.

The trustees are more comfortable, and the political costs are lower, when the trust lends its expertise to local and regional planning programs. When projects have threatened migratory bird habitat, the PRT has become involved. When a new highway interchange was proposed, a PRT representative attended meetings and worked with the county to redesign the project and develop a mitigation plan. The PRT has also worked on environmental impact statements for local water projects. For example, PRT staff prepared the biological portion of a plan for a water storage project. The PRT has also been involved in a number of broader resource planning processes. Recently, it worked with other nonprofit conservation organizations, irrigation districts, natural resource districts, and the Department of the Interior in a tristate memorandum of understanding process involving Colorado, Nebraska, and Wyoming. The three states agreed to work on resolving the impasse over water development and endangered species in the Platte River basin.

It is surprising that, of all possible activities, education has been the most controversial among the trustees. In fact, a proposed use of trust land for a nature center offering educational programs is one of the few instances in which the trustees failed to achieve unanimity. The executive director first proposed a nature center to the trustees in 1985. Although the facility would have been located on trust property, the operation would have been managed by a different organization. The idea drew criticism, based on the idea that "human uses were not Trust responsibilities."[26] Eventually, the proposal was adopted, but only because unanimity was not required. The nature center has been established, but continuing dissension among the trustees has prevented the PRT from becoming involved in further educational programs.

Given the PRT's political environment and the specifics of the trust declaration, it is not surprising that the trust has emphasized scientific research as the core of its activities. This seems a prudent path toward achieving trust purposes. Carefully supplementing the trust document with a series of well-supported policy statements and management plans, the trustees have proceeded prudently, demonstrating the compatibility of agriculture and wildlife. And, as befits an organization with a strong trust culture, the trustees have worked assiduously to increase trust assets in order to sustain their activities.

Of all the organizations discussed in this volume, the PRT most closely reflects trust principles as described in chapter 2. In it, we can see trust principles, the trust document, and the IRS requirements for a 501(c)(3) organization weave together to answer basic questions of structure and operation. The trust purposes led to a staff-centered operation heavily reliant on science. More difficult choices in the document regarding accountability have given the original litigants a continuing role in trust accountability, while the trustees have elected to minimize contact with the public. Liberal investment guidelines have enabled the trustees to nearly triple the trust's assets while funding staff and a range of activities, including purchasing thousands of acres of land. Much of the success of the organization appears to reflect the clear presence of trust principles in agency culture and decision making.

The PRT is important to our analysis for two reasons. First, all the basic elements of the trust are clearly laid out, visible in the operation of the organization. Despite their diversity of backgrounds, the trustees have been carefully educated in trust obligations, and they have worked hard to fulfill them. Second, those same principles appear to have played a significant role in the successful blending of the trust's public and private roles. Even though the trustees have explicitly decided to limit public participation in their activities, the trust has been effective in acting simultaneously as a public and private organization.

The PRT was established as a private organization. It is funded by private dollars and is not under the supervision of any public agency or official, although the governor appoints one of three trustees. The PRT has chosen to operate as far from the public eye as possible. Its decisions are made in closed meetings, and it relies on science rather than public preferences in making them. Conversely, the trust is charitable and operates as a nonprofit corporation; hence, its purposes are officially deemed "public." The trust enjoys a beneficial tax status that constitutes a public subsidy of its operations. It was created to administer funds paid in consideration of adverse impacts on whooping cranes and other migratory waterfowl, which are clearly public resources.

Although the public is held at arm's length, the organization is never far from politics. The PRT is known as a de facto conservation agency on the Central Platte. The PRT is the primary actor protecting habitat and defending the declining habitat against further incursion. The trust has run a successful acquisition program where both the FWS and Audubon failed, in part because it shaped its goals and activities to the surrounding agricultural economy.

This dual nature of the PRT is not unique in this era of dispersion and devolution of government authority: many private organizations have enormous public roles. But trust principles have played an important role in the PRT's effectiveness. The trust principle of undivided loyalty has pushed the trustees to remain focused on the purposes of the trust, and it has provided some protective cover and the basis for a legal defense when they have done so in the face of political hostility.

The trustees' loyalty to trust purposes has become an important element of their accountability—not to the local public, perhaps, but to the broader interests reflected in the PRT's founding. However, there are risks in the PRT's lack of a public face. There may come a time when state issues so challenge the trust that some public support and recognition may be needed. Meanwhile, the PRT is a best-case example—it seems to be prudently and effectively balancing risks and benefits, using its trust status and resources to act as an effective public-private agency.

PART II: GOVERNMENT TRUSTS

This part discusses three organizations that make use of a trust to put government activities outside the normal agency model discussed in chapter 1. A mitigation bank in Dade County, Florida, combines professionals from federal, state, and local agencies in a marble-cake board of trustees that could become a model for devolution of government programs. The *Exxon Valdez* Oil Spill (EVOS) Trustee Council, established following the infamous Alaskan oil spill disaster, is run by trustees drawn from the highest levels of federal and state agencies. The Department of Hawaiian Home Lands (DHHL), the oldest of the three, was established by Congress in the early 1920s to administer a trust created to "rehabilitate" native Hawaiians following the devastation wrought by Westernization and annexation.

These three trusts provide quite different reflections of the changing face of government. Only the DHHL is formally a government agency. And although the DHHL has a considerable independent endowment, its position within the web of state politics and standard bureaucratic lines of influence and accountability has left it vulnerable to domination by processes that do not appear to impact the other two organizations. The other two exist somewhere off the organizational charts, related to but not part of the agencies that provide the trustees.

Government trusts have several things in common. First, they are all managed by what we call government trustees. Government trustees are not selected by private groups or parties. They are either appointed by an elected official—the U.S. president or relevant state governor—or serve ex officio as a function of their employment in a government agency. Government resources also fund these trusts. The Dade trust is not endowed by developers' voluntary contributions; it manages funds paid by the developers to the county to mitigate damages caused to public resources in the process of making a private profit from development.

Similarly, although Exxon sends checks to the EVOS trust, the money does not, even approximately, belong to Exxon. It is paid as compensation for damage caused by Exxon to federal and state property. Hence, Exxon is not a settlor or trustor in the sense described in chapter 2. It was required by the court to make the federal and state governments whole after its gross negligence caused a major disaster. Similarly, the DHHL corpus includes lands and rents from lands specifically dedicated by the federal government and managed by the state government to "rehabilitate" native Hawaiians.

Perhaps because of their proximity to government bureaucracies, these three trusts are the least like the trusts described in chapter 2. Trust principles are frequently inchoate, rarely discussed. In the Dade case, the term never comes up outside the organization's formal and never used title. Similarly, although a "trustee council" administers the EVOS settlement funds, the trustees' obligations have not discernibly shaped EVOS trust activities. In the DHHL case, the beneficiary and trust purpose are clear, but for most of the trust's history, they have had almost nothing to do with DHHL activities.

Although trust principles are not evident in the current operation of these trusts, they were utilized in all three cases to establish the organization. For example, the EVOS trust was established under provisions of the Clean Water Act and has provided careful, thoughtful management of significant funds intended to accomplish a specifically identified purpose. The EVOS result compares admirably with the ambiguity in several of the states presently anticipating settlement funds from the tobacco litigation. The DHHL was established with the same goal of protecting funds from legislative misallocation.

The trust's contribution to avoiding normal legislative and appropriations processes should, however, serve as a warning flag. The legislative response to these trusts has not been uniformly welcoming. Legislatures tend to regard trusts spending public money with a gimlet eye. This attitude creates two risks. One is that the legislature will meddle. The other is that the trust will ignore its peculiar status and, as in the DHHL case, not do what it is supposed to do. However, if there are reasons to keep funds separate from the legislative appropriations process—and our cases provide several—then a trust is a useful format for doing so.

One can also find ample reasons for wanting to avoid Washington and to devolve authority to lower levels of government. The federal Departments of Justice and the Interior appear, through the small knothole of these case studies, as less than desirable partners. Way down the Interior totem pole, a national park scientist has been an effective participant in the Dade trust. And in Alaska, far from the Beltway, the secretary of the interior's personal representative, sitting in for an assistant secretary, has been, in several incarnations, an estimable EVOS trustee. However, when the department itself is involved, particularly when the department's attorneys are involved, the agency's record is less salutary.

Almost a century of interior secretaries have approached native Hawaiians with the same care and undivided loyalty that they have exhibited with regard to Native Americans on the continental United States. The Department of Justice has been, if anything, worse than Interior regarding the DHHL. It has also been a confounding force in the EVOS program, parlaying a minute role in fund disbursement into a veto over EVOS trustee decisions. To the extent that Interior Department lawyers are drawn into a project to avoid the legislature, analysts might fairly wonder whether the effort was worth it. Certainly no one in partnership with the federal government can count on being an equal partner. But it is possible to design around the federal government's least attractive tendencies if one is aware of them.

It is not clear, however, that trust principles have a decisive contribution to make in that effort. What role can they possibly play if basic trust principles are inert and the federal elephant tramples all the grass? The answer is threefold. First, each of these trusts has a corpus. Unlike the pretend trusts discussed in chapter 1, each of these organizations ties a specific pool of funds to the achievement of a defined purpose. This endowment, even in the DHHL's deeply impaired past, puts the organizations in a different position from that of most government agencies: the trusts are not wholly dependent on appropriations for their programs. (Those looking to improve government operations in general by allowing agencies to keep fees would put government agencies in a somewhat similar position and therefore ought to be interested in these cases.)

Second, important resource management issues fall under the joint purview of numerous agencies. The Dade and EVOS cases are very promising in terms of utilizing a slight dusting of trust principles to bind a collaborative multiple-agency endeavor, facilitate needed cooperation, and provide a basis for authority sharing.

Third, by allowing agencies to operate outside of their habitual settings, the trust mechanism allows agencies to transcend not just the legislature but also their own assumptions, standard operating procedures, and unexamined policies. The EVOS experience with land acquisition strategies is quite instructive. The EVOS trust has also proceeded under the keen eye of external auditors—both certified public accountants and the General Accounting Office. The experience with the former in particular has proved enlightening for the federal managers.

Unfortunately, when a government trust is not permitted to operate outside of a standard political setting, trust principles appear to achieve little. The DHHL case is a valuable check on the assumption that one can achieve something new or different in terms of institutional arrangements or expectations simply by dedicating funds in a trust. The DHHL is a particularly compelling tale of what can happen in a trust when normal trust enforcement mechanisms are turned off. If the organization is undistinguishable from other state agencies, trust principles cannot accomplish much.

What is most striking about these organizations is their lessons in the area of trust accountability. All score high on basic disclosure forms of accountability. These three organizations produce the most elaborate financial statements of any trusts we have seen. In terms of political accountability, we see three different models. The Dade trust has operated wholly within the penumbra of its organizing agencies and the county government and has been accountable through existing political mechanisms. Its invisibility has caused the participants some concern. In the DHHL and EVOS cases, the issue is not one of flying below the radar; it is that the normal routes to accountability are not relevant or do not work. Recent DHHL history has been completely dominated by the beneficiaries' efforts to use standard trust mechanisms to raise questions about serious misallocations of trust resources. The beneficiaries failed almost completely in that effort. The settlements ultimately reached to restore breaches were achieved by legislative action. Trust principles provided a context for a moderately successful political battle.

The EVOS trust has paid enormous attention to what we call political prudence. The trustee council was under great pressure from Alaskan Natives to reflect their interests in spill restoration programs. As long as the native villages were in a position to stymie major EVOS programs, the council was imaginative and creative in pursuing politically prudent programs. Now that the Alaskan Natives' ability to disrupt trust programs has largely ended, the outreach and involvement that once characterized EVOS activities appear to be ending as well.

The organizations have taken three different approaches to issues of perpetuity. Dade will sunset when its money runs out, the DHHL expects to continue forever, and the EVOS trust has recently struggled with decisions regarding a permanent endowment. Only the first of these decisions clearly makes sense. Given its purpose, the Dade trust will and should go out of existence when there is no more development to mitigate. Neither of the other two choices appears particularly well integrated with basic trust principles. Nevertheless, the cases provide ample opportunity to consider what we have described as the conservationist preoccupation with perpetuity.

Finally, the DHHL, despite its obvious problems and inadequacies, suggests that there are some long-term consequences for even pretending to establish a trust. The notion of loyalty to the beneficiary, if not undivided or even discernible, remains in the charter, and it may emerge to play a fruitful role somewhere down the road. That has not happened yet, and it is not clear that it will. Nevertheless, trust principles did help beneficiaries shape a moral and empirical claim for restoration.

There is almost no discussion of the trust mechanisms described in chapter 2 in the narratives that follow. When trust principles have been mentioned, as in the efforts to restore the DHHL trust, they have had limited effect. So, if these organizations are the least trustlike of the ones we studied—or, in the DHHL case, a trust only in the breach—what do they contribute to our analysis? When government agencies, even those with a limited history of cooperation, are forced to manage common resources jointly, the trust is a convenient and effective template for describing, in a sympathetic and credible way, the basis for joint action. The lessons and cautionary notes provide guidance for thinking about how to improve the template in the design of future power-sharing arrangements.

CHAPTER FOUR

Dade County Wetlands Trust: Trust Light

If the Platte River trust is a classic trust—an easily recognizable product of the expectations and principles outlined in the second chapter—the Dade County Wetlands Trust[1] is at the opposite end of the spectrum. Its structure and operations loosely embody trust principles and adapt them to fit the particular needs of a coalition of resource management agencies mitigating wetland destruction in Dade County, Florida. There is no real trust document, no designated trustees with terms and duties officially assigned, no corpus managed to produce a predictable annual income, and no commitment to continue in perpetuity to pursue clearly articulated trust purposes. When the money is gone, the trust will simply go out of business.

The trust did not, however, spring rapidly into existence, as did the Platte trust, as part of the end to a hotly contested lawsuit. The Dade County Wetlands Trust is an organization developed and administered by state, federal, and local officials, bureaucrats from different agencies with different missions, political contexts, time horizons, legal authorities, and institutional priorities. It gradually emerged from a multiagency special area management plan (SAMP) and an accretion of options, analyses, maps, vegetation inventories, habitat models, and kindred indicia of contemporary public resource management in the United States. Its existence is certified by county legislation and a memorandum of understanding that sunsets every five years unless it is renewed.

The Wetlands Trust fund was "created for use in acquiring, restoring, enhancing, managing, or monitoring wetlands."[2] Two-thirds of the trust's money is focused on the restoration of wetlands on federally owned land, in Everglades National Park. However, most time is spent on projects supported by the other third of its income—primarily awarding grants to departments of state and local governments in the Everglades basin charged with restoring and protecting wetlands. The Dade County trust operates as a mitigation bank—the money that developers must pay when they destroy wetlands is used to restore or create wetlands elsewhere as an offset.

Students of the trust instrument can learn much about the flexibility of the trust as an organizational tool from its particular configuration in

61

Dade County. Trust principles provided a convenient and agreeable institutional template to culminate and describe years of negotiation and planning among disparate agencies. The Dade setup is extremely informal—it has no staff, headquarters, or letterhead and is at times barely discernible. The trust is a spend-down trust, and its life expectancy is tied to full build-out in the rapidly developing area around Miami. When development is "complete," there will be no more mitigation, no more income, and, one presumes, no more trust.[3] This flexibility and informality have allowed the trustees to pursue trust purposes with a minimum of fuss and bother and ought to be seen as a virtue of the trust concept. The decision to go "light" on institutionalization of the trust has worked in the Dade context, but not without some risk and cost. Even in Dade's brief history, its light structure has left the trust vulnerable on occasion.

Our discussion begins with some details on the founding context of the trust, the Miami–Everglades National Park dichotomy that defines Dade County, and the planning and negotiations that led to a set of interlocking legislation, agreements, and delegations of authority that resulted in what we call the nonstructure of the trust. How the Dade trust format works in practice is the focus of the second section. The third section emphasizes potential weaknesses of this lightly built structure.

GETTING STARTED

In the early part of the twentieth century, nearly all of Dade County in southern Florida was wetlands. Beginning in earnest in the 1920s, the eastern portion of the county has been incrementally drained to make room for expanding Miami and its suburbs. The western part of the county—perhaps surprisingly, given Miami's considerable growth—remains in wetlands, much of which is in Everglades National Park.[4] Prior to 1985, privately owned agricultural land separated the Everglades from encroaching development.[5] Most of the area was designated agricultural under the county master plan, and more intensive uses were disallowed. Some of the lands were farmed, others not; but suburban sprawl had not reached the park.

This relatively stable situation changed in July 1985, when the Dade County Commission expanded its urban development boundary (UDB) westward. This shift in policy exposed critical wetlands—including an area known as the Bird Drive Everglades Basin—to development. The Bird Drive area is 12.5 square miles (8,300 acres) between Miami and the park on the Tamiami Trail and includes both seasonal agriculture and physically unaltered wetlands. Particularly important, the Bird Drive area contained

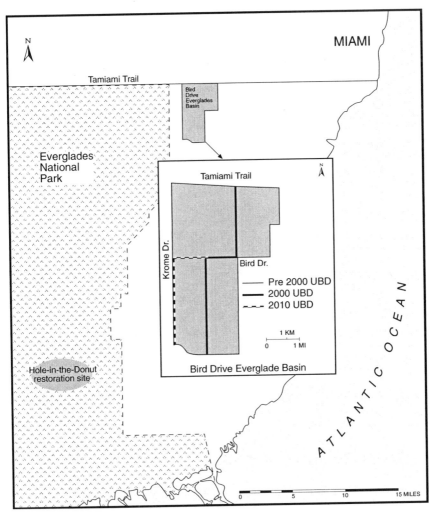

The map shows the relationship between Miami and Everglades National Park, the old and new urban development boundaries, the location of Bird Drive Everglades Basin, and the location of the Hole-in-the-Donut restoration site in the park. (Cartographer: Victoria Zaluda)

short hydroperiod wetlands, which are a crucial transitional habitat between the longer hydroperiod wetlands to the west and the eastern uplands.[6] Originally integral to the Everglades system, the Bird Drive area had been largely isolated from surface water movement by a proliferation of canals, levees, and dikes. Nevertheless, the Bird Drive area continued to provide valuable wildlife habitat.

Special Area Management Plan

Shortly after the UDB expansion, the Army Corps of Engineers received an application to build a public high school on Bird Drive area wetlands. The applicant failed to propose mitigation for the ecological impacts, and the Corps denied the permit. Subsequently, the Corps expressed concern over the county's drawing large areas of wetlands into its UDB. It requested that the county act as local sponsor for a SAMP, which is a standard Corps tool—both a collaborative interagency planning effort and a resulting set of policies.[7] The Corps' suggestion had some teeth. Had the SAMP process not been established, the Corps suggested that it would prepare an environmental impact statement for Miami's expansion.

In 1987, the county Department of Environmental Resources Management (DERM) became the sponsoring local agency for the SAMP effort. Included on the committee were professionals from an array of federal, state, and local agencies involved in permitting and regulating development in freshwater wetlands—the Corps of Engineers and DERM, plus the U.S. Environmental Protection Agency, the U.S. Fish and Wildlife Service, the Florida Department of Environmental Protection (DEP), the Florida Game and Freshwater Fish Commission, the South Florida Water Management District, and the Dade County Planning Department. Two advisory committees—a technical advisory committee and a public advisory committee—proceeded with a full panoply of workshops; wildlife, vegetation, and physical resource analyses; hearings; and comment periods.

The SAMP group considered two approaches to Bird Drive mitigation. One option was to designate part of the Bird Drive basin as mitigation for the development of the rest of the site. The other was to allow the development of the entire Bird Drive area and require mitigation activities outside the basin. These deliberations were interrupted in 1988, when the West Wellfield Policy Advisory Committee concluded that it was necessary to locate a wellfield in the Bird Drive area. During the protracted process of obtaining a permit for the wellfield, it became apparent to the SAMP planners that the Bird Drive wetlands would not survive withdrawal of water.[8] Because it would not be possible to use any part of the Bird Drive area for mitigation, the SAMP team would have to find a location for off-site mitigation.[9]

This was not a speedy process. Over the next three years, the SAMP participants evaluated eight mitigation sites and, after many further documents were prepared, identified a preferred alternative. The SAMP team's first idea was to focus mitigation activities on acquisition and restoration of an area called Frog Pond, located immediately east of the Everglades National Park boundary and containing the headwaters of Taylor Slough. However, the landowners were unwilling to sell the property, and in any event, purchasing it would have been difficult for the SAMP team. The SAMP group's failure to pursue the preferred alternative hints at a constraint imposed by the trust's funding source. Mitigation money would become available only in small bites, as sites within the Bird Drive area were developed, and it would take considerable time to build up significant funds. Recognizing that piecemeal land acquisition is not effective in rapidly developing areas of the county, the SAMP team refocused on a mitigation option known as the Hole-in-the-Donut.

The Hole-in-the-Donut is a 9,880-acre site within Everglades National Park. It had been farmed since 1916,[10] and about half of it had been rock-plowed beginning in the early 1950s (this involves crushing the natural limestone rock to make a more suitable substrate for vegetation). Farming ceased when the National Park Service purchased the entire area in 1975. The areas not rock-plowed returned to native vegetation, but the others rapidly became thickly infested with exotic vegetation, most notably Brazilian pepper *(Schinus terebinthifolius)*. Restoring the Hole-in-the-Donut was important not only to reclaim wetlands but also because the Hole-in-the-Donut had become the largest seed source in south Florida for the invasive plant. The restoration required removing the rock-plowed substrate and recreating the proper microtypography for the short hydroperiod wetland. A pilot project in the early 1980s had been coordinated by Everglades National Park, DERM, and the Army Corps of Engineers. The sixty-acre project had demonstrated the likely success of restoration techniques.

In January 1992, the SAMP planners held a series of meetings on the proposed wetlands mitigation in the Bird Drive area and revised its proposals based on one last round of public input. In early April, they decided to use the Hole-in-the-Donut as off-site mitigation for destruction of wetlands in the Bird Drive area, and they proposed that a trust be established to hold and allocate the mitigation money. However, it took three more years for the trust to get up and running.

Trust Creation

Within three months, the Board of County Commissioners adopted an ordinance that was the first step toward implementing the SAMP. The ordinance created the Freshwater Wetlands Mitigation Trust Fund "for use in acquiring, restoring, enhancing, managing or monitoring wetlands." Almost before the ink was dry on the statute, Hurricane Andrew swept through Florida. Everglades National Park was closed for a year. The hurricane slowed but did not stop the process of putting the trust pieces in place. In order for the SAMP to work, a number of certifications and interagency agreements had to be put in place. First, the state of Florida had to certify Everglades National Park as a mitigation bank. After submitting an application that required extensive technical information, the national park received its permit.

Second, in order to create a mechanism for the work to be accomplished within the park, the Department of the Interior had to approve a cooperative agreement between the Park Service and the National Park Foundation. The foundation is a nonprofit organization and is the entity that actually funds and contracts for the Hole-in-the-Donut restoration work.

Third, each agency involved in the SAMP process had to sign off on the trust creation and agree to participate. Although all the SAMP participants and their organizations were deeply involved in the drafting process, the formal memorandum of understanding (MOU) is between DEP and DERM. The MOU has a five-year term, and the whole agreement must be reconfirmed twice a decade. Fourth, the state and the Army Corps of Engineers had to delegate wetlands permitting authority to the county.

Even before all those steps were taken, well before it went into operation, the trust expanded its focus in two ways. First, although the SAMP process had focused on the Bird Drive area, the statute adopted by the Board of County Commissioners provided that the fund could include all monies accepted by the county as wetlands mitigation payments. The SAMP team agreed to expand its area of operation to receive payments for wetlands destruction beyond the Bird Drive area, throughout the county. Second, although the Hole-in-the-Donut was the final choice, the U.S. Fish and Wildlife Service objected strenuously, and not unreasonably, to spending all the mitigation money on land that was already in public ownership and at least technically protected. With no further analysis, the SAMP group simply decided that two-thirds of the money would be for the Hole-in-the-Donut, and the remaining one-third would be spent on land acquisitions identified by SAMP members. All this occurred before the trust became fully operational. The Everglades project is reported in trust documents as the Hole-in-the-Donut project. The other funding is captioned "held in trust."

The last step in establishing the trust was to determine the mitigation ratio. The ratio has two components. The first concerns the amount of land necessary to mitigate the acreage being lost. Throughout the country, this ratio tends to vary between 1:1 and 3:1, based on various factors, such as the habitat quality being lost. In the Dade case, the ratio was set at 1.5:1— for each acre destroyed, one and a half acres must be mitigated. The second component of the mitigation ratio is the price per acre, which may vary from year to year. This amount was set at the restoration cost of one acre of the Hole-in-the-Donut—initially, $18,000 per acre, although it has increased slightly with actual costs and is presently $19,802 per acre of restoration. The rate is set by the National Park Foundation and is based strictly on project costs; there is no administrative overhead added for the trust.

For example, if a project is going to impact ten acres negatively, fifteen acres of wetlands mitigation must be provided as an offset, for which the project developer would pay $297,030.[11]

This accretion of agreements and documents is not what we are referring to when we call Dade a "light" trust. It was not a simple matter to put the trust and its program into place. However, the process is a familiar one, largely having nothing to do with the trust part of the operation. It may become even more so in an era of devolution. Even after traversing all those slippery slopes, the trust that was founded is not very different from the process that had been under way for almost a decade. For example, none of the documents mentioned above identifies trustees, nor do they provide for terms of office, duties, salaries, or anything similar. Representatives of the original SAMP agencies now simply convene occasionally to manage what became a trust; they are the U.S. Army Corps of Engineers, the U.S. Environmental Protection Agency, the U.S. Fish and Wildlife Service, the Florida Department of Environmental Protection, the Florida Game and Freshwater Fish Commission, the South Florida Water Management District, the Dade County Planning Department, and the Dade County Department of Environmental Resources Management. The group receives monthly updates and meets at least yearly to evaluate grants and undertake trust business. It has not sought nonprofit status and takes advantage of its context within a nest of government agencies for tax purposes—it pays no taxes on receipts.

Trust Management

Most of the day-to-day paper management is undertaken by the county. The MOU between the county (DERM) and the state (DEP) directs the county to take the lead on most trust activities, as it had in establishing and administering the original SAMP process. DERM handles all financial matters, negotiates contracts, prepares minutes and reports for the group, and is the lead organization for overseeing trust projects. Initially, DERM absorbed the work and was not reimbursed by the trust. However, when the workload grew beyond what the existing staff could provide, DERM hired a person in part to manage the trust program. This was accomplished with a minimum of discussion. The DERM coordinator, in his monthly communication with the SAMP committee members, simply noted that the trust was "no longer a part time effort but one that requires someone's full time attention. To this end DERM, after consultation with some of you, has decided to create a new position specifically to manage the trust fund and the contracts for all projects selected by the SAMP Committee."[12]

Since the trustees grew out of the SAMP process, it should come as no surprise that there was no founding corpus either. The trust was created *in anticipation of* forthcoming mitigation payments. Because the payments are to be expended as they are received, this funding pattern has implications for the projects the trust can undertake at any point. The Hole-in-the-Donut funds are transferred fairly soon after receipt to the National Park Foundation, and the other one-third, which has been in the area of $2 million per year, is held in trust pending expenditure on approved projects.

The held-in-trust funds are invested as the ordinance establishing the trust directs—according to the county's detailed investment policy.[13] This policy defines types of risks and strategies to deal with them and seeks to maximize return, although doing so is secondary to safety and liquidity. It details prudence and ethical standards, authorized instruments, and portfolio composition. Although the county receives and holds the money, none of the trust funds can be commingled with other county funds. The wetlands trust funds are usually invested in high-liquidity, short-term instruments, and interest earnings have ranged between 3.2 and 6.3 percent.[14] Under the terms of the DERM-DEP memorandum, all interest earned on the account is turned over to DERM to cover the costs of administration. By 1996, this amounted to about $100,000 a year.

For an organization involving so many federal entities, receipts and disbursements are notably uncomplicated: all funds are paid to the DERM office, which forwards them to the county accounting department. Mitigation payments from developers are accepted and credited to the trust ledgers. The National Park Foundation submits bills to the trust as portions of the restoration work are completed. DERM directs the accounting department to make payments, either to the National Park Foundation or to other grantees—and it does. This may seem a small and obvious point, but in other trusts involving the federal government (notably EVOS, discussed in the next chapter), the story is not so simple.

ACTIVITIES AND ACCOUNTABILITY

The trust has two primary activities. The bulk of its funds supports restoration of the Hole-in-the-Donut, with the National Park Service and the National Park Foundation actually doing most of the restoration work. The group of agencies reviews the work plans and periodic reports, and periodic payments are approved. The Hole-in-the-Donut restoration is expected to cost approximately $60 million—approximately what the SAMP planners estimated would be the trust's total income over its lifetime. The original agreement to fund the Hole-in-the-Donut work is for twenty years, with two possible five-year extensions. If the work is still not complete at that point, all costs, mitigation ratios, and so forth will be recalculated for other mitigation sites. The work proceeds on large areas at a time. Currently, one can view three completed restoration sites, each at a different stage of vegetative recovery in the donut.

More of the group's attention is devoted to the selection, oversight, and reporting of the projects funded with the remaining one-third of the money. The held-in-trust (HIT) funds are spent through a grants program with significant limitations. Initially, the list of those who could submit proposals included only the SAMP agencies plus departments of Broward County, Monroe County, and Collier County; Biscayne National Park; Big Cypress National Preserve; and public universities and colleges. Very quickly, the group added the U.S. Department of Agriculture and the Miccosukee and Seminole tribes of Indians to the list and removed the Florida DEP and the universities and colleges. The educational institutions were removed because the trust was interested in short-term applied research—not the kind of inquiry that most university professors are prepared to devise. The group also feared that the application process would become political, with university officials or local politicians calling to urge them to fund a certain project.

The SAMP group also imposed a number of additional requirements, such as a 25 percent match for trust funds received and a guarantee that long-term monitoring and management of the restored sites will be provided by the applicants. Finally, the group agreed that a minimum of 50 percent of the HIT fund must be used for acquisition, a maximum of 25 percent can be used for land management planning, and a maximum of 25 percent can be used for wetlands enhancement or exotic species removal projects. When a HIT project is approved, the trust guarantees funding for only two years at a time to ensure that it does not exceed trust income. In addition, under pressure from the state legislature, which viewed the approximately $2 million HIT fund as an end run on its ability to allocate funds within the state, the groups has agreed that money left in the account at the end of the year will be allocated to land acquisition.

The HIT projects are selected by unanimous vote. This is not a rule, and it is not stated as a requirement in any of the founding documents. It simply works out that way: permits from virtually all the participating organizations are required for any project undertaken with the granted funds.

For all its informality, the Dade County trust has one of the most exacting public accountability mechanisms we have encountered in our study of trusts. Unlike many of the organizations we look at in this book, this trust was created after a protracted process of workshops, public hearings, and public comment. In addition, the trust's work goes forward as an integral part of government activity within the county, subject to the continued cooperation of a diverse array of agency participants. Finally, every five years, the trust agreement between DERM and the state DEP must be renewed. This provision is unique among the trusts we studied and could provide an opportunity for a new set of elected officials and their appointees to reshape the trust significantly. The first reauthorization was simply a formality—a letter was sent from DEP to DERM at the appropriate time—but the potential for close scrutiny of trust activities is important.

Given the potential for mischief,[15] some SAMP participants are concerned that the public does not know enough about the trust and its activities. Outside of public agencies and the development community, the trust is not well known. The group would like the Dade County public to be more aware of how development on wetlands is being mitigated. Informing the public about the trust would also, it hopes, strengthen political support for the trust if future challenges are made. Accordingly, the group plans to begin production of an annual report that would broadcast trust activities and policies.

FUTURE PROSPECTS FOR THE DADE COUNTY TRUST

SAMP participants have enjoyed the informality and personal relationships that constitute so much of the trust structure. However, challenges to the trust's mode of operation have raised important questions about this light approach to organizational issues. Moreover, the SAMP members wonder whether they should create more formality and a clearer set of rules and procedures to ensure the continued effectiveness of the trust. Many of the founding members of the trust are still participating. Where, they wonder, will the trust be in five, ten, or twenty years? Who will be running it? What should they do now to protect the organization and its purposes?

These questions were sharpened by a proposed in-stream mining operation in the county. Initially, the company attempted an end run around the county's mitigation program. A bill introduced in the state legislature would have allowed the company to bypass the mitigation payment requirement altogether. That effort failed, but it precipitated a brief period of unanticipated and unwelcome political visibility for the trust. A second legislative proposal would have required the mining corporation to pay a per ton fee on gravel removed. It was estimated that over the life of the mine, the proposal could have produced an additional $180 million for the trust.

This sounds like a wonderful windfall, but the SAMP team viewed it as a problem. Most obviously, the $180 million would vastly outstrip the current plans for the organization and its activities. The Dade trust is a spend-down trust and can function with minimal staff, structure, and formality because it does not have much money and will not last long. The estimated life of the proposed mine would have extended the life of the trust to as long as seventy years. The group believed that such an expansion of its term and resources would have required a significantly different approach to the trust program. Participants were particularly concerned that the mining company sought to take advantage of the trust's informality by proposing that it should have its own trustee.

The SAMP group made preliminary plans to place a greater emphasis on public education regarding the trust, to publish an annual report, and to try to develop public support for its programs. Ultimately, the mining issue was resolved by legislation that bypassed the trust altogether and divided any income from the mining operation between the state and the South Florida Municipal Water District.

At present, the Dade County trust has maintained both its minimal structure and its low-profile approach to accountability. It is not clear that this was the best outcome. To some extent, the Dade trust was forced by its decision to forgo any investment in structure to also forgo the mine mitigation funds. Clearly, planning a trust for a finite period to operate with a small amount of money and exposure is not the same thing as building an organization that can withstand public scrutiny and political hostility. However, there is no necessary virtue in a minimal structure and a low profile. It seems reasonable to wonder whether the Dade trust collaborators might not have done a superior job managing the larger funds. The structural decision to forgo even the possibility of an expansion seems unnecessarily restrictive.

The Dade SAMP group is a splendid example of using a trust to achieve real power sharing among diverse government agencies at all levels. The complexity of its founding arose, for the most part, from the requirements of mitigation banking rather than from the trust. Many contexts in which a trust might be appropriate could easily require similar efforts. Since the founding, however, the operation has been smooth and simple. Thus far, the Dade participants have been fortunate. They have used an almost invisible trust structure and minimal formalities to manage a rather large amount of money—a projected $60 million over the life of the trust. They can do this, it appears, in part because they have relied on inchoate trust principles and in part because the organization is a loose overlay on numerous well-structured, highly accountable government agencies. We are not convinced that avoiding the risks and responsibilities of the mining mitigation was necessary. Nevertheless, as it stands, the Dade trust provides useful insight into the ease with which trust principles can work to allow power sharing and joint decision making among federal, state, and local professionals.

CHAPTER FIVE

Exxon Valdez Oil Spill Trustee Council

The *Exxon Valdez* oil spill (EVOS) symbolizes for many Americans the destruction that corporate irresponsibility and our consumption-oriented society wreak on the natural world. In March 1989, 11 million gallons of crude oil were released when the Exxon tanker ran aground on Bligh Reef and were spread over 600 miles during a storm three days later.[1] The spill contaminated approximately 1,500 miles of Alaska's coast, killing birds, fish, shellfish, and mammals and disrupting the ecosystems that sustain the social, cultural, and economic life of the region.

The EVOS trust arises from the fact that the oil spill contaminated land and killed thousands of marine creatures that are owned, managed, or held in trust by the federal and state governments: the spill fouled beaches in a national forest, four national wildlife refuges, three national parks, five state parks, four state critical habitat areas, and a state game sanctuary.[2] We emphasize government lands and resources because the EVOS Trustee Council is responsible *only* for funds paid by Exxon in settlement of *civil* claims for damages to resources held, managed, or owned by state and federal government agencies. Almost all other claims for damages are still pending.

A relatively obscure section of the Clean Water Act provides that if an oil spill is the result of willful negligence or misconduct, the owner or operator of the vessel is liable both for any costs incurred by the state or federal government in cleaning up the spill and for any costs incurred by the federal or state government "in the restoration or replacement of natural resources damaged or destroyed." Related provisions in the Superfund Act provide that the state or federal government shall act "on behalf of the public as a trustee" and retain any funds recovered from the responsible party for use "only to restore, replace, or acquire the equivalent of such natural resources" as were damaged in the spill.[3]

With only this to guide them, the federal and state plaintiffs established the EVOS Trustee Council in the process of settling their civil claims against Exxon.[4] The EVOS trust is the 900-pound gorilla among the trusts we studied: publicity is so intense, the land and resources so spectacular, the ethical issues so profound that it is hard to view the EVOS Trustee Council as a model.[5] Moreover, the council has had so much money to spend so quickly that the trustees have not, until the most recent stages of program planning, focused on the fact that the EVOS Trustee Council is a trust. Never-

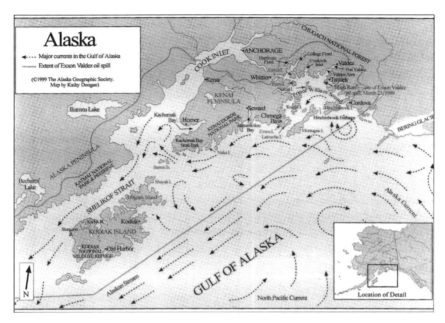

The oil spill area is part of the Gulf of Alaska and includes portions of Prince William Sound, the Kenai Peninsula, lower Cook Inlet, the Kodiak Archipelago, and the Alaska Peninsula. (Reprinted with permission from "Restoring Alaska: Legacy of an Oil Spill," *Alaska Geographic* 26, no. 1 [1999])

theless, its experience is an excellent source of insight into and guidance on structuring organizations in far simpler contexts.

This chapter focuses on four major elements. First, because the trustees are all drawn from the upper echelons of federal and state agencies, the EVOS case raises interesting questions about structuring trusts that involve such agencies. It also provides a unique and useful lens into the operations of the agencies involved. Second, Alaskan Natives are not included as trustees. Political prudence required, however, that they be intimately included in EVOS decision making. Innovations to involve villagers and to use traditional ecological knowledge in EVOS programs provide important models for responding to historic and contemporary exclusions. Third, the management of EVOS funds is hamstrung by restrictions that are standard procedure for managing *any* funds received in settlement of federal civil claims. The EVOS trust's stunning inability to pursue even a modest financial management program heightens attention to fund management issues, especially when dealing with the federal government. Finally, the EVOS trustees have wrestled with their decision to hold some of the settlement funds more or less permanently and to convert them into an endowment. Focusing on trustee council decisions regarding this "reserve" enables us to explore perpetuity issues and the potential importance of trust principles in future EVOS affairs.

TRUST STRUCTURE

The state and federal governments were encouraged by the provisions of the Clean Water Act to proceed jointly against Exxon. At the same time, they were suing each other over division of the anticipated litigation spoils. The memorandum of agreement (MOA) in which Alaska and the federal government resolved their differences is one element of a complex set of settlements of the governments' civil and criminal complaints against Exxon. Because the MOA formally established the EVOS trust and gave direction (albeit sparse) regarding the goals and structure of the EVOS Trustee Council, we focus on that element of the settlements.[6]

The state-federal civil settlement is frequently discussed in terms of a billion dollars, but the figure is misleading. After damage assessment, cleanup, and litigation expenses were deducted, only $700.4 million of the billion that Exxon paid in civil damages was included in the EVOS trust corpus. It was to be paid over a ten-year period concluding in September 2001.[7]

The document was less clear about the beneficiary. The MOA simply states that the cotrustees will act "*for the benefit of* natural resources injured, lost or destroyed as a result of the Oil Spill."[8] Although programs were not limited to the oil spill area, the council's almost unalloyed focus during the first decade of operations has been there.[9] The trust purpose is more controversial. Many have argued that restoration of natural resources and habitat is the sole purpose of the trust. Nevertheless, in the final restoration plan, the trustee council pushed the definition of the purpose to include the "services" provided by the natural resources on which the villages and the local culture and economy depend.

The MOA designates the federal and state governments as cotrustees of the funds. The president and the governor of Alaska were each to designate three trustees. Although they can choose anyone, the trustee council is made up of high-ranking representatives from agencies whose resources were affected by the spill—the Alaskan Departments of Environmental Conservation and Fish and Game, U.S. Forest Service, National Marine Fisheries Service, and Department of the Interior (representing both the National Park Service and the Fish and Wildlife Service).[10] In addition, Alaska's attorney general is included on the council. There are no terms of office for trustees; they serve at the pleasure of the executive who appoints them.

The MOA requires that all decisions be made by "the unanimous agreement of the Trustees." Although this rather harsh requirement was a source of considerable concern at first, most observers agree that the requirement has evolved into an essential ingredient of EVOS trust effectiveness. Since unanimity is required, an individual trustee is reluctant to be the deal breaker. "You can see the wall you are about to hit," commented one observer, "and therefore you make special efforts to avoid it."

The composition of the council is controversial among Alaskans, who believe that there ought to be native trustees as well. The point arises because so many EVOS trust activities are intimately related to the land, culture, and livelihood of the native peoples of the spill area. The standard riposte is a legalistic one: the trust arises from the settlement of federal and state damage claims, not from native claims, many of which are still pending.[11]

The trustee council responded, in part, by giving nontrustees a substantial role in EVOS programs. The MOA specifically directed the council to provide for "meaningful public participation" in the injury assessment and restoration process, and the trustees focused major attention on ensuring full involvement of native communities in the spill area. These efforts may not be an adequate substitute for inclusion at the decision-making level, but they provide instructive examples for improved public involvement programs.

The MOA gave the new council only a short time to get up and running: it allowed ninety days following receipt of any damage payment to establish an organization. This mandated haste may have led founding trustees to make a specific commitment to "organize within existing structure where feasible" and to use as little of the trust funds as possible on administration.[12] The results were not inspiring: the trustees soon regretted their reliance on committees made up of agency personnel and hired an impressive professional staff. The improvements were almost immediate and were reflected in the final restoration plan, which continued to guide EVOS activities for the rest of the decade.

The initial committee structure was made up of personnel from the land management agencies who worked to ensure that each agency got "its share" of the EVOS program.[13] However, the agency-dominated council also initiated an extensive and extremely effective planning process designed to solicit opinion from the spill area, the state, and the nation in establishing priorities for the trust. Over the course of the planning process, the council evolved into a significantly improved organization. A professional executive director and director of operations were hired in October 1993. The fundamental accomplishment of the new staff was to separate the trustee council from the participating agencies. The shift in tone resulting from this structural change is apparent in the minutes of EVOS Trustee Council meetings. Well-briefed trustees increasingly focused on policy decisions. However, distinguishing EVOS programs from agency priorities is still not easy. As late as 1995, the Public Advisory Group (PAG) asked the executive director to develop criteria to differentiate more clearly between oil spill–related projects and normal functions of the EVOS trustee agencies.[14] After several drafts and discussions, they abandoned the effort.

RESTORATION PLAN

The first major achievement of the reconstituted trust structure was the publication, in November 1994, of the final restoration plan. The vocabulary and format are similar to those of other government planning documents, but both the tone and the substance are different from earlier, agency-dominated drafts. EVOS trust staff invested heavily in outreach to affected villages. Their effort is reflected in the plan's emphasis on restoring "reduced or lost *services* (including human uses) provided by injured natural resources." This might include "subsistence, commercial fishing, recreation (including sport fishing, sport hunting, camping, and boating), and tourism . . . that were affected by injuries to fish and wildlife. Injured services also include the value derived from simply knowing that a resource exists."[15]

The plan adopted by the new organization describes four areas of activity. First, although the final plan differs from earlier drafts in its emphasis on services, the dominant chord in all the documents is land acquisition. In EVOS parlance, the term *habitat protection* translates as buying land. Acquisition attracted the most public comment and support and will consume the largest portion of EVOS trust resources. Almost 90 percent of those commenting during the planning process, irrespective of where the respondents were located, commented on the acquisition proposals, and of those, over 90 percent favored acquisition.[16]

The plan contemplated two approaches to land acquisition—one focused on large parcels, several of which were purchased before the plan was adopted, and one focused on small parcels (small in this instance meaning less than 1,000 acres). The small parcel nomination process is open ended, and the EVOS trust staff will continue to evaluate transactions on a continuing basis, even after the restoration reserve is established. The large parcel program focused from the outset on fifteen specific landholdings.[17] The council planned to acquire 645,000 acres, for which it anticipated spending $339 million in EVOS funds and $56 million from other sources. At the end of 1999, the program terminated, with all but one of the anticipated transactions having been accomplished.[18] The plan underscored that the

EVOS trust would not hold or manage any of the land acquired. Areas are selected and transactions are funded by the EVOS trust, but the land is acquired and managed by the most appropriate state or federal agency. Second, the plan addressed a persistent drag on credibility: the quality of the science surrounding the spill. Early EVOS programs were tarred by public perceptions formed during the difficult period immediately following the disaster. Secretive and adversarial damage assessment "research" was undertaken by a full spectrum of potential plaintiffs for use in the lawsuits that followed. Transcending the emotionally charged postspill environment has been a gradual process for EVOS administrators and researchers. As a first step in that direction, the plan emphasized peer review in its massive research and monitoring program.

Third, the plan is emphatic about the importance of transcending mere public involvement in planning to achieve a continuing dialogue with the public. "Public participation is not a once-a-year government activity limited to commenting on draft documents. Rather, to the greatest extent possible, individual projects should integrate the affected and knowledgeable public in planning, design, implementation, and review."[19]

Finally, the plan introduced the idea of a permanent endowment. The plan asserts that because complete recovery will not occur for years, and because it takes many life cycles to obtain meaningful information about the impact of the spill on many populations, restoration could take several decades. To ensure that funds will be available to meet future needs, the trustees set aside $12 million from Exxon's 1994 payment and anticipated doing so annually until the payment period ends in 2001.

The major accomplishment of the professional staff was to separate the EVOS organization from the agencies that make up the trustee council.[20] Following adoption of the plan, trustee council activities centered primarily on land sales negotiations and grant review and approval. The general outlines of the plan are tied to continuing activities, and most decisions are formalized, in the process of elaborating an annual work plan.

LAND ACQUISITION

The land acquisition programs will ultimately consume approximately 60 percent of available settlement funds. Typically, the small parcels have been acquired at appraised value from private parties without much public comment. The large parcels are acquired, often at several times appraised value, from native corporations and are a focus of diverse and continuing controversy. As of the end of 1999, the small parcel program had acquired 7,100 acres for $19 million.

Although it is normal to speak of EVOS trust land transactions, the lands are actually acquired by one of the council's constituent land management agencies. EVOS staff and relevant agency personnel negotiate a purchase—depending on the situation, either a rough outline of a transaction or a detailed agreement—with a potential seller. The trustee council then authorizes expenditure from the settlement funds. When the deal is basically agreed to, the case is transferred to the designated acquiring agency to complete the transaction.

In spite of the agency acquisition, a typical EVOS large parcel deal looks more like a land trust project than a government agency land transaction. The EVOS trust has no authority to condemn land,[21] and the MOA does not add to or alter the land acquisition authority of any of the agencies involved. Nevertheless, the federal and state agencies involved in the trustee council have evinced a flexibility regarding the timing and specific details of a transaction that is not consistently apparent in their own land transaction programs. Part of the success that the EVOS trust has enjoyed arises from the fact that the money for each acquisition is already in hand and does not depend on contentious or competitive legislative appropriations.

However, it is also worth noting that in the context of EVOS trust acquisitions, the government agencies have let go of some dearly held policies and assumptions: the acquisitions are not limited to appraised value, and they do not insist on acquisition of title in fee simple. The EVOS council has approved purchases for *more* than fair market value.[22] It works assiduously with sellers to craft a package of land sales, timber and conservation easements, areas with and without public access, and other title arrangements that meet the present and future needs of the seller as well as the habitat protection requirements of the settlement. These adjustments have included granting the seller continuing rights for home sites, lodges, and other specified uses in designated areas of the acquired parcels.

As anticipated in the restoration plan, the agency that acquires the land holds title to it. The management regime for each parcel is defined by the purposes of the EVOS trust, any agreements made with the seller, and the statutory mandate of the acquiring agency. However, it is instructive to note that the council members do not wholly trust one another to manage in accordance with their mutual expectations. To ensure that the managing agency continues to meet the expectations of the trustee council, the "nonacquiring government" holds an easement on the acquired property. When the Forest Service, for example, acquires a parcel, the state government holds an easement on it. This strategy is designed to ensure some control should the acquiring agency stray.

Control may not, however, be possible. For example, in late summer 1999, Alaska congressman Don Young introduced a bill that would allow a native regional corporation, Chugach Alaska, to take title to sites recently

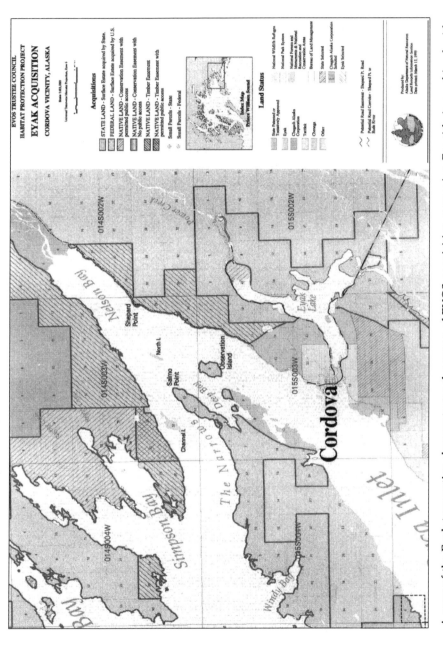

EVOS TRUSTEE COUNCIL
HABITAT PROTECTION PROJECT
EYAK ACQUISITION
CORDOVA VICINITY, ALASKA

Scale 1:63,360
Universal Transverse Mercator Projection, Zone 6

Acquisitions

STATE LAND - Surface acquired by State.

FEDERAL LAND - Surface Estate acquired by U.S.

NATIVE LAND - Conservation Easement with
permitted public access

NATIVE LAND - Conservation Easement with
No public access

NATIVE LAND - Timber Easement

NATIVE LAND - Timber Easement with
permitted public access

◆ Small Parcels - State

✦ Small Parcels - Federal

Index Map
Prince William Sound

Land Status

National Wildlife Refuge

National Park System

National Forests and National
Recreation and
Conservation Areas

Bureau of Land Management

State Selected

Chugach Alaska Corporation
Selected

Eyak Selected

State Patented or
Tentatively Approved

Eyak

Chugach Alaska
Corporation

Tatitlek

Chenega

Other

∿∿ Potential Road Easement - Shepard Pt. Road

∿∿ Potential Road Corridor - Shepard Pt. to
Rude River

Produced by:
Alaska Department of Natural Resources
Land Records Information Section
Date printed: March 15, 1995

A map of the Eyak transaction demonstrates the range of EVOS acquisition strategies. Fee title is combined with easements with and without public access, timber easements, and a variety of reservations for village shareholders to develop individual and community resources. (Courtesy Alaska Department of Natural Resources) acquired by the federal government with EVOS funds. During the native land selection process outlined in the Alaska Native Claims Settlement Act (ANCSA), Chugach had tried to select the lands as historic or cemetery sites. However, village selection of the same sites took priority. After the villages sold the land to federal agencies, the Young bill proposed giving Chugach a second chance at them. Were the Young bill to pass, the state easement on the land would continue to protect it from development, as would its status as historic or cultural, but the opportunity for public access, for which the EVOS trust paid a substantial premium, would be lost. The proposed legislation does not provide for compensation to the trust.

In spite of the overwhelming support for the planned acquisitions, controversy around the EVOS trust purchases is intense. Part of the debate arises from the simple fact of spending $375 million to acquire land for government management in a state and region that is already largely publicly owned. Federal and state governments at the time of the disaster owned approximately 80 percent of the spill area. When the full set of anticipated EVOS trust transactions comes to fruition, public ownership in the spill area, state and federal combined, will reach approximately 90 percent. Questions about the appropriate balance of public and private landownership in the area are durable, important, and deeply felt. Not unrelated, it is wholly appropriate to wonder whether federal and state agencies are capable of managing sensitive lands for habitat restoration.

Moreover, it is not always clear how acquiring upland habitat protects the marine species affected by the spill. What, one could ask, does acquiring forestland have to do with protecting habitat for herring or sea otters? In some cases, the connection is clear, especially when the affected species or service is related to rivers that cut through the upland areas to the coast. Or when a marine habitat is under pressure from a spill, preventing siltation from logging could help the recovery of the habitat. Frequently, however, the connection between the land acquired and the habitat of affected species and services is less apparent.

These are important questions. However, the large parcel transactions are controversial primarily because the vast majority of land is being acquired from native corporations. To understand the participation of village corporations in the EVOS trust land acquisition program, it is necessary to know at least a little about the provisions of ANCSA.[23] To facilitate the development and shipment of oil reserves discovered in Alaska in the 1960s, Congress enacted the Alaska Native Claims Settlement Act in 1971. The act extinguished long-recognized but never-addressed native title to land and resources in Alaska. In return, it conveyed to the natives about $1 billion and approximately 44 million acres of land. Congress established 12 regional and more than 200 village corporations, quite distinct from extant native governments and organizations, to receive the compensation.[24]

Village corporations own large amounts of land in the spill area. Although lands may "be perceived as 'belonging' to the whole village, only those who are shareholders in the corporation in fact own them."[25] Thus, those who live in a village but are not shareholders cannot vote on a proposal to sell village lands. This group of nonvoters includes both non-natives and natives who were born after ANCSA passed ("afterborns"), for whom ANCSA made no arrangements regarding shareholding. However, shareholders who no longer reside in a village are entitled to vote on a land sale. The rifts between native culture and the values and priorities of a for-profit corporation are myriad and have been extensively commented on.[26] The problems and perceived inequities resulting from ANCSA are an important element in the public, particularly village, response to the EVOS trust land acquisition program.

A proposed EVOS trust acquisition is typically subjected to a vote of the affected shareholders.[27] This creates a defensible argument that the villagers are "willing sellers." However, some observers question the legitimacy of this impression, given the disconnect between the for-profit values of the corporation that negotiated the sale conditions and the values of the native culture, and between the village residents and the voters. Others question the sellers' willingness from another angle. The EVOS settlement came early in the cacophony of litigation that followed the spill. Villages caught in the rounds of legal maneuvering and appeals had still received no settlement for their damage claims by the time the large parcel program was completed, yet they experienced negative impacts on subsistence resources, economic opportunity, and cultural coherence as a result of the spill. Some village residents perceived that the trustee council got its share, while the natives had to sell their land to get any timely compensation.

Given our nation's history, it is appropriate that Americans should look carefully at programs that separate indigenous people from title to and control over their land. But it would be wrong simply to presume that the EVOS trust transactions are a bad deal for the villagers. Nor should observers discount the village boards' and shareholders' careful assessment of their own best interests that preceded all decisions to sell. Many concluded that the EVOS trust land acquisitions created an unprecedented opportunity for native villages because it gave them a chance to achieve enormous economic benefit from their lands while protecting them as well. By selling their land to the EVOS trust, the villages achieved a substantial income without having to endure the changes to their environment or culture that would accompany an influx of loggers, second home owners, tourists, or other resource developers. With few exceptions, the sellers involved in large EVOS trust transactions have taken great pains to deposit their funds in tightly protected perpetual trusts to ensure that the benefit

Table 1. Large Parcel Acquisitions

Parcel Acquired	Acreage	Total Price (Incl. Interest)	Trust Fund	Other Sources[1]
Afognak Joint Venture	41,750	$74,133,824	$74,133,824	$0
Akhiok - Kaguyak, Inc.	115,973	$46,000,000	$36,000,000	$10,000,000
Chenega	59,520	$34,000,000	$24,000,000	$10,000,000
English Bay[2]	32,537	$15,371,420	$14,128,074	$1,243,346
Eyak	75,425	$45,000,000	$45,000,000	$0
Kachemak Bay State Park Inholdings	23,800	$22,000,000	$7,500,000	$14,500,000
Koniag (limited term easement)	55,402	$2,000,000	$2,000,000	$0
Koniag (fee title)	59,674	$26,500,000	$19,500,000	$7,000,000
Old Harbor[3]	31,609	$14,500,000	$11,250,000	$3,250,000
Orca Narrows (timber rights)	2,052	$3,450,000	$3,450,000	$0
Seal Bay / Tonki Cape	41,549	$39,549,333	$39,549,333	$0
Shuyak Island	26,665	$42,000,000	$42,000,000	$0
Tatitlek	69,814	$34,719,461	$24,719,461	$10,000,000
TOTAL:	**635,770**	**$399,224,038**	**$343,230,692**	**$55,993,346**

[1] For the acquisition of Kachemak Bay State Park inholdings, funding from other sources consists of a State of Alaska contribution of $7 million from the Exxon plea agreement and $7.5 million from the civil settlement with the Alyeska Pipeline Service Company. For all other parcels, funding from other sources consists of a Federal contribution from the Exxon plea agreement.

[2] The first closing on the English Bay acquisition occurred in November 1997 and resulted in the purchase of 29,636 acres for $14.1 million. Subsequent closings will occur in the future to complete the acquisition.

[3] As part of the protection package, the Old Harbor Native Corporation agreed to protect an additional 65,000 acres of land on Sitkalidak Island as a private wildlife refuge.

At the end of 1999, the large parcel program was complete. The trustee council had acquired interest in 75,000 acres at a cost of $45 million in trust and other funds. (Courtesy EVOS Trustee Council) of the transactions will continue to be an economic resource for the villages for generations to come. To achieve the economic benefit of development without the environmental and cultural destruction that frequently accompanies it could be viewed as a unique opportunity created by the spill disaster that the village corporations are wise to embrace.

This is, however, no response at all to those who believe that land, and the ability to control it, is an essential ingredient of group and individual identity and well-being. We have not encountered anyone involved in the process who seemed comfortable with the impact of the land acquisition program on Alaskan Natives. Clearly, some will always regard the spill settlement as another step in the centuries-long process of dispossessing indigenous people of their land and culture. Certainly, there are many examples of both well- and ill-intentioned individuals who pursued policies that had dispossession as their explicit or only slightly concealed goal. And for that reason, the controversy surrounding EVOS trust land purchases is probably both unavoidable and appropriate.

SCIENCE

EVOS trust investment in science is also probably inevitably controversial. The EVOS trustees estimate that by the time the restoration plan phase of the trust winds down, somewhere between $217 million and $247 million will have been spent on research, monitoring, and general restoration.[28] This huge investment has not purchased the uniform enthusiasm of the scientific community. Articles in major periodicals such as *Scientific American*[29] raise serious questions whether the money is being well spent.

Much of the negativity is based on reports from pre–EVOS trust damage assessments. Nevertheless, the questions raised about "good science" even under the fully evolved EVOS trust administration are important. The restoration plan directs funds toward applied inquiries that will guide investment in restoration. This emphasis will always create a tension between the EVOS trust and the scientific community. These predictable tensions are potentiated by large pots of money. Because the EVOS trust awards enormous research grants in a competitive program (during a period of declining federal investment in research), and because enormous investments are shaped by scientific findings, intense debate over all aspects of EVOS trust inquiries are likely to continue.

Predictable fractiousness within the scientific community is accompanied by understandable conflict between what appears "right" to the scientist and what the people in the villages need and want. For example, for village dwellers and subsistence hunters—indeed, for most people, whether they lived near the oiled coast or not—simply removing the oil was a high priority. Restoring the services provided by the natural resources is an important element of the trust purpose. Moreover, it is not politically prudent for the council to ignore the needs and expectations of spill area residents who shape the trust's political environment. So, for example, the EVOS trust agreed to spend almost $2 million in the summer of 1997 on programs employing de-oiling compounds, which in some cases can be harmful to intertidal organisms.[30]

Finally, Exxon may benefit from doubts about the findings of EVOS trust researchers. As long as the $5 billion private settlement against Exxon remains on appeal, and as long as the MOA's $100 million opener remains on the horizon, we are likely to hear continuing criticism of EVOS trust inquiries.

PUBLIC ACCOUNTABILITY

Although the EVOS trust scientific legacy remains controversial, its innovations in the area of public involvement are not in doubt. MOA direction requiring the trustees to develop "meaningful public participation in the injury assessment and restoration process" focused the trustee council's initial efforts on traditional agency-like public involvement. In addition, the MOA specifically required that a public advisory group be formed to advise the trustees about assessments of damage, allocation of available funds, and the conduct and coordination of restoration activities. After much controversy about how to structure the group, the trustee council chose members based on their affiliation or familiarity with a particular issue of concern to the trust—aquaculture, developed tourism, subsistence, and the like. Although no arrangements have been made to ensure that the "representative" of a specified interest consults with or in any formal sense "speaks for" the group from which the member is drawn, the goal of interest representation is clear. Several public-at-large members were subsequently added to the original group.

It is not clear that the PAG approach to accountability has been a useful element or that the effort is worth transporting to other contexts. Some observers believe that the PAG has been valuable as a forum where those from different interests can engage in a discourse that is broader than each group putting out its "100 percent position." Others believe that the group is unnecessary. One PAG member argues that in Alaska, public officials are so accessible that it is not necessary to have a screen or comment group.

It does seem clear, however, that the PAG has been overshadowed by the EVOS trust staff's aggressive efforts to involve affected groups deeply in EVOS trust programs. The trust is charting new territory in its efforts to develop processes and protocols for integrating the villagers and their tra-

Residents of Chenega Bay in Prince William Sound prepare a boom to trap any oil that is washed off the beaches near their village. Chenega Bay residents teamed up with the Alaska Department of Environmental Conservation in 1997 to clean about half a mile of beach still oiled eight years after the *Exxon Valdez* spill. The project was undertaken to allow residents to return to beaches traditionally used for subsistence hunting, fishing, and gathering. (Courtesy Alaska Department of Environmental Conservation)

ditional ecological knowledge into research projects based on Western science. Local villagers are frequently the only source of baseline information on what existed before the disaster.

EVOS trust staff and agencies also work with villagers to help them develop their own applications for trust funds. Local leaders worked with Alaska Department of Fish and Game scientists to design a proposal for a program that involves subsistence hunters in the collection of tissue samples from harbor seals. The Alaska Native Harbor Seal Commission based in Cordova hired a biologist to train the hunters in how to collect the samples. In addition, this program brings village young people together to show them traditional ways of dealing with the animals.

It seems reasonable to speculate that the EVOS trust has worked so hard at public accountability because its land acquisition programs are so controversial. And while these efforts have been diverse and imaginative, their success has been spotty. Traditional ecological knowledge is a new and poorly defined field, and the council programs have not consistently achieved the anticipated level of villager involvement and training. However, EVOS public involvement only vaguely resembles NEPA-inspired equivalent programs run by the government agencies that make up the council. Even if many EVOS trust efforts turn out to have been merely worthy experiments, its programs will still have been instructive.

FINANCIAL MANAGEMENT

Given the intensity of the scrutiny surrounding most aspects of EVOS trust affairs, concern about the financial arrangements seems surprisingly subdued. Perhaps because the EVOS trust has so much money, most public observers are largely unconcerned about why there is not more money or how it is spent. Staff, however, have always been deeply concerned by the numerous ways their hands are tied in both the management and the expenditure of EVOS trust funds.

In the restoration plan, the trustee council estimated that when the ten-year payment period ended, the trust would have received about $14 million in investment income. Even allowing for the facts that Exxon deposits the funds annually and that much of the money is expended on programs as it comes in, the cash on hand at any time in the trust account has always been around $100 million. How does that translate into total earnings of about $1.4 million per year?

The discussion of prudence in chapter 2 might lead one to suspect that the trustees are not appropriately prudent in managing trust funds, but the problem lies elsewhere: the EVOS trust is a spectacular victim of standard procedures for managing funds recovered by the federal government in damages. Funds are not paid to either the state or federal treasuries or to the trustees, but rather are deposited in a joint account in the Court Registry Investment System (CRIS). Specifically, Exxon sends its annual payments not to the trustee council but to the U.S. District Court for the Southern District of Texas.[31] All the funds deposited with CRIS are held in government treasury bills with maturities of 100 days or less. This is not an aggressive investment policy designed to balance risks and returns or to produce significant returns. Nor is it a diversified portfolio that would meet the standards of most endowment managers.

That is bad enough, but the situation is actually worse. CRIS transactions are undertaken by a local firm that charges "a fee of .025 percent added to the cost of securities purchased by CRIS."[32] In addition, although all the investment work is done by the local firm, the clerk of the court charges a separate registry fee. The court takes 10 percent of the income for use in its own administrative account.[33] This may be a worthy public investment, but it is not related in any way to the settlement agreement, to the actual costs the court incurs in holding EVOS trust funds, or to the notion of a trust. Neither the piddling returns on the EVOS trust funds nor the court's inflated charges have attracted much attention outside the EVOS trust staff, perhaps because there is so much money available.[34] Moreover, those who oppose additional land acquisitions by state and federal governments view the constraints on the money available to the EVOS trust as positive. After the 1994 elections, the Alaska Senate delegation was in a position to improve the CRIS situation and was reluctant to do so for that very reason. Nevertheless, the standard operating procedure would strangle a less well endowed program and cannot be regarded as anything other than idiotic.

Management of the funds is not the only problem confronting the EVOS trustees. They also have a surprisingly difficult time when they try to spend any of it. First, the federal and state attorneys general must jointly certify that an expenditure is compatible with the terms of the settlement agreement and request CRIS to release any money allocated by the trustee council. The Alaska attorney general is a member of the council and supports EVOS trust decisions. On occasion, the federal Department of Justice does not. Although they have no formal part in council decision making, Justice officials have used their role as intermediary in the disbursement process to second-guess the council. Frequently called the fourth federal trustee, Justice dawdles and occasionally simply refuses to request the release of money.[35]

Once the money is released from CRIS, there is still another wrinkle. Funds released for federal agency expenditure do not go to the council or to the appropriate agency. Instead, they are deposited in the Natural Resources Damage Assessment and Restoration Fund (NRDA, pronounced "nerda"). NRDA invests the proceeds to earn interest that is available to the council without going back to CRIS. The fund managers are limited to government bonds but attempt to purchase investments with maturity dates scheduled to match when the agencies will need to spend the money. Similarly, money to be spent by Alaskan agencies is transferred to a special Oil Spill Settlement Fund. Like NRDA managers, the state fund officials invest in instruments based on the agencies' liquidity needs, but they are not limited to government instruments. The state fund has, not surprisingly, produced considerably more returns than the NRDA investments on approximately the same level of holdings.

Although Byzantine, the NRDA and state fund arrangement provides a modicum of relief from the CRIS situation. Money transferred from CRIS to NRDA or the state is no longer subject to the outrageous CRIS skimming of returns. Accordingly, EVOS trust staff have tried to minimize the amount of time that funds languish in the CRIS account, moving them over to NRDA or the state as rapidly as possible.

But the spending constraints are still not over. The state is not allowed to expend funds without a legislative appropriation. Although the Alaska attorney general concluded early in the process that expenditures of trust funds do not require appropriation, the council has found it politically prudent to involve the legislature anyway. Initially, the legislature enacted annual legislation approving EVOS trust expenditures. Since 1996, EVOS trust expenditures have been included as a line item in the budget of each state agency authorized to spend the money. Although the legislature initially balked on a few EVOS trust proposals, the process has boiled down to a reliable annual approval routine for EVOS trust activities. Nevertheless, the prospect of rejection makes EVOS trust staff nervous, and the process is not wholly consistent with basic notions of prudent, independent trust management of resources. The federal government is not so restricted and simply appropriated the funds permanently by passing a single statute.[36]

In this unfortunate maze of confusing restrictions and requirements, there is one interesting ray of light: the federal and state agencies are required to submit to the trust's external audit. Government resource managers have not generally been required to keep track of their investment of time, administrative support, and other expenses in the precise context of project-by-project accountability. This, some argue, has contributed to a rather loose approach to tracking public funds. EVOS trust auditors discovered appalling basic problems in agency accounting: extensive data entry errors, agency accounting systems unable to separate general administration expenses from project funds, and agencies' failure to allocate personnel to projects accurately. For example, auditors discovered that at one point, 45 percent of the salary for the budget analyst in the National Oceanic and Atmospheric Administration's regional office was charged to administrative expenses for an EVOS project. Part of the problem, the auditor concluded, was that much of the accounting for federal agencies is done in Denver. Hence, the agencies do not have control over the accounting activities or access to records much of the time.[37]

Every step of the way, receiving, spending, and accounting for EVOS trust funds was bumpy at first. However, as things have become routine, few of the rules and procedures regarding the handling of funds appear to have had a discernible impact on EVOS programs beyond causing the trust staff occasional dyspepsia.[38] It is difficult to estimate what the EVOS trust could have earned if the funds held in its accounts had been less restrictively invested. But because the trust has received annual payments from Exxon and has spent most of the funds soon after they were received, the forgone income is probably less than one might fear. As the end of the payment period (2001) nears, the issue of investment returns focuses less on the funds used for acquisition and restoration and more on how CRIS policies will affect the long-anticipated restoration reserve.

PERMANENCE

In the EVOS trust context, the issue of permanence is called the restoration reserve, or simply the endowment. In part because one of the large parcel acquisitions did not go through, the total amount now available for the reserve is approximately $170 million. The original idea was that the funds would be held to fund long-term restoration proposals that would "potentially benefit any resource or service injured by the oil spill."[39] It was also widely anticipated that the trustee council and the administrative structure would sunset, and a new governing structure would manage a new set of programs. The intervening years have permitted some shifting of perspective and allowed potential claimants to devise a marvelous array of proposals for spending the growing pot of money.

The council established an artificial deadline for reserve decisions—the tenth anniversary of the spill—and approached the deadline with some urgency. Alaskan senator Frank Murkowski, chair of the U. S. Senate Committee on Energy and Natural Resources, refused to consider legislation moving EVOS trust funds out of the CRIS system unless he was assured that the money would not be used to extend major land acquisitions into the indefinite future. Without the prospect of improved returns on the reserve funds, however, the council's plan for an endowment was stymied.

Murkowski's position combined with human nature to focus attention on dividing the pie rather than on devising a new organizational structure. A typically elaborate EVOS public involvement effort focused attention on options for the reserve about eighteen months before the deadline. Fewer than 20 percent of the more than 1,360 responses even commented on future administration of the funds.[40] Everybody wanted to talk about the money, and most had in mind a project that would benefit their own interests. Academics at the University of Alaska lobbied extensively to create endowed chairs and support their research. Village groups mounted a major campaign supporting a community set-aside of $20 million for expenditure on village-oriented programs and priorities. The Sierra Club, Alaska Center for the Environment, and Alaska Rain Forest Campaign mounted a similar effort in support of allocating 75 percent of the reserve to land acquisition.

In the end, the trustee council was no more interested in administrative issues than the public. Its March 1999 resolution concerning the restoration reserve left to future discussion any changes in the current structure. The trustee council will continue to operate in the foreseeable future. In addition, the Council made two crucial decisions about the fund itself. First, it rejected a spend-down or term arrangement and decided to establish a permanent endowment, spending only earnings from investments. Second, it made a crude allocation of the money. Funds supporting a continuation of the small parcel acquisition program were capped at $55 million. The rest of the money is available for long-term monitoring, research, and stewardship. The council implicitly deferred decisions about community set-asides and grants to the University of Alaska until later in the endowment planning process.

Presuming a 5 percent return on investments, which is what the council calculated in its 1999 reserve planning, the council's allocation decision unleashes only $2.75 million per year into the area's real estate market. Compared with the heyday of the large parcel program, this is small potatoes. It was apparently satisfactory to Senator Murkowski. His Senate committee rapidly reported a bill that would lock the council's allocation decision into law. It would also permit the release of EVOS trust funds, including the restoration reserve, from the CRIS morass for investment by NRDA or other accounts "outside the U.S. Treasury." Investments are permitted, under the Murkowski bill, in "income-producing obligations and other instruments or securities that have been determined unanimously by the . . . trustees for the Exxon Valdez oil spill to have a high degree of reliability and security."[41]

Under the reserve, the council will experience a significant change in persona. It seems obvious that a professional organization oriented toward negotiating large land acquisitions and running a major grant-making and public-relations program is no longer necessary. One manifestation of this pending shift is already visible to the staff. EVOS trust culture is evolving more clearly in the direction of trust principles. For most of its history, the EVOS trustee council has not operated specifically in contemplation of itself as trustee of a trust corpus. Perhaps because they were largely land managers to begin with, or perhaps because their money was simultaneously so munificent and so unproductive, members viewed themselves more in terms of what we described in chapter 2 as a "sacred trust." Although the council was directly responsible for the trust corpus, its members were explicit that they were not acting in a fiduciary capacity except for the resource. Thus the EVOS trust is not the most trustlike of our case studies. But it does comport with the MOA's definition of the beneficiary: the agreement directs the state and federal governments to act as cotrustees "for the benefit of natural resources injured, lost, or destroyed as a result of the Oil Spill."

The pendency of the restoration reserve is changing that understanding. The council is now specifically moving toward managing funds, not restoring resources. What this means in terms of administration is not yet clear. Extensive planning for a Gulf ecosystem monitoring (GEM) program that will consume the residual share of the endowment is well under way. Preliminary documents presume but do not evaluate important changes in EVOS trust orientation. The council is expanding its focus beyond the oil spill area to include monitoring and research throughout the northern Gulf of Alaska. More important, the GEM proposal constitutes a major change in the trust's purpose. The plan specifically rejects restoration of injured resources and services and adopts as its new mission fostering a "healthy and biologically diverse marine ecosystem" through "greater understanding of how its productivity is influenced by natural changes and human activities." Restoration projects related to the lingering impacts of the *Exxon Valdez* spill will "diminish over time. . . . As the effects of EVOS fade and as GEM matures, the selection of research projects will increasingly arise out of the results of the long-term monitoring program." As part of morphing into a long-term ecological research program, the proposal largely abandons the element of EVOS programs that focused on services provided by natural resources in favor of a basic research program. The proposal reframes the trust's commitment to Alaskan Natives and the villages, focusing not on involving them but on communicating scientific results to them. Lack of "timely, accessible, and understandable" communication of scientific results "can compromise the success of a program like GEM," the plan notes.[42]

This redirection would, of course, erode the original reason for establishing the restoration reserve, which was to ensure that restoration—including restoration of services, not simply research—would continue after Exxon payments ceased. As time passes, the GEM documents assert, the influence of the Exxon disaster is more and more difficult to separate from previous and continuing natural and human-induced changes. Yet the underlying statute, the MOA settlement, the restoration plan, and the provisions of the Water Pollution Control Act are clear that the trust's purpose is restoration, not research. The trustee council may yet learn that the trust documents endure to define endowment priorities.

Although the EVOS trust's most telling experience with trust principles may lie in the future, some interim observations are appropriate. Many of the lessons relate to the preeminent position of government bureaucrats in decision making. The trustee council began with a familiar inclination: to minimize administrative costs and make do with what was readily available. The EVOS trust's early experience reminds us that skimping on administration is not necessarily prudent. The professional staff was almost immediately successful in creating an effective organization that functioned in cooperation with but wholly separate from its constituent organizations.

The EVOS trust's experience with CRIS is a special subset of the agency self-dealing problem apparent when the federal government is involved in a trust. Those who establish a trust related to the settlement of civil damages involving the federal government need to pay close attention to the management of funds, not simply after they have the corpus in hand but at the earliest phases of the settlement process.

Conversely, the EVOS trust experience suggests that working in the trust format has been edifying for the agencies involved. The agencies' ability to adapt themselves to a seller-friendly style of land acquisition strategy is instructive. The EVOS trust experience casts an interesting light on what the agencies view as immutable constraints on their land acquisition programs. Those contemplating a donation or transfer of land to a government agency would do well to consider the overlapping easement arrangement that the EVOS trust staff developed to address concerns about future management of acquired lands.

The EVOS trust experience is also instructive in the area of accountability. Beginning in 1996, the EVOS trust and its grantees have been audited annually. This process has been a bit of a cold shower for several of the agencies. Those audit reports provide a valuable lens into some of the most pervasive problems in government accounting and an abbreviated but stark contrast between public and private expectations. Moreover, the agencies' ability to make the changes necessary to comply with trust requirements, when properly motivated, demonstrates that they are capable of establishing systems that can achieve fairly normal businesslike accounting.

The GEM changes in public involvement also raise important issues about the other branch of accountability—in general and with Native Americans in particular. With public attention on the issue less intense than at the trust's founding, perhaps the council is wise to consider a less elaborate public process.[43] It may well be that the EVOS trust's emerging political situation does not justify continuing major investment in general public or Alaskan Native involvement. The present GEM plan does not, however, reflect the advances in attitude and approach achieved in the EVOS trust's own experience. We are tempted to attribute this unfortunate deviation back to the agency norm to the ascendancy of science in the GEM proposals. It should not surprise us that a shift from restoration to basic research de-emphasizes humans. However, it is clear that the EVOS trust's experience with trust principles is still unfolding, arguably just beginning, and worthy of continuing attention.

CHAPTER SIX

Hawaiian Home Lands:
The Bad News–Good News Trust

The Hawaiian Home Lands trust was established in 1921 to support home-steading by native Hawaiians.[1] Unlike wildlife and other beneficiaries that cannot speak on their own behalf, native Hawaiians are politically astute human beings.[2] Yet this fact has not made it easy to enforce trust principles. The Hawaiian Home Lands are in an uncomfortable institutional position, slung awkwardly between the shoulders of the state and federal governments. Efforts to use trust principles to balance the playing field in favor of the beneficiaries have been complicated by the fact that the federal Departments of Justice and the Interior hold many of the key cards. Sadly, the federal government has been the major perpetrator of trust breaches and has yet to play a positive role in achieving trust purposes. The Hawaiian Home Lands have long been managed by state agencies that are responsive to powerful political forces. The current manager, the Department of Hawaiian Home Lands (DHHL), is wholly embedded within the state bureaucracy. For most of its history, trust purposes and obligations have had limited impact on the Hawaiian Home Lands.

The good news, if any, is that trust enforcement is not wholly dependent on the courts. Restitution of misappropriated trust resources did not rely on trust enforcement mechanisms but drew instead on the symbolic weight of native Hawaiians' quest for sovereignty.[3] Trust notions played a small but significant role as a positive symbol during restitution—a verbal hammer wielded by the increasingly sophisticated beneficiaries in diverse legislative and administrative battles. The positive outcome leads us to suggest that the basics of trust management could play an important role in future Hawaiian Home Lands management.

We are not sanguine about the future of the Home Lands trust as a trust. Half a decade after the major settlements, the trustees have yet to adopt a plan for investing the refurbished corpus or for deciding how to

Research for this chapter forms the backbone of Stacey Dinstell's two December 1999 master's theses, the first in the College of Natural Resources, the second in the College of Environmental Design (City and Regional Planning). They are entitled, respectively, "The Hawaiian Home Lands Trust: A Conservation Trust for the Benefit of Native Hawaiians" and "Conservation Trust Planning: Lessons Learned from Hawaii's Ceded Land Trust." Both projects were supported by a grant from the Agricultural Experiment Station.

fit Hawaiian Home Lands programs to the new resources. Absent a major reorganization of state government, the trust will continue to be, from many perspectives, just another state agency. Nevertheless, trust principles could provide managers with a set of guidelines and priorities—and an approach to decision making—that could be of enormous utility when managing trust resources in DHHL's intensely political setting.

We begin with a brief history of the land and the territorial period in Hawaii. First, it is important to trace the land now in the Home Lands corpus through a number of trusts—public, implied, and express[4]—in order to understand both the native Hawaiians' moral and legal claims and the plethora of organizations and expectations that emerged from the American annexation of Hawaii and statehood. Second, efforts to repair and replenish the trust are used to show how enforcing trust terms failed, but also how trust notions were used in the restoration of the corpus. Traditional trust enforcement mechanisms discussed in chapter 2 are of little use in the context of a government trust. Finally, we review current DHHL activities and explore future trust management issues, emphasizing where trust principles could and should play an important role in planning for a new era of Hawaiian Home Lands programs.

DIVERSE TRUSTS FROM CAPTAIN COOK TO STATEHOOD

Those familiar with the federal government's pursuit of its trust obligations to Native Americans in the continental United States will find much that is familiar in the Hawaiian Home Lands story. Here, our recapitulation of the sorry tale is necessarily narrow, focused on tracing the land presently in the trust corpus. Indigenous landownership in Hawaii began with a kind of public trust, with land held by the Hawaiian king for the gods, and commoners holding usufructuary or use rights that became increasingly well defined over the course of a century. The land that concerns us was seized and then ceded to the United States at annexation and, subject to some major constraints, dedicated to the benefit of the islands' inhabitants. The Hawaiian Home Lands trust was carved from the ceded lands in 1921.[5]

Precontact Hawaii operated under a quasi-feudal system: the king held all the land "in trust" on behalf of the gods and for the benefit of all. Land not specifically claimed by the royal family was allotted to chiefs, who partitioned it among their followers and ultimately the common people. When Captain Cook arrived in 1778, the islands were governed in four separate kingdoms. Preferring to deal with a single monarch, Cook helped King Kamehameha I unite the islands. After unification, Kamehameha retained the ancient land system. However, he also took the first steps toward the fee simple ownership familiar to outsiders. For example, land of a deceased chief was to remain with his heirs rather than reverting back to the *ali'i nui*, the paramount chief.

In the ensuing decades, Hawaiian culture was overwhelmed by an invasion of missionaries, agriculturists, traders, and merchants. Steadily gaining power and influence, but feeling hampered by the inability to own private property, Westerners clamored for revisions in the land system. In the mid-nineteenth century, changes appeased the Europeans but at the same time strengthened and protected the rights of both the Hawaiian royalty and the commoners. Hawaii's first constitution adopted by Kamehameha III in 1840 transformed Hawaii into a constitutional monarchy. The document reiterated that although all the land on the islands belonged to the king, it was not his private property. Rather, it belonged to the chiefs and people in common. Land could not be conveyed away without his consent, but under the 1839 Bill of Rights, tenants could not be subject to arbitrary removal.

Protection of tenants' rights was central, as well, in the 1845 formation of a land commission that was established to investigate all claims of private individuals, whether native or foreign, to real property. The minister of the interior was authorized to issue a royal patent extinguishing the king's private rights to the land but not the rights of the tenants, as the king still had no right to convey away the rights of Hawaiians without their consent. With such obstacles, land still could not be freely bought and sold.

Westernization continued when, in 1848, the Great Mahele identified and separated the rights of the king and chiefs. The king retained all his private lands but quitclaimed his interest in the remaining lands to the chiefs and the government. The king's private lands were still subject to tenants' rights. Tenants of these lands were entitled to fee simple title to one-third of the lands possessed and cultivated by them, when either the king or the tenant desired the division. Through such divisions, Kamehameha III intended that private titles conveyed to Hawaiian natives would protect them against Western acquisitiveness. More than 12,000 claims were recorded in large volumes known as the Mahele book. Immediately after the Mahele, Kamehameha III divided his lands into crown and government lands to prevent confiscation of the royal properties.

Under the Mahele, the lands of the king, chiefs, and government were still encumbered by tenants' rights, making land sales complicated. The Kuleana Act of 1850 attempted to clarify these rights. The act gave common people an opportunity to seek fee simple title to their cultivated land and house lots. Unaccustomed to the idea of private ownership of land and distrustful of Western law, they understandably made no rush to do so. Only 8,200 titles were formalized on less than 1 percent of the land area.[6]

Legislation passed in the same year authorized the sale of land in fee simple to resident aliens. Although the Great Mahele and subsequent acts introduced the concept of fee simple ownership to Hawaii, government and crown lands continued to be held by the sovereign on "behalf of the Gods and for the benefit of all."

By the late nineteenth century, a small group of Westerners had acquired title to more than 320,000 acres of land previously held by the Hawaiian government.[7] Nevertheless, both the crown and the commoners continued to hold substantial rights in land, and Westerners continued to view the monarchy as a barrier to their aspirations. In 1887, a group of Western plantation owners staged a coup. The Bayonet Constitution, which they imposed, gave them much of the monarch's power and established a property requirement for voting that essentially terminated native Hawaiian participation in government.[8]

Queen Lili'uokalani ascended to power in 1892 and attempted to revise the constitution that had disenfranchised Hawaiians. But American businessmen in Hawaii formed a Committee of Public Safety and requested military support from Washington to extinguish a rebellion that did not exist. Marines and sailors landed on the islands, ostensibly to protect the U.S. legation and to secure the safety of American life and property. In fear of her supporters' lives, Queen Lili'uokalani surrendered to the United States. Thus empowered, a newly formed provisional government simply declared itself owner of 1.8 million acres of government and crown lands that the Hawaiian monarchs had tried so hard to protect.

Although President Grover Cleveland demanded that the monarchy be restored, the United States officially recognized the Republic of Hawaii in 1894. The utility of Pearl Harbor as a vital stopover for both troops fighting the Spanish American War in the Philippines and the growing trade in the Far East made annexation especially timely and attractive. With no congressional aid in sight, loyalists to the queen attempted to overthrow the Western government. Lili'uokalani was charged with treason and held prisoner for nine months. She formally abdicated the throne but continued to appeal for redress. President William McKinley signed a Resolution of Annexation in July 1898.[9]

Under this resolution, native Hawaiian title to and rights in the land were simply ignored. The United States accepted cession of approximately 1.8 million acres, without the consent of or compensation to the Hawaiian people. These became known as the ceded lands. At annexation, Congress provided that all revenue or proceeds from the ceded lands would be "used solely for the benefit of the inhabitants of the Hawaiian Islands for educational and other public purposes." These provisions resemble the statehood grants of school and other institutional lands now managed by most western states as trusts.[10]

Although a U.S. attorney general opinion in 1899 concluded that the annexation resolution created a "special trust relationship" between the federal government and the islands' inhabitants,[11] the ceded lands themselves were not definitively a trust. The annexation resolution contained other provisions that were decidedly untrustlike. Congress provided that any part of the ceded lands could be "used or occupied for the civil, military or naval purposes of the United States, or . . . for the use of the local government."[12] In addition, although U.S. public land laws were not in effect in Hawaii,[13] homesteading by the general public was allowed on the ceded lands. The 1900 Organic Act, which established a government for the Territory of Hawaii, began the bifurcated management of the ceded lands: title remained in federal hands, but the territory possessed, controlled, maintained, and managed them, at its own expense.[14]

The Hawaiian Homes Commission Act of 1920 (HHCA) separated approximately 203,000 acres from the ceded lands and dedicated them to the rehabilitation of native Hawaiians.[15] Most of the land was to be open to homesteading by native Hawaiians, but existing leases on 26,000 acres were to continue, providing funds that could be used, in part, to support the homesteading effort. Although the ceded lands were not viewed as a trust, the HHCA clearly created one. As noted in chapter 2, it is not necessary to use trust terms specifically in order to create a trust—whenever a property owner identifies property to be managed for the benefit of another, a trust can be implied. This occurred in the case of the Hawaiian Home Lands. Congress dedicated land and revenues to benefit native Hawaiians and established the Hawaiian Homes Commission (HHC) to serve as trustee. However, the trust was established in a complex land transaction involving expiring preannexation land leases. The circumstances of its founding obscured trust principles and established the framework for management problems that continue to this day.

It is typical to gloss the creation of the Hawaiian Home Lands as a humanitarian act benefiting native Hawaiians, and this is not wholly unreasonable. Testifying on behalf of the proposal, Secretary of the Interior Franklin K. Lane reminded the committee that "the native[s] of the Islands, who are our wards, . . . and for whom in a sense we are the trustees, were living in poverty and dying off rapidly." Nevertheless, the confluence of events that gave rise to the trust is less than uplifting.[16] The key fact is that between 1917 and 1922, preannexation leases on more than 200,000 acres of ceded lands were due to expire. The land would then become open to homesteading by the general public. Most of the acreage was usable only for pasturage and had been leased to cattle ranchers in large tracts. However, about 26,000 acres of the expiring leases had been intensively developed for sugar cane and were quite valuable. Both rancher and plantation owner lessees were anxious to maintain their leases and end the threat of homesteading.[17] With their encouragement, a delegation of Hawaiian notables traveled to Washington to seek support in Congress.

The delegation did not find a uniformly uncritical embrace in the nation's capital. Congress supported continued homesteading as a way to "Americanize" the islands and counter the growing Japanese influence in the region. Moreover, many in Congress shared Lane's concern regarding the native Hawaiians. Congress allowed the planters to retain their valuable agricultural leases without the threat of general homesteading, but only in the context of native Hawaiian "rehabilitation."

Congress amended the Territorial Organic Act to protect the sugar cane leases, effectively terminating homesteading by the general public in Hawaii. But Congress also established a trust to facilitate homesteading by native Hawaiians. It did so implicitly, by dedicating public lands to the rehabilitation of native Hawaiians. Native Hawaiians were to have exclusive rights to homestead on the areas under the expiring leases. Again protecting sugar interests, Congress excluded the cane lands from what became known as Hawaiian Home Lands or "available lands." The sugar interests continued to lease them as before, although a portion of the rent was allocated to support the program and provide loans to homesteaders. But the trust did not get all the cane lease revenues. Only 30 percent of the money was to be deposited in the Hawaiian Home Loan Fund established to receive receipts. The rest went to the territory's general treasury. In addition, Congress established a trustee, the five-person HHC,[18] to manage the land and funds, oversee the homesteading, provide training to homesteaders, develop infrastructure, and make loans to support settlement.[19]

Not unexpectedly, the trust was in trouble from the beginning. Powerful interests continued to treat the Home Lands as if they were still available for appropriation as ceded lands. Territorial governors withdrew and transferred land for federal agency use and other public purposes. More seriously, the structure of the fund removed any incentive to seek fair market value for the leases. The amount that could be deposited in the fund was capped, initially at $1 million. Any revenues beyond that were to be turned over to the territorial government. Although the cap was occasionally raised, there were periods during the territorial era when the trust received no revenue.[20] The fund also created a conflict of interest within the Hawaiian Home Lands program that continues to this day: although most of the land was supposed to be available for native Hawaiian homesteading, leasing it to paying customers was the only way to fund the program. Trust administrators learned early to ignore fair market value and undivided loyalty to the beneficiary and instead to serve the needs of the federal government and established economic interests.[21]

Finally, Hawaiian homesteaders had access only to remote and essentially uninhabitable lands. The act also barred the homesteaders from patenting land. Title to the Home Lands was to remain with the United States, and native Hawaiians paid $1 per year for a ninety-nine-year lease term. This limited the homesteaders' ability to obtain commercial loans and left them dependent on the Home Lands trust for financial support.[22]

It is clear that Congress created a trust when it established the homestead program in 1921. However, territorial and federal officials did not treat it as a trust.[23] The cane planters' goals were met, but the putative purpose of the trust—to rehabilitate native Hawaiians by providing support for homesteading—was not achieved. The available lands were uninhabitable without major infrastructure investments, but the trust structure prevented prudent management of leases on trust lands that would have funded such improvements. Hence, the program precipitated little actual homesteading by beneficiaries.

Statehood in 1959 created an opportunity to make improvements in the program. Title to the lands in the trust corpus was transferred to the new state, the Hawaiian Homes Commission Act was adopted as a part of the state constitution, and the Hawaiian Home Lands program was expressly defined as a trust, with the state serving as trustee. Unfortunately, institutional arrangements created lasting problems. The federal government retained absolutely crucial oversight responsibilities, including exclusive but discretionary authority to sue for breaches of trust. Only the federal government can freely sue to protect trust principles, but it is not required to do so. It never has.

State-level decisions created further impediments to effective trust implementation. The HHC continued to act as trustee on behalf of the state, but its role was redefined by the creation of a new cabinet-level agency of state government: the DHHL was established to manage trust programs. The new agency seriously confused the role of trustee. The same individual who serves as chair of the HHC also serves as executive head of the DHHL. These two roles are in conflict, and the commission's ability to act as a trustee directing the DHHL is fatally compromised. The DHHL is an executive agency of the state government, dependent on the legislature for operating revenues, the governor for political visibility, and the attorney general for legal advice and representation. The commission has not established independent authority to define policies and direct the activities of the DHHL.[24]

ACCOUNTABILITY IN TRUST MANAGEMENT

Beginning in the late 1970s, long-standing complaints regarding the Home Lands trust were formalized in a series of investigations and reports.[25] From the stinging indictment of Hawaiian Home Lands trust management, a consensus emerged regarding the basic problems.

The most obvious failure of the trust was the continuing inability of native Hawaiians to secure homesteads. In 1979, only 25,000 acres, or approximately one-eighth of the available land, was being homesteaded by beneficiaries. About 3,000 leases had been awarded, and more than 6,000 beneficiaries remained on waiting lists for homesteads.[26] Fifteen years later, there were nearly 13,000 applicants on waiting lists. More than 3,000 of those applicants had been on the list for at least ten years, with nearly 600 of them joining the list prior to 1970. The trust simply was not fulfilling its purpose.[27]

Although native Hawaiians were not using the available lands, the lands have never been idle. Home Lands were being used illegitimately or illegally. The DHHL 1976–1977 annual report indicated that a total of thirty-one executive orders or proclamations allowed 16,863 acres, or almost 9 percent of the Home Lands, to be diverted to such uses as airports, schools, parks, game reserves, and other public facilities. Federal agencies, including the U.S. Navy, U.S. Army, and Federal Aviation Administration (FAA), controlled vast acreage of land and paid virtually no rent. In 1977, these three entities were paying an average rental of 45 cents per acre.

Why is the trust not enforced? Keeping the trustee in line ought to be fairly straightforward: if the federal government is abrogating the Hawaiian Home Lands trust, it should be simple for the courts to draw that conclusion and enjoin or order a remedy for the harm. However, this has never happened. The problem is the same as it was in the beginning—a catch-22 division of responsibilities between the federal and state governments.

Any discussion of who is responsible is confused because trustee responsibilities are divided between the federal and state governments. In addition, these responsibilities appear to be of two types: first, the role of trustee of the Home Lands, and second, the federal government's ill-defined and rarely honored "trust responsibility" to Native Americans, and the unclear extent to which that applies to native Hawaiians. The issue also turns on timing. Who was responsible at what point? Many of the breaches of the trust occurred during the territorial period, when all responsibility for the Hawaiian Home Lands resided with the federal government. Regarding that period, the federal government has denied having a trust responsibility for the Home Lands. Because of federal statutes of limitations, the courts are unlikely to alter that questionable assertion. Since statehood, it has been difficult to enforce the trust; although the state is trustee, only the federal government has enforcement authority.

Enforcement problems are clarified in a family of cases in which the Keaukaha-Panaewa Community Association and the Hou Hawaiians attempted to sue the state as trustee. When the DHHL agreed to exchange Home Lands trust lands to facilitate construction of a flood-control project unrelated to trust purposes and transferred land, beneficiaries sued. The

U.S. Court of Appeals concluded that native Hawaiians had no private right of action, that is, no right to sue to enforce duties and obligations imposed by the Admission Act.[28] In 1984, the association amended its claim and tried again. The court held that the Admission Act created federal rights; therefore, the beneficiaries could file suit under federal civil rights law.[29] This can only be applied prospectively, however, and does not provide an opening to address past abuses of the trust. In other cases, access to the courts has been restricted by limitations regarding the naming of defendants, sovereign immunity, and remedies available.[30] For enforcement purposes, it was as if the trust and trust enforcement mechanisms did not exist.

It has been even more difficult to bring the federal government to heel. After a confusing bit of waffling, the federal government simply denies that it is a trustee, either for the Home Lands trust or for native Hawaiians generally. In 1979, a Department of the Interior solicitor concluded that the federal government was responsible for the Home Lands trust prior to statehood and that its trust responsibility carried forward thereafter.[31] However, subsequent secretaries of the interior have refused to acknowledge pre- or post-statehood trust responsibility, and in 1989, the 1979 statements to the contrary were rescinded. In 1993, the solicitor of the Department of the Interior formally declared that the federal government did not serve as trustee for native Hawaiians before or after statehood and was not a trustee for the Home Lands trust.[32] That conclusion created such controversy that the statement was later rescinded,[33] but nothing has taken its place.

Because they were having no success suing on their own behalf, beneficiaries tried to frame a federal trust responsibility for native Hawaiians more generally that might force the Department of Justice to sue, as the statehood act contemplates, to enforce the trust. The court rejected the argument, concluding that the United States "is permitted, but not required, to bring enforcement actions."[34] The federal government has successfully avoided responsibility.

Although a small window to sue to enforce native Hawaiians' rights under the 1921 Homes Commission Act and the Enabling Act remains open under federal civil rights acts, the courts have not provided an effective forum for beneficiaries concerned about breaches of the Home Lands trust. Any restitution that has been made has come through a more explicitly political process.

COMPENSATION AND RESTITUTION

It would overstate things considerably to say that trust principles provided a basis for enforcing long-ignored breaches of the trust. Nevertheless, the trust made it possible for beneficiaries to argue that specific lands should have been available and specific rents should have been paid. Because they were not, the beneficiaries' quest was for restitution of relatively easy to identify rights that had long been ignored. This is not the same as enforcing the trustee's obligations, but the structuring of the issue was clearer than if the beneficiaries had been seeking to right historic but difficult-to-identify or -quantify moral wrongs.

State Action

Repair began in 1984 when Governor George Ariyoshi canceled twenty-seven gubernatorial orders and proclamations that had transferred land out of the Hawaiian Home Lands trust for state and county uses. Ariyoshi's action returned approximately 28,000 acres to the trust corpus. In 1988, the state legislature enacted the Native Hawaiian Trusts Judicial Relief Act, which initiated a protracted process for further restitution. The statute had the effect of dividing complaints about the trust along two dimensions—those that occurred before and after the 1988 statute, and those that involved injuries to individual beneficiaries as opposed to more general breaches of the trust.

Pre-1988 Breaches. In lieu of what we would consider normal enforcement mechanisms, the 1988 statute defined a planning process. The governor created an interagency task force to review and verify DHHL claims for land and lost value of land during state administration of the trust.[35] In 1992, the legislature paid the trust $12 million for the uncompensated state use of some trust lands. By 1993, a process for replacing misallocated lands and resolving disputed set-asides of Hawaiian Home Lands had been identified, and the state had begun paying fair market rent for the lands it will continue to hold.[36]

All the outstanding claims on behalf of the trust were resolved by the passage of Act 14 of the Hawaiian legislature in 1995: $600 million is to be paid to the DHHL in $30 million annual installments for twenty years.[37] The statute established the Hawaiian Home Lands Trust Fund in the treasury to receive the payments and interest from trust investments. Management of the funds was left almost entirely to the DHHL's discretion. The act provides only that the agency is "to have fiduciary responsibility toward the trust fund, and provide annual reports to the legislature and beneficiaries." With all state breaches supposedly resolved, any further claims against the state for the period 1959 to 1988 on behalf of the trust were prohibited.[38]

Pre-1988 Injuries to Individuals. In a separate 1991 statute,[39] the legislature established an individual claims review panel to evaluate claims from beneficiaries alleging that they were personally harmed by DHHL decisions. The legislature would review and approve awards or other action proposed by the panel. This process is currently stalled. After the panel submitted a first round of proposals, the legislature got cold feet. Concerned that the panel was addressing too broad a range of claims, it passed a new law creating a new group to redefine the claims that the panel was authorized to address. The new panel was promptly found to be unconstitutional,[40] but the old one continued to hear claims. Under the terms of the 1991 statute, it was to sunset at the end of 1999, and the governor vetoed a bill extending its life. As of June 1999, the panel had reviewed about half of the 4,327 claims originally filed. Although it recommended damages in 509 cases, no claims have been paid, and the rest remain in limbo.[41] Pre-1988 individual claims appear unlikely to be resolved.

Post-1988 Claims. Regarding claims arising after the 1988 act, the state waived sovereign immunity and allowed a broad range of interested parties—native Hawaiians, native Hawaiian organizations, the Office of Hawaiian Affairs, and qualified successors to homestead lessees—to sue in state court to seek remedies for both individual harms and breaches of the trust. The waiver was heavily qualified, however. The act allows a plaintiff only two years after an alleged breach to bring a complaint, provides that litigation is an option only after exhaustion of all administrative remedies, and does not apply when a remedy is available elsewhere. Finally, the statute stipulates that the courts can award land or monetary damages only to restore the trust and cannot make awards to individuals, save for actual damages suffered. A decade later, these opaque provisions have yet to be tested in court.

Federal Action

The 1995 Hawaiian Home Lands Recovery Act resolved all claims involving federal misuse of Home Lands trust resources.[42] The claims will be paid not in cash but in surplus federal land. The secretary of interior was directed in section 203 of the act to determine both the value of lands and the value of lost use of lands that had been designated available in 1920 but were subsequently transferred to the federal government.[43] The DHHL submitted to the Department of the Interior a list of 1,772 acres of land that met the specifications of section 203. Secretary of the Interior Bruce Babbitt allowed claims for $80 million—$50 million for the current market value of the land and $30 million for back rent and interest. In the fullness of time, land worth that amount, approximately 950 acres, will be made available to the DHHL. The process is essentially a land exchange, with the federal government retaining the land from the trust and conveying land of equal value to the DHHL in its place.

A second potentially important part of the act authorized claims that were not otherwise covered. The secretary was encouraged to take a broad perspective, using equitable as well as legal approaches to the topic. Nevertheless, Babbitt took a very narrow view of the federal government's responsibilities and rejected all of the DHHL's claims. Among the reasons given was that even if the federal government had paid rent when it should have, the money would not have gone to the trust because of the funding cap limits. In all, the Recovery Act was a good deal for the federal government. The DHHL even had to pay for the land appraisals required under section 203.

Restitution of historical breaches of the trust is now legally complete, although individual historical claims are in limbo, and future claims by both individuals and the trust proceed on a very narrow path under state law. The federal government continues to hold, unexercised, the clearest authority to sue to enforce the trust. Nevertheless, the trust is, if not whole, at least much restored and free to pursue its purposes. It is difficult, however, to look to the future with confidence. The DHHL still does not have its house in order. Although it has moved unquestionably in recent years toward recognizing its obligations to native Hawaiians, it is not clear that it is well positioned to use the restored trust corpus prudently to serve the beneficiaries.

THE FUTURE OF THE HAWAIIAN
HOME LANDS TRUST

The Home Lands trust began with seventy-five years of untrustlike treatment of trust lands, funds, and beneficiaries. Although the DHHL now appears to be highly motivated to serve the beneficiaries, the future of the DHHL as a trustee is not assured. After nearly forty years of acting like a state bureaucracy, it continues to do so—specifically abjuring the prudent attention to resources and programmatic planning that is required of trustees. It continues to serve established interests with below-market rentals, for example. It is accountable to the beneficiaries in a political way—acceding to beneficiary pressures and preferences—rather than in the context of a fiduciary relationship. We do not, however, conclude that trust principles are irrelevant to the future of the Hawaiian Home Lands. Indeed, we believe that they could be of enormous value as the DHHL tries to start anew after decades of intense political struggle to make the trust whole.

To understand the role that trust principles might play, it is important to understand DHHL activities. Homesteading remains the core of the DHHL mission, although the program has never resembled the family-farm model that operated in the western United States. The trust makes land available to native Hawaiians primarily for residential use. As needs have evolved increasingly toward suburban housing, the DHHL has worked with developers to plan and construct "master communities." The DHHL is responsible for developing infrastructure—water, roads, and utilities—

Less than 5 percent of DHHL leases are granted for what appears to be traditional homesteading. This 300-acre pastoral homestead was let in 1952 to Ekela and Alfred Andrade. They continue to run cattle on their lease. However, the more typical Home Land development constructed today resembles a housing project anywhere else in the United States. (Photo: Stacey Dinstell)

to make home sites habitable. The DHHL has also become a guarantor of housing loans or, in many cases, the lender of last resort for beneficiaries who have been awarded home sites and need additional resources for construction and financing. For beneficiaries who lack the resources to purchase DHHL contractor-built homes, the DHHL has begun to work, on a small number of sites, with Habitat for Humanity.

The DHHL land management programs are presently divided among three operating divisions. The Land Management Division is responsible for managing 80 percent of the trust lands. That includes lands that are managed to produce revenues for the trust, about 38 percent of the corpus.[44] It also includes land that is presently lying fallow or is included in forest reserves, a whopping 42 percent of the corpus.[45] The Homestead Services Division manages both the homesteaded lands, the remaining 20 percent of the corpus, and the homesteaders. It screens and processes homestead applicants; manages loans, transactions, and legal documents; and facilitates conveyances. In addition, the division "supports and empowers" the homesteaders through community-based projects that "preserve, beautify and secure" neighborhoods.[46] The third operating division, Land Development, is responsible for developing trust lands for both homesteading and income-generating purposes. Finally, the DHHL Planning Office oversees social and educational services to homesteaders. For example, DHHL scholarships support the educational advancement of high school graduates. Over $200,000 in scholarships was awarded in 1998–1999 to help native Hawaiians achieve economic self-sufficiency.

From the perspective of trust principles applied to achieve undivided loyalty to the beneficiary and accountability in management, many aspects of the current organization are troubling. A state auditor study of the DHHL raised a number of important issues,[47] questioning whether the HHC is acting effectively in the capacity of trustee. As noted earlier, the chairperson's role is conflicted, encompassing responsibilities as both the operating head of the DHHL and the chair of the HHC. The commissioners are therefore compromised in their ability to act as trustees. The auditor concluded that the commission does not have a process for planning, nor does it appear concerned about fitting program goals to present and future trust resources. It acts more or less as a rubber stamp for the chairperson and cannot even ensure that its decisions are carried out.

Unfortunately, the commission has emphatically rejected the auditor's recommendations that would aim the organization toward more effective planning and implementation. The DHHL's priority is to place beneficiaries on homesteads. The commissioners argue that committees proposed by the auditor to aid planning would not help achieve that priority and have simply spent settlement funds to expedite homesteading.[48] They have not developed a process to define the trust's programs and goals in terms of newly expanded resources. Instead, the commission continues to assume, for no apparent reason, that federal assistance will make up whatever shortfall occurs between trust resources and homesteading aspirations.[49] But the federal government is not a reliable partner in the DHHL enterprise. Close attention to the basic principles of trust organization would help the DHHL identify and address issues fundamental to the future of the trust.

Trust Purpose

The commission defines its mission in terms of "deliver[ing] land to native Hawaiians." Before the restitution process was completed, DHHL staff estimated that it would require in excess of $1.2 billion to provide infrastructure on available lands, and an additional $1.2 billion to construct 16,000 homes to serve those on the waiting list at the time. Even those crude and outdated estimates are instructive—they represent roughly three times the resources foreseeably available to the trust. And they do not include the full array of DHHL programs.[50]

Table 6-1 Homestead Applications and Awards, 1988–1998

	1998	1996	1994	1992	1990	1988
Homestead applications pending, cumulative total	29,702	28,641	26,023	23,536	20,001	17,643
Homestead leases awarded, cumulative total	6,547	6,350	6,059	5,889	5,778	5,803
Leases awarded in previous two years, total	197	291	170	111	–25	

Source: DHHL Annual Reports, 1988–1998.

As Table 6-1 demonstrates, the trust has always had far more qualified homestead applicants than it could serve, given the funds available to support the program. In the most recent decade for which we have data, 744 leases were granted to homesteaders. However, more than 12,000 applications were filed.[51] The commission must think critically about the purpose of the trust and develop some priorities that are reasonable in terms of trust resources.

Beneficiary

Surprisingly, an important element of clarifying the trust purpose is to specify the beneficiary. The HHCA of 1921 stated that those with at least 50 percent of their blood quantum derived from those inhabiting the island when Captain Cook arrived were entitled to homestead on the available lands. But since the trust cannot serve even all those on its applications list, which native Hawaiians will be the trust's priority? Many of the intended beneficiaries do not need trust resources to establish a home for themselves and their families. Others are too poor to qualify for loans that would enable them to buy or build homes and take advantage of the program. Though well intentioned, working with Habitat for Humanity for a few of the poorest applicants does not solve the larger problem.

The need to clarify the beneficiary definition was amplified in a recent DHHL decision regarding the heritability of homesteads. Although one needs a 50 percent blood quantum to qualify for a homestead award, the DHHL now permits anyone with 25 percent native Hawaiian blood to succeed to or receive transfer of a homestead lease. While it might be churlish to turn a homesteader's heir off a leasehold, it is clearly not acceptable to favor those who would not qualify for a lease over the stated beneficiaries of the trust still on the waiting list. Trust principles suggest the importance of developing a policy for determining how many and which of the applicants the trust can effectively serve. A beneficiary needs study that was commissioned in 1995 was intended to provide information on the size of the beneficiary class, their housing preferences and needs, and their qualifications for financing. The results of the study have yet to be translated into a planning process for targeting trust programs.

Undivided Loyalty

Numerous indications suggest that trustees and employees alike could benefit from a richer understanding of the concept of undivided loyalty. For example, it appears that the DHHL routinely grants leases on the trust's revenue-producing lands at rentals referred to appropriately as "nominal." It may be politically prudent to make such commitments to schools and churches, but the trustees need to analyze individual leases carefully, weighing risks and returns to ensure that the trust is not funding public benefits beyond the purposes of the trust. Similarly, it may be reasonable to offer reduced rents to corporations that provide direct benefits to the homesteaders. For example, one might justify a nominal rental to a utility company providing service at a remote homestead location. However, the trustees must evaluate the trade-offs to ensure that the reduced rent is, over the term of the lease, a cost-effective means to procure the benefit.[52] Also troublesome are references in the annual reports to the need to go gently on valued lessees during times of economic stress. This desire to "work with" established lessees could, after an analysis of risks and benefits, prove to be prudent. However, given the troubled history of the trust, it seems at best a poor policy to trumpet this intention routinely in the annual report.[53]

Prudence

Five years after the settlement, the commissioners have not developed a financial investment and management strategy. This does not mean that the DHHL does not plan—it ambitiously plans to develop specific sites. Nevertheless, the commissioners must have a financial plan that will both maximize the trust corpus and give them a rough indication of the resources available over time to ensure that contemplated projects do not exceed future resources.

In addition to this long-term analysis, DHHL trustees need to look carefully at day-to-day program management. For example, 42 percent of the trust's land lies fallow. Although some of the land is developable and the commission has plans to do so, much of it is economically impractical to develop. The commission cannot yield to beneficiary pressure to not diminish the land base. The commission must develop a feasible strategy to exchange the unusable granted lands to create a more productive corpus. Similarly, it is clear that the DHHL loan program is not prudently administered. The agency provides loans to beneficiaries and guarantees loans made by alternative lending sources for the replacement, construction, and repair of homes and the payment of real property taxes. These DHHL programs are clearly tied to trust purpose. Unfortunately, the delinquency rate on DHHL loans is just under 50 percent annually.[54] It appears that the DHHL has allowed the homesteading beneficiaries to develop a culture surrounding the loans that suggests that because the money is from the DHHL it does not have to be repaid.

Accountability

The DHHL story defines a difference between being politically accountable to beneficiaries and acting effectively on their behalf as a trustee. The DHHL is politically responsive to the homesteading beneficiaries—it pushes ahead with homesteading and allows established homesteaders to transfer their leases and avoid loan repayments without regard to the impact on potential homesteaders—all without a careful analysis of the trust's long-term prospects. This responsiveness is arguably an improvement over the DHHL's long history of deference to powerful economic interests in the state, although it appears to be in addition to rather than in lieu thereof. Although political accountability to the homesteaders is an important element of trust activities, it cannot be allowed to overwash the trustee's obligation to prudently manage the trust corpus and plan to achieve trust purposes. If the DHHL were to devote time and attention to clarifying trust purposes and beneficiaries, it would be able to take a more balanced approach to accountability.

Perpetuity

Finally, the DHHL would do well to consider its own life expectancy.[55] It might seem self-evident that the trust intends to be perpetual. How else can one view an organization that grants century-long leases? However, the trustees might consider for how long it is prudent to maintain a state agency to dispense about seventy-five homesteads a year, and whether the resources available thereafter justify a continuing effort to create new homesteads. They might also compare the present rapid build-out program with a slower expenditure of trust resources in order to serve beneficiaries of the next generation. Certainly the policy of allowing nonbeneficiaries to acquire Home Lands leases must be considered. Similarly, the first leases will be expiring fairly shortly. Where do they figure into the equation? These questions must be answered in the context of an improved definition of who the beneficiaries are and what constitutes appropriate DHHL purposes.

The DHHL story is primarily about the relationship between structure and accountability. In any charitable trust, enforcement mechanisms are impaired. In this peculiar federal-state institutional melange, the DHHL's were near totally disconnected. Trust enforcement was impossible as a result. This does not mean that trust principles were meaningless in the fight to restore the trust, just that they did not help in ways that chapter 2 would have predicted. If there are enforcement advantages in having a trust somewhere in an organization's structure, the same is not necessarily true of accountability. The DHHL story is also about the difference between undivided loyalty and political responsiveness. The DHHL clearly responds to pressure from some subsets of the homesteading beneficiaries. But that is not the same thing as undivided loyalty to all the beneficiaries.

The DHHL may yet learn to use the basic trust structure to sculpt a prudent planning approach to its recently restored corpus. The DHHL cannot long avoid addressing the difficult questions that the settlements have created. Trust principles cannot answer them, but they can serve as a guide for defining and resolving the issues in a structured and defensible manner. It seems unlikely, given the trust's history and institutional setting, that the beneficiaries can force the commissioners to act prudently in the analysis and management of trust resources and programs. Caught between two governments, the DHHL is overly accountable to the state's political forces and not at all likely to be pushed toward trust principles by the federal government. However, it does not seem overly optimistic, given what the DHHL employees and beneficiaries have accomplished in terms of trust restitution, for them to aspire to a DHHL that proceeds on something approximating a trust.

PART III: GOVERNMENT-PRIVATE TRUSTS

The North Dakota Wetlands Trust and the Great Lakes Fishery Trust were both established, much like the Platte River trust discussed earlier, with compensation paid by a developer for damage caused by a proposed project. In the North Dakota case, the damage was anticipated. The trust was established as an element of negotiating legislation authorizing the Garrison diversion water project in the upper Midwest. In the Great Lakes trust, an electric power company paid compensation for damage to fish resulting from pumps at a power plant, as an element of gaining approval to continue operating.

What distinguishes these government-private trusts from those in the previous section is that private parties are involved as trustees. These trusts do not merely put a government agency on a longer, slightly peculiar leash, as do those discussed in Part II. They involve private organizations in exercise of governmental authority. Environmentalists had successfully halted the Garrison project by litigation and had been challenging the Great Lakes power plant in court for almost a decade. Both the Garrison legislation and the Great Lakes settlement included the environmentalists, along with government trustees, as participants in decision making about the agreed-on funds. The Platte River trust, although it is discussed in chapter 3 as the classic trust, is appropriately referenced in this part, as it too is a government-private trust. However, it is shaped a little differently from the other two—it includes not only the successful private plaintiffs as trustee but also the private developer-defendant.

These private entities share decision making with trustees who are appointed by government officials or employees of government agencies. State, federal, and tribal governments are involved, but the government-appointed trustees are not necessarily employed by government agencies. In the North Dakota case, the governor appoints private citizens. They are, however, undeniably from the governor's address book, and by general agreement, they represent affected water and agricultural interests.

The underlying disputes thus provide a convenient answer to a complex question that arises in many partnerships: who should be included in the arrangements? The power sharing in these cases arises from the participants' shared interest in a resource—a wetland, a fishery, or a threatened habitat. This interest does not have to be ownership. It can be political veto power or some other "legally cognizable" or protected interest. For example, in the Great Lakes fishery dispute discussed in chapter 8, federal, state, and tribal groups all asserted ownership interests in the resource. The environmental groups had no ownership claim except for a remote interest as citizen beneficiaries of the public trust. However, their group goals and concerns gave them standing to sue.

The major insight to be gained from these organizations is that although they all have problems, none of their limitations seems to arise from the public-private sharing of power. These public-private trusts are also an important element of devolution of governmental authority. The trust instrument provides a convenient vehicle for shaping this rapidly expanding sector of our changing approach to government. The Platte trust puts the best possible face on these organizations. The North Dakota and Great Lakes trusts present fundamental problems that can shed light on both the likely consequences of the present emphasis on partnering and the role of trust principles in ameliorating them.

The major issue addressed in the following chapters is trust structure. The cases demonstrate the need to be mindful when designing the board of trustees, making sure that it fits with the purposes of the organization. At the most basic level, the North Dakota trust suggests that it is important to pay attention to the trust documents and make sure that the institution is reasonably adapted to the territory in which it will operate. In both these trusts, those involved in the dispute—plaintiffs and co-defendants— were given a continuing role in selecting the trustees. This is an important element of the trusts' accountability—one can hope that the boards reflect a built-in balance relevant to the trusts' purposes. However, this approach to accountability can create havoc with the notion of undivided loyalty. The Great Lakes and North Dakota trusts are particularly instructive regarding the challenge of giving partisan politicians a role in choosing trustees. Whereas undivided loyalty fits quite nicely with the sacred trust obligations discussed in chapter 2 and the civil servants running the Dade and EVOS trusts in Part II, legislators and governors appear to have a different standard. This creates apparently insurmountable problems for the DHHL, and it may do so for the North Dakota trust as well.

However, it is not productive for trust mavens to wring their hands about politicians meddling in trust affairs. The private entities appointing trustees are no less looking for representatives than are the elected officials. And, if the trust format is to be relevant to the changing landscape of conservation organizations outlined in chapter 1, it has to account for the polarized political environment in which many of the trusts must operate.

The public-private organizations in this part provide guidance on ways to include, and not to include, political realities without throwing the basics of trust arrangements into total disarray.

This same political interface puts an interesting spin on the notion of accountability. There is no question of mere bookkeeping and disclosing, although the public-private trusts we studied are far less concerned than the government trusts about providing basic financial information. The challenge is to find a way of achieving public accountability for public funds. The successes of the Great Lakes organization and the difficulties encountered in North Dakota provide ample instruction for doing that.

The question of appropriate trust activities is also pressing for both the North Dakota and the Great Lakes trusts. The political environment in North Dakota is such that it has been hard for the trustees to agree on anything. When they have begun to move, they have run afoul of the governor and odd state laws that were not considered in the founding of the trust. In the Great Lakes context, the problem of activities is less fraught but no less pressing: how can an organization spend $70 million in a relatively short period when it is required not to duplicate or displace funding for existing programs? This is a variant on the problem encountered by the EVOS trust when it tried to avoid overlap with the constituent agencies' missions. It is hard to make a unique contribution in a crowded field. We find it curious, viewing the Great Lakes and North Dakota trusts together, that environmentalists are extremely tolerant of "indirect" conservation in the relatively benign setting of Lake Michigan but are considerably less tolerant of the truly embattled North Dakota organization's attempts to do *anything*. The juxtaposition highlights the need to think more broadly about what constitutes appropriate conservation activities.

Trust principles, and lawyers' familiarity with them, made it easy to set up the organizations discussed in this part. The North Dakota trust glided into existence with deeply flawed documents and has suffered ever since. The Great Lakes trust has had a less troubled, albeit briefer, history, but it is not clear that the organization adds much to the mix of public and private entities working to enhance Lake Michigan fisheries. These stories raise questions about when and under what circumstances building not just an organization but a trust is an appropriate way to spend public funds.

CHAPTER SEVEN

North Dakota Wetlands Trust: What's Trust Got to Do with It?

Wetlands preservation is a subject of intense dispute,[1] and perhaps nowhere is the dispute more polarized or intractable than in North Dakota. Yet for a brief period in the mid-1980s, a burst of optimism for ending the "wetlands wars" overtook key protagonists and led to the creation of the North Dakota Wetlands Trust (NDWT). The enthusiasm was short-lived, however, and the NDWT story is about caution and realism when thinking about a trust. Forming an organization is not necessarily an appropriate way to express even the best of intentions. And although it is relatively simple to start a trust, its emphasis on undivided loyalty may not be the right framework for achieving an organization's goals.

In the NDWT case, the most serious problems arose from the fact that the NDWT was established as a by-product of an intense battle over the Garrison diversion water development project. Formation of the NDWT proceeded in a disjointed series of "inside the Beltway" negotiations that omitted key interests. Furthermore, the NDWT has not one trust instrument but three founding documents. The combination is inconsistent on key points involving trust purposes and undivided loyalty, and the expectations for the organization are out of touch with general and specific contours of the trust's territory.

Because the context is particularly important, we begin the NDWT story with a brief explanation of prairie potholes and the controversy over their protection in North Dakota. The second section extracts from the trust's disjointed founding documents some observations about the intersection between trust purposes, framers' aspirations, and institutional design. Undivided loyalty is an unshakable trust basic, but it becomes fragile and obscure when the trust purposes are murky, the directors emphasize responsiveness to their own appointers, and the political environment is hostile. The third section focuses on trust activities. A smooth beginning was undone both by North Dakota statutes ignored at the founding and by shifting political winds. Several years later, a new board had partially righted the situation, but the trust remains vulnerable to capsizing with each change in the political cycle. Our concluding section uses recent discussions about expanding both the Garrison project and the trust as an opportunity to ponder when forming a trust makes sense. Trust principles

115

have not played an important role in the NDWT thus far. And although we are not discouraged by the NDWT's programs or prospects, we do not see how trust principles might make a difference in the future.

THE FOUNDING CONTEXT: POTHOLES

The Prairie Pothole Region lies in the northern prairie in the center of the North American continent. At one time it included more than 20 million acres in the north-central United States and Canada. Prairie potholes are small, constantly changing marshes that typically contain both vegetation and open water. Potholes have distinct vegetative communities based on a five- to twenty-year cycle of forming, degrading, and drying. Most are smaller than a football field, but they can be several hundred acres in size, and they range in depth from a few inches to a few feet. The potholes only appear to be independent bodies of water—the region is better described as a single massive underground lake.

A stunning 75 percent of the migratory waterfowl in North America depend on the prairie pothole ecosystem for at least one stage of their life cycle. Ducks—mallard, pintail, blue-winged teal, gadwall, green-winged teal, canvasback, redhead, ring-necked duck, lesser scaup, hooded merganser, ruddy duck, and wood duck—are the most prominent users. Other birds— snow goose, grebe, rail, coot, American bittern, killdeer, willet, marbled godwit, Wilson's phalarope, black tern, marsh wren, yellow-headed black-bird, red-winged blackbird, and savannah sparrow—also depend on the potholes. Different species use different types of potholes. For example, dabbling ducks use ephemeral marshes, while diving ducks use seasonal and semipermanent potholes.[2]

Not unexpectedly, the prairie pothole ecosystem is imperiled. Half the potholes in North Dakota have been destroyed, and many more are so degraded that they have little biological value. Pothole drainage has been curtailed by recent legislation. Even when a pothole is not drained, how-ever, plowing up to their edges eliminates surrounding terrestrial vegeta-tion and allows damage from siltation, tillage, and pesticide use.[3]

Conservation of the potholes is hard to achieve for a variety of rea-sons. Family farmers who have maintained their political clout in North Dakota work 95 percent of the state's land. The state is a curious mix of strong beliefs in private property rights, hostility to the federal govern-ment, and economic dependence on federal commodity and farm assis-tance programs. Corporations are no more popular in North Dakota than the federal government is. Populist legislation enacted in 1932 prevents corporations, other than limited family corporations, from owning land.[4] Recent amendments have broadened that law to constrain the purchase

Snow geese occupy temporary wetlands in La More County, North Dakota, during their spring migration in 1998. (Photo: Craig Bihrle, North Dakota Game and Fish Department)

and holding of farmland by nonprofit conservation organizations. Moreover, despite the state's respect for private rights, the governor has great authority over the voluntary arrangements that private landowners can make with conservation organizations.

State politics are dominated by agricultural and water associations. Although both are concerned with farming, their approaches are different. The water development community can be described as relatively progressive; it concedes the legitimacy of environmental objectives and is willing to work with environmental interests to meet its own goals. The agricultural community tends to be distrustful of the water interests and hostile to environmental concerns. One farm organization staff person observed, "The water development community is willing to work with the wildlifers—we don't."

The environmental community in North Dakota is almost nonexistent, dominated by government agencies. The Fish and Wildlife Service (FWS) is the major actor. It has purchased fee title and perpetual conservation easements on more than 1 million acres of wetlands. Neither of the two state agencies concerned with wetlands issues—the Game and Fish Department and the Parks and Recreation Department—has attempted

Potholes are not remote from agricultural life in North Dakota. This picture shows a seasonal pothole near a farmhouse in Wing, North Dakota. (Photo: Craig Bihrle, North Dakota Game and Fish Department)

conservation programs on the scale of those of the FWS. The private conservation community is limited. The North Dakota chapter of the Wildlife Society, an organization of wildlife professionals, has been the most active in monitoring and advancing wetlands issues within the state. The National Audubon Society owns and manages one refuge, and the Nature Conservancy has a small program, primarily in the southern area of the state, away from the potholes. Finally, from the safe distance of Washington, D.C., the National Wildlife Federation (NWF) maintains an active interest in North Dakota's resources.

Most of these groups and agencies have been major players in the debate over the Garrison diversion. Garrison looms large in the mythology of the wetlands wars but is merely one blip in a controversy that has engulfed North Dakota for more than half a century. The core of all the disputes is the relationship between draining wetlands and increased flooding. The cycle began in the early 1950s, when federal programs encouraged the draining of wetlands. Serious flooding followed. The problem is passed downstream when one flooded landowner installs drainage to pass the water on to the next. North Dakota legislation in the 1950s required a permit for private drainage of wetlands and adopted a moratorium on drainage in especially hard-hit areas. Landowners, state agencies, and the local water resource boards have ignored the requirements.

The Garrison diversion is the part of the Pick-Sloan Missouri Basin Project that was to solve North Dakota's problems.[5] First approved in 1944, Garrison stalled in the early 1960s because of its enormous cost. In 1965, Congress approved a much-reduced project,[6] but as time passed, support for the project eroded further. Concerned about canals' impact on their operations, farmers formed a committee to oppose the project. Environmentalists objected as well and used the newly minted National Environmental Policy Act (NEPA) to delay the project. Carter administration officials thought that they had killed it, and the Reagan administration, unimpressed with the project's high cost, did nothing to revive it.

Meanwhile, national wetlands conservation efforts prospered. "Swampbuster" legislation in 1985 denied eligibility for almost all federal farm program benefits to growers who either converted or planted on converted wetlands.[7] The North American Waterfowl Management Plan, approved in 1986, anticipated a major venture in the prairie pothole region: acquisition of 74,000 acres per year, and restoration of another 350,000 acres per year.[8]

Just when the Garrison diversion appeared to have sunk of its own weight, a perverse miracle occurred: in 1985, California Democrat George Miller became the first avowedly environmentalist chair of the House Subcommittee on Water and Power. Miller conceived the idea of proving that a really bad water project could be made acceptable to environmentalists.

Garrison was chosen as the guinea pig, and negotiations on authorizing legislation began. The North Dakota water development community got the message: water development could proceed if it addressed environmental protection. Diverted by Swampbuster, the North Dakota farm interests withdrew from the Garrison debate and did not rejoin it.

NWF staff suggested including in the Garrison authorization an organization that would break down the divisions in North Dakota. The federal and state governments would contribute $13.2 million to an organization patterned after the Platte River trust, which the NWF had also helped create. The NWF's draft outline of an organization was quickly accepted by the Garrison negotiators and added to the proposed legislation with only slight modifications.

THE FOUNDING DOCUMENTS

Three documents are key. The first to become "official" is a statement of principles signed by some but not all of the relevant parties as a side deal during the legislative process. The second is the NWF proposal, enacted as part of the Garrison diversion authorization. The third subsumes the statutory language and adds provisions called for in the legislation. It was imposed by the Department of the Interior on protesting charter directors just after they had been appointed.[9] Each of the three contains slightly different information, and the disjointed process left the directors with a number of major problems.

Statement of Principles

The Statement of Principles to Support the Agreement for Reformulation of the Garrison Diversion Unit arose during the Garrison legislative debate. The North Dakota governor feared that the environmentalists would turn at the last minute and oppose the project. NWF staff offered a peace pact as a side agreement to the Garrison negotiations: a statement of hope for resolving North Dakota's wetlands wars. In this document, the environmental community reiterated support for the modified Garrison project, and the state and water interests committed to developing legislation calling for no net loss of wetlands. Unfortunately, the optimistic group of signers did not include state farming interests. Moreover, the statement is not legally binding, and it was not integrated into the proposed legislation. Thus, even before the statute was enacted, much of the NDWT's difficult fate was sealed.

The statement nevertheless evinces a real opening in the North Dakota wetlands debate:

This agreement is intended to launch a new partnership among the parties to improve the management of water and wetland resources within North Dakota. It signifies a good faith and vigorous effort to end the institutional and political conflicts over wetland acquisition and management programs, including the Small Wetlands Acquisition Program.

An example of this new partnership is the Wetlands Trust authorized by the Garrison legislation. The Trust is to be cooperatively funded and managed to complement existing state and Federal wetlands programs, by developing innovative approaches to the preservation, enhancement, restoration, and management of wetlands in private, as well as public, ownership.

The parties agree to work towards the development of "no net loss of wetlands" policies and guidelines for the state, in conjunction with the development and management of North Dakota's water resources and in recognition of the needs and concerns of farmers. The parties support the enforcement and improvement of existing state wetland and drainage laws.[10]

These high hopes were not mere posturing. Within a year, the Garrison coalition was successful in selling the North Dakota legislature on no-net-loss legislation. It was not aggressive compared with other state programs—indeed, it had major loopholes—but it was a major breakthrough in North Dakota.[11] Participants still marvel at their success, describing it as "all the stars lining up at the same time."

Garrison Diversion Legislation

The second trust document, the NWF proposals as folded into the legislation approving the Garrison project, gives general but legally binding guidance to the trust. The purpose is broad: to "preserve, enhance, restore and manage wetland and associated wildlife habitat." The document assigns no mandatory activities, but some of the framers' ideas about the purpose are expressed in suggested programs. The document provides that, at their discretion, the directors may (1) acquire lands and interest in lands, with the consent of the owner and the approval of the governor; (2) acquire water rights pursuant to the laws of North Dakota; and (3) finance wetlands preservation, enhancement, and restoration and wetlands habitat programs.[12] These formal purposes are muddied by similar language in the statement of principles that directs NDWT directors to find "innovative approaches to wetlands protection," with sensitivity to the "needs and interests of the water and agricultural communities." Even though the statement is not binding, the directors have generally read the two documents together, treating the intentions described in the statement of principles as informal purposes.[13]

The admixture of formal and informal purposes has made it difficult to identify the trust beneficiary. Because the NDWT is a charitable trust, its beneficiary is technically the general public. A clear trust purpose is therefore especially important in helping directors identify clear parameters for decision making. This clarity is absent in the NDWT case. Because 90 percent of wetlands are in private ownership, conservation activities are necessarily focused on modifying private agricultural practices. But the combined documents provide poor guidance to directors in choosing programs. It is often hard for both directors and observers to discriminate between innovative, cooperative protection of wetlands and subsidizing of agricultural operations. The statement's emphasis on cooperation with and sensitivity to historic opponents of wetlands protection erodes the directors' ability to proceed in accordance with the most fundamental trust obligation: undivided loyalty to a clearly identifiable beneficiary.

The beneficiary-purpose problem is exacerbated by the NDWT's approach to directors. The legislation and the statement of principles do not mesh regarding the directors. The legislation provides for six.[14] One is appointed by each of the three environmental groups involved in the dispute: National Audubon Society, National Wildlife Federation, and North Dakota chapter of the Wildlife Society. The other three—half of the board—are appointed by the governor, who has selected individuals from the water and agricultural communities.

Fortunately, decision making is relatively simple. Most trust decisions require a simple majority of the board. Nevertheless, the legislation's approach to board balance is problematic. It supports, in part, the statement's aspiration for the trust, which was to provide a forum to resolve disputes and develop cooperative protection programs. Thus, it was important for the directors to speak for—and, in an important sense, to *learn* for—the different interests in North Dakota wetlands issues. But this representation function is not compatible with the trustee's basic obligation of undivided loyalty. Worse, other elements of the legislation head in the opposite direction, setting a two-year term of office.[15] It also allows the appointing authorities to request the resignations of sitting directors.[16] The directors were denied the stability and time in office that would have allowed them to develop and communicate a shared vision of a new era in wetlands management.

Interior Department Grant Agreement

The North Dakota Wetlands Trust Grant Agreement is the third trust document. Created by the Department of the Interior, it is a composite of the statutory provisions and its own. It has been particularly costly in the area of the trust corpus. The Garrison coalition agreed that the NDWT should have an investment principal of $13.2 million deposited, over a protracted period, by the federal and state governments. Twelve million dollars was to be paid by the Department of the Interior, the implementing agency for the Garrison project, beginning with $2 million in the first year (1986).[17] North Dakota committed to paying $1.2 million. The statute provides only that the state's payments would begin after 1990, four years after the trust began operations, and it left the Department of the Interior to negotiate a payment schedule with the governor of North Dakota. In 1991, a year after its payments were to have begun, the state finally agreed to a schedule under which its contribution will not be completed until 2013. The state's successful stonewalling of its obligations has sent a clear signal to the directors and all outside observers that the NDWT is a vulnerable, low-priority program. More than a decade after the trust was established, the NDWT still has not received the originally agreed-on sum.

Although it did not develop a state payment schedule, the grant agreement did impose investment restrictions, limiting the trust to U.S. Treasury instruments. The restrictions directly contradict the legislation establishing the trust, which requires the interior and treasury secretaries to consult with the governor of North Dakota to establish investment requirements that "shall ensure that such amounts are invested in accordance with sound investment principles." A trust portfolio restricted to U.S. Treasury instruments is not in accordance with any reasonable definition of sound investment principles.

Both the governor and the newly appointed directors sought modifications to the investment guidelines, but the Department of the Interior refused any important changes. The governor also pressed to allow the North Dakota State Bank, a state agency, to hold and invest the money, but again Interior refused, insisting that the principal be deposited in a federally insured member institution of the Federal Reserve System. The directors reluctantly accepted the agreement in December 1986, and with their signatures, the North Dakota Wetlands Trust was fully born. The first federal payment of $2 million was made on the last day of the year.[18]

The good news about the trust's founding is easily stated but difficult to assess: after decades of dispute, environmentalists and the North Dakota water development community had achieved a real breakthrough. The new vision was expressed in the NDWT creation and, shortly thereafter, in the passage of no-net-loss legislation. Unfortunately, agricultural interests did not participate in either the dialogue or the jubilation that followed. Moreover, the disjointed process of founding the trust did not produce an auspicious launch for the new organization. The statement of principles combined with the statute to create sufficient ambiguity about trust purposes and the beneficiary to make it difficult for the directors to distinguish between trust purposes and subsidies to local farmers. This, in turn, has made it difficult for the directors to take direction from, or later refuge in, trust principles' insistence on undivided loyalty.

Problems were apparent from the start. The governor's appointees claim that the environmental directors experienced difficulty in finding cooperative and innovative solutions. Clearly, their actions were closely scrutinized by an environmental community legitimately concerned about the intentions of the North Dakotans on the board.[19] Similarly, some environmental directors report that the directors from North Dakota were always looking over their shoulder, wondering how the governor would react. The NDWT directors were soon buoyed by the success of the no-net-loss legislative effort. However, as the political environment shifted, problems rooted in the founding almost derailed the organization.

TRUST PROGRAMS AND ACTIVITIES

Because the NDWT's resources were initially quite limited, the trust started slowly. For the first few years, the directors did all the organizational work themselves, because they believed that they could not afford staff assistance. Nevertheless, they began the tedious process of incorporating as a 501(c)(3) organization and initiated an extensive program planning process. True to the Garrison coalition's aspiration that the organization would serve as a focus for consensus-building dialogue, the NDWT adopted an open approach to decision making. The directors began with a series of public meetings and took seriously the guidance offered.[20] Moreover, in spite of the anticipated criticism from their appointing powers and respective communities, charter directors from both "sides" worked to find projects that contributed to trust purposes.[21]

The charter directors were proceeding, as best they could, in the spirit of the statement of principles. However, their devotion to the details of the operation did not include any training in trust principles. The directors followed the Interior document in referring to themselves not as trustees but as directors.[22] They proceeded, and continue to do so, without any apparent awareness of the peculiar nature of the organization they were running or their obligations as its directors. In July 1987, they produced the "North Dakota Wetland Trust Guidelines."[23] As advised by the public, the directors decided *not* to spend trust income on staff, research, public relations, acquisition of long-term easements, payments for temporary habitat improvement, or maintenance of any natural area. Instead, the original guidelines focused on acquisition of wetlands and associated habitat. The directors developed both an elaborate process and thirteen criteria to guide land acquisition. The criteria reflect the basic NDWT commitment to achieving habitat protection while being sensitive to the needs of farmers. The process provides adjacent landowners, county commissioners, water resource and soil conservation districts, state agencies, and the executive branch an opportunity to comment on proposed acquisitions. While this might seem excessive, the directors considered it imperative for the organization to function in a transparent manner and for its programs to exist harmoniously within the state. Finally, because the governor had to approve all acquisitions of property interests, they knew that acquisitions required both public and gubernatorial support. However, the initial acquisition program was ambitious within those constraints.

The directors also decided to retain title to the fee land the trust purchased. But the directors decided that the trust would not *manage* any of the lands it acquired; instead, they executed management agreements under which public agencies would pay most management costs. This decision gave the NDWT a low profile as a landowner and minimized responsibilities and expenses, but it also precluded the trust from earning income or using the properties for demonstration purposes.

Because major land acquisition efforts would be delayed until the trust had sufficient funds, the directors initiated two other programs—one supporting farmers' efforts to create wetlands, and the other a small grant program. In 1987, the directors initiated a Create-a-Wetland (CAW) program. The effort was designed to "improve water management, . . . crop yields, . . . [and] water quality; create migratory bird habitat; demonstrate cooperation between landowners and wildlife interests; and provide an opportunity for long-term change in wetland management on private lands."[24] When it began on an experimental basis in one county, the NDWT paid for the installation of gated culverts to retain spring runoff on formerly drained wetlands, thereby creating seasonal wetlands. The trust paid participating farmers an annual per acre fee (usually $10) for three years for the flooded acres.

Although the program continues to be an important NDWT activity, early controversy among the board regarding CAW illustrates problems with undivided loyalty. One of the directors instigated the program and was both a leader in anchoring the program in his county and a participant. Although he did not vote on the project when the board considered it, it is difficult to avoid the conclusion that he had a conflict of interest. But the "cooperative spirit" of the trust convinced him, and ultimately most other directors, that it was necessary for him to participate if the trust was asking other landowners in the area to do so. Wondering whether the program was merely a subsidy to farmers, dissenting directors then questioned the program's contribution to ecological improvements.

To address the issue, the NDWT did something unusual in the context of the programs we studied: the board hired a consultant to evaluate the program. The study found that although agricultural production increased on the lands enrolled in the program, significant adjustments were needed if the effort were to achieve the habitat goals. The NDWT made changes to the program and extended it to landowners in another county.[25] The directors continue to hope that programs like CAW demonstrate that wetlands protection is compatible with agricultural land use. The directors have not discussed this issue in terms of trust principles, but it clearly raises them.

The second early focus was a small grant-making program. The initial requests tended to be small, and the trust income was adequate to fund most of them. For example, the NDWT gave numerous full and partial grants to various counties to purchase no-till drills for farmers.[26] The directors hope that farmers will test the no-till drill and decide to switch to it permanently. However, because many of the directors are themselves farmers in the prairie pothole region, the potential exists for conflict of interest. Further, when the directors simply "hope" that farmers will switch to no-till drills, extending the grants appears questionable in terms of undivided loyalty. Nevertheless, by the early 1990s, grant-making activity had increased so much that the directors were concerned that the trust would be viewed as merely a grant-making organization rather than one that develops and implements projects itself. The directors wanted to be more proactive in developing the projects.[27]

The burgeoning grants program is one reason that the directors decided in 1990 to engage the services of a consultant to act as part-time executive director and perform administrative and managerial tasks. Most directors did not believe that their income or level of activity justified a full-time position. Also, by using a consultant, they did not have to provide office space, equipment, or other staff support. The arrangement gave the trust access to biologists and other consulting specialists, but only as needed. The contract was renewed on an annual basis.

The new executive director also developed and proposed projects to the board. For example, the Maple River Drift Prairie Project identified an area of biological concern where it was politically possible to work. The NDWT would acquire the land in partnership with other groups and then "work with landowners to provide technical assistance and economic incentives which allow them to develop and maintain farming and grazing practices that will improve the biological diversity of wetlands."[28] The trust was soon planning to develop a long-term easement for the project. In spite of all its financial problems and constraints and its organizational design flaws, and without any reference to directors or their obligations, the NDWT was off and running.

A second land acquisition project, Kenner Marsh, began in January 1989 and ultimately became one of the trust's major success stories.[29] It also raised an unforeseen problem. While acquisition negotiations were under way in Kenner Marsh, the directors became aware of the implications of corporate farm law for their activities.[30] The statute was designed in the 1930s to prevent corporations (other than family-owned corporations) from owning farmland.[31] It was amended in 1981 to apply to conservation organizations as well, providing that no organization chartered in North Dakota after 1985 could own farmland in the state. Conservation organizations that were chartered before 1985 could acquire land only with the governor's approval after a public review process.

It is not clear why the Garrison negotiators envisioned land acquisition as a trust activity without determining the precise circumstances that would require the governor's permission. Surely that provision of the legislation ought to have set off warning flares among the environmentalists. Unfortunately, it did not.[32] The original coalition held together long enough to procure an amendment to the Corporate Farm Law that allowed the trust to pursue land acquisitions. However, it limited NDWT holdings to 12,000 acres. It also prohibited the trust from conducting farming operations on its lands and imposed significant public involvement requirements.[33] Although the directors' own acquisition procedures had more or less anticipated the other constraints, the belated "discovery" of the statute and the need to work for amendments was another hurdle for the NDWT.

Stalled but not halted, the directors completed the Kenner Marsh program and acquired several other important parcels. However, the portents were not positive. Finally, a particularly complex transaction at Rush Lake took the momentum out of the trust's land acquisition program altogether. Numerous agencies and private landowners were involved in working out scientific issues (determining, for example, how much land is needed to restore minimum lake levels), management issues, and financing. Just before the directors' final vote on the project was to have occurred in January 1994, a newly elected governor appointed new directors, and the project was killed. Thereafter, the land acquisition program withered. As of this writing, the trust has purchased 4,154 acres, all initiated by the charter directors.

The Rush Lake collapse was one element of a major shift in the political climate in North Dakota and, indeed, the nation as a whole that surrounded the 1994 elections. Among other things, the elections rejuvenated the state's farmers. No longer preoccupied with defensive reaction to burgeoning wetlands laws and regulations, North Dakota's farming associations adopted the increasingly fashionable "wise use" nomenclature and went on the offensive. They interested themselves intensely in the NDWT's affairs.

The changed climate caused major alterations in the trust. The governor's were not the only new appointments. Two of the environmental groups changed their representatives as well. As 1994 began, five of the six directors were totally new to the organization, and several were inexperienced in water and wetlands issues. Such major turnovers create serious challenges for small organizations.[34] Worse, from our perspective, the new directors knew no more about the notion of undivided loyalty than had the charter board. The new governor's new directors understood their position as one of representing the governor and their respective constituencies. For example, one director stated, "The governor gave me the job, and I should do what he wishes." But the same is true of the environmental directors. One environmental appointee stated, "I wouldn't vote for something my organization was against." Fortunately, the part-time executive director could orient the new directors to NDWT programs, but she could not introduce trust principles, because she did not know about them herself.

Organizational momentum and activity ground to a crawl. At the executive director's urging, the directors agreed to begin a formal planning process that included weekend retreats and professional facilitation. The first year was difficult, as the directors could not agree to very much. The resulting strategic plan[35] emphasized private land incentives and conflict resolution and de-emphasized land acquisition. One strange objective was to "expend up to 25% of annual income on short-term projects which have long-term educational and demonstration value."[36] A second odd goal focused on conflict resolution that involved communication of success stories, creation of more partnerships, and educational programs. Cooperative approaches, originally an addendum to the trust documents, evolved into a major trust purpose.

Conflicts over educational programs are symptomatic of the rifts between "direct" environmental protection and gradual reorientation of farmers that almost immobilized the board. One might have assumed that projects concerned with education would be noncontroversial. Because they do not require the governor's approval or incite the ire of the agricultural community, the external politics of educational programs are less complicated. However, the internal politics are intense. The board that was designed to encapsulate the state's wetlands wars is deeply divided on the issue. Some environmental directors oppose investing large sums in educational projects that do not achieve direct wetlands protection. The governor's appointees consistently support it.

External criticism echoed the internal divisions. The agricultural community remains hostile to the trust and criticizes it for attempting nearly any wetlands protection activity other than education. For environmentalists, the directors are not pursuing conservation activities directly enough. The NDWT came under unrelenting criticism from virtually all elements of the attentive public.

In response to public criticisms and internal disputes, the beleaguered directors hired a consulting firm to perform an evaluation of the trust in 1997. The evaluation lists a number of achievements: 53,339 acres of wetlands on public and private lands were protected, restored, or enhanced, and 4,154 acres acquired; 170 landowners signed wetlands agreements, and 578 farmers participated in field tours of conservation practices; 31,000 acres of privately owned agricultural land have been improved for habitat or removed from agricultural use; and flood control was increased by 4,501 acre feet.[37] The report also notes that nearly $800,000 was paid to landowners and communities in the form of real estate taxes and conservation incentives.[38]

The evaluation is imperfect and probably overstates the accomplishments of the trust, particularly after the new directors were appointed. However, the analysis is unusual in the annals of the organizations we studied and valuable for putting criticisms in perspective. There is no support for the allegation that the trust is too focused on education rather than "direct" conservation programs. Spending on acquisition, restoration, and enhancement far exceeded spending on education. Moreover, the data do not support a broad-brush conclusion that the trust is inappropriately skewed away from wetlands conservation toward subsidies for agriculture. Even if one considers the entire $800,000 paid in taxes and for conservation incentives as supportive of farmers and farm communities, the amount is still only 20 percent of the total trust expenditures. Moreover, in a region where 95 percent of the wetlands are privately owned, it is not clear that conservation can be achieved without substantial payments to property owners. Finally, NDWT expenditures are considerably less than the investments that its programs have leveraged. During the period of evaluation, the trust spent $1.9 million on wetlands projects but attracted an additional $3.5 million.

The evaluation made it clear that the NDWT had been providing information, services, and benefits to wetlands and habitat protection that were not available prior to the trust's establishment. Environmentalist critics and directors both preferred a more direct approach to wetlands protection. However, in a region so hostile to conservation programs, and in the face of political pressure and outright gubernatorial vetoes, more aggressive, direct wetlands protection activities may not be feasible. Perhaps what the NDWT accomplished is all that can be expected.

It is also clear, however, that between the new directors' 1994 plan and the most recent one promulgated in 1997, something changed. One current director observed, "You get tired of banging your head against the wall—conservation is tough in North Dakota. You tend to start doing what you can." The board appears to have weathered a period of upheaval and emerged on a more positive, confident path. One symbol of the trust's renewal is the directors' decision to hire a full-time executive director and three support staff. Initial estimates that administrative costs would approximately double to about $250,000 did not deter the board. However, the directors expect the new executive director to raise money from foundations or donations to make up the difference and support a more aggressive array of programs.

The directors also adopted a revised version of the strategic plan in June 1997 for the period 1997 to 2000. The goals are clearer and more concrete, and they show an increased focus on and knowledge about wetlands resources: restore a major wetlands area for habitat and water management benefits, complete the Maple River Drift Prairie Project within four years, improve management of existing trust lands.[39]

This new momentum does not necessarily presage a happy ending for the NDWT. Even when the directors are able to agree, their efforts can be frustrated by external conditions. For example, the new-era directors agreed to acquire long-term easements as part of restarting the stalled Maple River Drift Project. The easements were designed to meet landowner concerns. For example, the trust offered thirty-, fifty-, and ninety-nine-year terms. Although he did not support the project, when outvoted, the chair of the board moved the paperwork forward, although he was also clear that all the governor had to do was "nod and wink" his disapproval to kill it. Even with willing landowners, the governor rejected the NDWT's application to purchase a ninety-nine-year conservation easement and stated that he would not accept a thirty-year term application either. The governor might, his attorney hinted, consider a fifteen-year easement. The directors, whether they considered that inadequate or detected a negative nod from the governor, halted the program.

The more serious problem is not the external frustrations. Twice in fifteen years a set of directors has come together across broad differences to plan and undertake a significant set of programs. The enduring risk is that they will have to keep doing that. The poorly planned structure leaves current directors as vulnerable to removal as were the charter directors during another political perturbation. This would require another set of directors to slug it out until they too develop enough experience as a group to begin to envision a new strategic plan. The presence of a professional staff could be important in tempering those swings somewhat. However, the staff is no less vulnerable to a disturbance than are the directors themselves.

For students of the trust, it is important to note that trust principles did not prevent or even focus comment on the NDWT's decline, and they have played no apparent role in its modest resurrection. The one trust element that appears to matter is that the NDWT has an endowment, constrained though it may be by the Department of the Interior's ill-advised investment restrictions. The trust does not want for funds, and it can plan its activities with confidence that it will not need a yard sale or a legislative appropriation to fund them. This is significant, but it does not make trust principles important in the NDWT. It would be wrong to say that the organization does not work—the NDWT has surmounted many problems to play a small but positive role in wetlands. However, it does not work *as* a trust or because it *is* a trust. The idea of a trust was an important element in the NDWT's hasty founding, but we have not really seen or heard of trust principles since.

EXPANSION OF THE NDWT?

It is appropriate to wonder whether the gains made by this organization have been worth the effort. This is more than an academic pondering. A second stage of the Garrison diversion project has been proposed, and $25 million additional federal funding for the NDWT has been discussed. A bill has been introduced to change the NDWT to the Natural Resources Trust.[40] Its purposes would be expanded to include the protection of grasslands and riparian habitats.

Environmentalists do not support the proposal. They question whether the NDWT should be given more resources when it has not expended what it already has, and when it is so constrained by the governor. The agricultural community has proposed an alternative, a separate conservation trust that would pay farmers to plant trees and undertake similar conservation activities on private land. The directors have not become involved. Their position is that if someone wants to give them more money, they will take it. But they are not going to try to get it.

We will ignore several aspects of this interesting debate. First, a list of design flaws to be fixed would repeat much of the discussion in Part II. The NDWT structure is poorly conceived and ill suited to support trust principles, achieve the coalition's goals, or sustain an organization in the difficult political climate of North Dakota. If a second round of legislation could, for example, establish terms of office that stagger the governor's appointments so that they cannot all be removed at one time, that would be helpful. However, opening the structure to reconsideration would also allow Congress to create new problems in the process of addressing the old. We are not optimistic.

Second, we are not interested in discussing whether those concerned about wetlands protection should accept $25 million for mitigation in place of the areas that will be destroyed by an expanded Garrison. The answer is, of course not. However, if project opponents conclude that the expansion is inevitable, they should be prepared to wonder whether expanding the NDWT or establishing a new organization ought to be included in whatever compromise they can strike in defeat. Our discussion may raise some fodder relevant to that debate, but we will not engage in it directly.

We understand why agricultural interests would like to be paid to plant trees, but we are not sure that even their relatively simple goal is best achieved by establishing or enhancing an odd public-private institution like a trust. We have a well-functioning mechanism in this country for funneling subsidies to interests, both powerful and aggrieved. This is not an arena in which government investment is fading and government hollowing out. We think that a heavy burden of proof rests with those who want to build an organization that will add a few small drops to that torrent. This is especially true when doing so drains the scarce human resources required to maintain voluntary public service organizations. Who would be the directors, and who is going to keep an eye on it? The NDWT spends public money with very little oversight from Congress and arguably excessive oversight from local farmers and the governor. We do not need a new organization, let alone two trusts, to encourage farmers to plant trees.

There are alternative ways to spend the small funds that were devoted to wetlands conservation in the Garrison legislation. The Garrison negotiators could have endowed a series of extension programs to bring water, agricultural, and environmental interests together to seek a new wetlands dialogue. Similarly, if they had wanted to support a modest wetlands acquisition and protection program, a small grant to the Nature Conservancy or a special earmarked fund for the FWS would have filled the bill quite satisfactorily.

More specifically, we see no reason to establish a trust unless the reasons for doing so fit reasonably well with trust principles. The trust is not just an organization; it is characterized, as discussed in chapter 2, by one person or people holding and managing resources for the exclusive benefit of another. The idea of undivided loyalty can provide a decision guide and a principled defense for unpopular decisions in a harsh political environment. If the directors—or the framers—are unable to conceptualize a clear purpose that will put a fairly sharp edge on the trustee's deliberations, they should probably stop right there. It simply does not make sense to build an organization around undivided loyalty to a deeply contested or undefinable abstraction.

We wind up with mixed conclusions about the NDWT. In spite of all the barriers—the failure of the framers to secure the state contributions and permit reasonable portfolio management, the inadequate design of board terms and accountability, and the organization's apparent ignorance of trust principles—the NDWT has accomplished much for wetlands protection in a hostile environment. It has developed a number of voluntary programs that are working their way into agricultural operations. It has taken small but unusual steps to evaluate its programs. It may not have pursued the environmentalist's preferred strategy of buying land and creating preserves, but that model cannot be applied everywhere. Working within the political realities in which it was created, and reflecting the sentiments of the state's population and politicians, the NDWT is creating its own model for wetlands and wildlife habitat protection in North Dakota.

We do not lament the NDWT simply because we might prefer a different or more familiar set of programs (and we are not sure that we do). We do, however, note the organization's distance from trust principles. Thus far, the major role that trust principles played in the NDWT was to make it far too easy to create the organization. Confidence in those principles lulled the Garrison negotiators into establishing a trust compromised by sloppy thinking about structure and purpose. However, there is clearly a need for an organization in North Dakota whose focus is on wetlands protection. For now, the NDWT is that organization. Trust principles estivate at the margins of its operations. At some future point, a board of directors may find it productive to dust them off and put them into play.

CHAPTER EIGHT

Great Lakes Fishery Trust:
Blending Governments and
Nongovernmental Organizations

The Great Lakes Fishery Trust (GLFT) was established in a now familiar context: it is one element of a court settlement in protracted litigation. Trust principles were not used to bind together those who had been on opposing sides of the dispute but, as in the EVOS case, to enable not always agreeable coplaintiffs to move together toward a settlement and subsequent management of a rather large damage payment. Thus, the GLFT displays the trust in one of its best applications—as a familiar template for allocating control over shared resources. The trust was useful in pulling an odd lot of organizations—state and federal agencies, tribal governments, and private conservation groups—together to manage common resources on more or less equal footing. The GLFT is barely beyond the formation stage, having been established only in 1996, but as an example of how public and private entities might structure organizations or run programs based on "partnering" agreements, it is hard to top.

One reason the GLFT is so instructive is that it has taken an interesting and frequently opposite approach to many of the same questions that have concerned the other trusts we studied. For example, the GLFT is currently planning, in spite of clear language in the trust instrument directing a perpetual trust, to go out of business in the year 2020. Second, whereas most of the organizations in this volume have worked assiduously to acquire land, the GLFT began with more than 11,000 acres in its trust corpus and has sought to dispose of those resources and not to acquire more. In so doing, the GLFT has had to balance its role as a land seller obliged to maximize returns to the corpus with its obligation to act with undivided loyalty to the fishery resources—a difficult but interesting compromise. Third, it is typically taken for granted that prudence requires trustees to avoid spending trust resources on administration. Almost without exception, trustees at least start by deciding to get by with as little structure as possible. The GLFT headed in the opposite direction, and its organizational density is striking. An exploration of its brief history suggests why that decision is prudent.

The GLFT is also distinctive among the trusts we studied in its approach to science and trust activities. Unlike the Platte River organization, which has defined itself largely in terms of research, and the EVOS trust, which appears headed toward an emphasis on large-scale marine science, the GLFT focuses on what its manager calls "things people can see." This focus persists in spite of the fact that the trustees wrestled with the role of scientific advisers institutionalized in the settlement. For example, researchers' preference for funding in perpetuity put the trust's scientific advisers on the opposite side of the trustees' decision to sunset in 2020.

Finally, and very much related to the role of science and research in trust activities, the GLFT is specifically directed to find a distinctive niche for itself. Several of the organizations in this volume have tried to think in those terms, but the GLFT is prohibited from spending trust resources to supplement or replace funding for "traditional" programs. The GLFT's effort to establish the trust as an independent organization—separate from the legislature, the scientific advisory group, the participating organizations, and others similarly situated—figures prominently in many of its organizational choices. The GLFT is particularly well heeled, but in the end it is simply one of many participants in the crowded field of Great Lakes restoration and enhancement.

We follow these issues through a chronological discussion of the GLFT, focusing first on the settlement and then on trust organization and activities. We conclude with two observations. First, we notice a dog that did not bark: why was it not more difficult to make an effective blend of disparate public and private groups? The GLFT makes it look easy. Second, we also note with pleasure the blessings secured by a well-thought-out trust document and a careful orientation in trust principles. Finally, we wonder again about science, research, and appropriate activities in the expenditure of restoration resources.

FROM ALEWIFE MORTALITY TO THE GREAT LAKES FISHERY TRUST

It is perhaps difficult to get as excited about alewife mortality as, say, whooping cranes or prairie potholes. The fish are small, relatively unattractive members of the herring family. They do not appear, at first blush, likely to precipitate nearly a decade of litigation on their behalf. But appearances can be deceiving.

Their most important feature, at least in telling this tale, is the alewife's tendency to get sucked into the pumps at the Ludington Pumped Storage Facility on the eastern shore of Lake Michigan. For three decades, the plant has been killing fish, including several species particularly cherished by anglers. The alewife is not among those; it looms large not for itself alone but because it is a primary food source of the larger, preferred fish species,

The alewife is a small herring, typically about six inches long. It has a greenish to bluish back, silvery sides with faint dark stripes, a spot behind its head, and a small patch of teeth on its tongue. (Photo: University of Wisconsin–Madison, Sea Grant Web site, and Shedd Aquarium, Chicago)

such as salmon. The sport fish populations have declined in Lake Michigan, and ecologists have attributed much of the loss to the decline of the alewife population. The alewife came to be seen as "salmon in disguise" and thus a focus of the Ludington dispute.

The GLFT was formed to receive and dispense the damages paid for fish mortality caused by the Ludington Pumped Storage Project. Two interlocking agreements resolved proceedings before the Federal Energy Regulatory Commission (FERC), litigation brought in Michigan state court, and state administrative proceedings. The agreements[1] provided a structure under which Consumers Power Company and Detroit Edison Company[2] could continue to operate while paying for past and future fish mortality caused by the operation.

The plaintiffs assembled slowly over the course of the eight-year proceedings. In 1985 and 1986, the National Wildlife Federation (NWF), soon joined by the Michigan United Conservation Clubs, challenged the Ludington Project before the FERC when its license was due to be renewed and in court on air pollution grounds. The two groups also intervened before the state Natural Resources Commission to block a "proposed settlement between the State of Michigan and the power companies pursuant to which the State was going to resolve all past and future claims for fish mortality from the facility for approximately $440,000."[3] By 1986, the state saw the enormous potential of the mortality claims, changed hats, and also filed suit to recover damages in state court.

The litigation turned on complex questions about fisheries biology, the extent and value of the damage to numerous fish species, and the effect of mitigation efforts. Scientific advisers accordingly played an enormous role, most clearly in connection with a barrier net erected by the defendants during the litigation. The net was installed to keep the fish from being sucked into the pumps. The early parties to the litigation formed the Ludington Advisory Committee to monitor and improve the net. It was the precursor of the scientific advisory team (SAT) created as part of the settlement agreement.

As the dispute ground toward closure, two new interests became involved. About eighteen months before the end of the process, the Department of the Interior (DOI) entered the negotiations to assert federal rights in the Lake Michigan fishery. About six months after that, several Native American tribes joined the proceedings to protect their own interests in the fisheries. As intermittent trustee[4] for the Native Americans, DOI supported recognition of the tribes' legal position.[5] The group of plaintiffs thus included an uncomfortable set of bedfellows. Some of the groups were habitual adversaries. None would allow the others to dominate the settlement. The plaintiffs' litigation team worked constantly to quell dissension and to keep their group of clients speaking with the same voice. Most particularly, it was necessary to convince officials from the state of Michigan that the Lake Michigan fishery was not their exclusive domain, that others had well-established legal rights to use the resource and protect their interests in it.[6]

As a settlement began to take shape, it became clear that practical and legal problems attendant to "dividing the spoils" among the fractious plaintiffs presented a major challenge.[7] The idea of a trust as a frame for the settlement was first presented by the NWF to the state of Michigan's attorney. It had instant appeal because it offered a neutral and familiar format in which each of the parties could both share control and surrender some, and it obviated the necessity for calculating what portion of the funds went to each of the parties. The idea of an independent organization with an exclusively ecological purpose also appealed to the scientists involved. The trust concept appeared even more promising after the late entry of the federal and tribal parties further complicated the pie and power sharing.

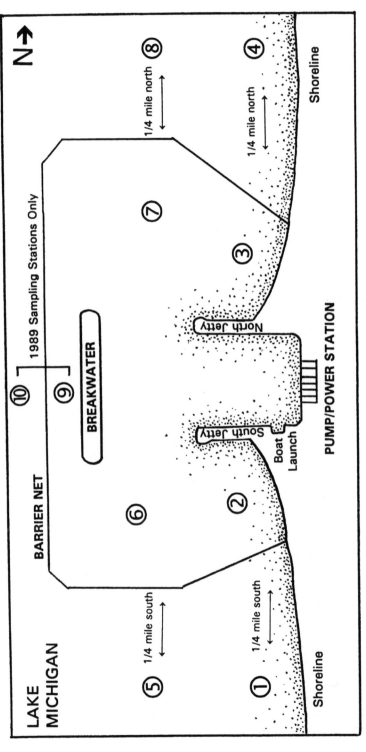

The barrier net erected by the defendants during the litigation plays an enormous role in settlement implementation. The net is not simply a strainer placed over the end of the intake pipe; its aim is to keep fish out of the entire area affected by the suction of the plant. Continuing efforts to improve the net could impact payments received by the trust. (Courtesy Detroit Edison)

Unfortunately, perhaps, the state legislature was not informed about the proposed trust until just prior to the signing of the settlement agreement. Although the legal team did not expect any opposition, numerous state senators thought differently. They saw the fish mortality as an injury to the state's public trust and argued that the damages ought to be paid to the general fund and be subject to the control of elected officials.[8] They argued that the proposed trust would be unaccountable and that its creation was an "end run" around the legislature. Following senate hearings, the settlement and the trust eventually proceeded,[9] but the problem of the legislature's interest in the funds has continued to influence trust decisions.

The settlement was complex, but for our purposes, it can be broken down into three primary components. First, Consumers Power agreed both to minimize damage to the fishery resources and to pay compensation for historic and continuing fish mortality associated with the Ludington plant. Second, the GLFT was created to manage and expend the damage payments. Consumers Power's payments are to continue for the period of the license granted to the plant, that is, until 2019. Third, the SAT, the successor to the Ludington Advisory Committee, which had participated in the litigation, was created to monitor plant operations, calculate annual fish mortality, and provide scientific leadership to the GLFT. Consumers Power's annual payments are based on a formula approved by the SAT. The settlement thus established a potentially competitive relationship between the GLFT and the SAT. Managing that relationship has been a conspicuously successful element of GLFT decisions thus far.

TRUST PURPOSE

The purpose of the GLFT is "to mitigate for the use and enjoyment of Lake Michigan fishery resources forgone as a result of the operation of the Ludington Project and to benefit the Great Lakes fishery by providing funding for the enhancement, propagation, protection and replacement of Great Lakes fishery resources."[10] The declaration suggests five permissible uses of trust funds: research; rehabilitation of lake trout, sturgeon, and other populations; protection and enhancement of fish habitat; public education; and acquisition of real property.[11] In the end, the document permits "any other" activities consistent with the settlement and approved by the trustees. It is interesting to note that, like the EVOS trust, the documents focused on rehabilitating resources, but from the outset, the trustees have used their discretion to emphasize public use projects.

Although the purpose is quite similar in scope and specificity to the North Dakota trust's formal goal, it is important to underscore a basic difference: the GLFT is not encouraged to enhance, protect, and restore the fishery while acting in supportive and sympathetic harmony with the power companies. There is no distracting overlay of subpurposes that erodes the clarity of the trust's mission. This does not mean that the GLFT does not have a political context. It clearly does, although the legislature's concerns have been nowhere near as compromising of trust purposes as the situation in North Dakota. But GLFT trustees can, even acting within a charitable trust's expansive notion of a beneficiary, define a relatively clear purpose and beneficiary to guide their decisions.

BENEFICIARY

The only question about the beneficiary is the geographic scope of GLFT operations. The trustees engaged the issue extensively. The Great Lakes are ecologically connected. Given the nature of the fish mortality problem and the reach of the settlement, trust activities could include a wide variety of affected interests, within and beyond both Lake Michigan and the state of Michigan. The trust is, after all, named after the Great Lakes fishery resources, not Lake Michigan or the Michigan shoreline. Although the settlement allows the trustees to undertake projects in any of the Great Lakes, the voting requirements give priority to projects that benefit the Lake Michigan fishery. Going outside of Lake Michigan requires support from five of the six trustees.[12] The trust has in fact funded projects in Lake Huron and work by organizations in New York, Indiana, Wisconsin, Massachusetts, and Oregon that was related to Great Lakes fisheries problems.

TRUSTEES

The trustees reflect the origins of the trust—all the plaintiffs are represented. One trustee is appointed by each of the six plaintiffs: the Michigan Department of Natural Resources (DNR), the Michigan attorney general, the U.S. Fish and Wildlife Service, the Tribal Council of the Grand Traverse Band of the Ottawa and Chippewa Indians, the Michigan United Conservation Club, and the NWF. Each trustee serves at the pleasure of the appointing plaintiff, and there are no terms of office.[13] Contrary to the EVOS and DHHL experience, some creativity was involved in representing the tribes' interests, even beyond those that participated in the litigation. Two nonvoting trustees are appointed by the tribal councils of the Little River Band of Ottawa Indians and the Little Traverse Bay Band of Odawa Indians— tribes recently recognized and therefore less involved in the settlement.

The GLFT's basic structure, Native Americans aside, does not sound very different from the provisions that brought the North Dakota trust so much grief. However, beyond merely representing each of the plaintiffs among the trustees with no set terms, the trust framers sculpted related provisions appropriate to the Michigan context that have helped the organization work with its potentially fractious board. For example, the GLFT has a permanently designated chair: the director of the Michigan DNR. This provision may simply acknowledge the state's insistence that its own interests in the fishery were paramount. However, the designation is more interesting than that. Oddly enough, the GLFT's approach to the chair allows the governor to have a role in appointing trustees while creating some insulation from partisan state politics. The provision builds on the fact that in Michigan, the governor appoints the commissioners of the DNR, who in turn select the director of the DNR. The governor has a role in selecting the GLFT chair and state trustee, albeit from one remove. To unseat the DNR appointee would require removing not just a trustee but the director of the department as well. Thus, although the state trustee is clearly connected to the governor, it is far more difficult for elected officials to meddle in trust affairs than in North Dakota, where the governor directly appoints three of the six trustees.

The settlement agreement is also more formal than most regarding voting: the trustees cannot do business by simple majority. The agreement of four—or two-thirds—of the trustees is required for most actions. Concurrence of five of the six trustees is required, as noted earlier, to approve expenditures for activities outside of the Lake Michigan basin. The same near unanimity is required for the acquisition or sale of real property,[14] and the assent of all six trustees is required to amend the trust documents.[15] However, as a practical matter, the trustees' mode of operation is consensus. They seek agreement by all trustees for all their actions, with the nonvoting tribal trustees fully participating in deliberations and decisions.

The DNR's close relationship with the trust was not entirely comfortable for the DNR. The settlement agreement had also given the agency a pivotal role in providing start-up support and structure for the new organization. The subsequent legislative objections to the trust required the DNR to distance itself noticeably from the GLFT. The DNR is dependent on the legislature and cannot afford to be seen as devoting state resources to trust activities that the legislature does not enthusiastically endorse.[16]

TRUST CORPUS

Although the need to separate the trust from the DNR appears to have inspired much of the GLFT's approach to structure, the mixture of assets that make up the corpus also contributed to the organizational decisions. The trust manages three types of resources: an initial lump-sum payment of $5 million; annual payments of up to $2.5 million for fish mortality; and, unusual for the trusts we are studying, approximately 11,000 acres of land, valued at the time of the settlement at roughly $7 million. The total future value of the trust corpus at its founding was considerable, in the neighborhood of $71 million.[17] Unlike the Dade and North Dakota trusts, the GLFT did not have to sit and wait for trust assets to build; nor, however, did it have a grace period in which to get organized before it had to deal with significant issues. The lump sum and the land gave the trust considerable starting funds. Although the annual payments will fluctuate like Dade's, depending on how well improvements in the net or other mitigation measures reduce fish mortality,[18] they constitute less than a quarter of the trust's starting corpus.

Despite the presence of the DOI in the negotiations, the funds are not managed, as are the EVOS trust's, by CRIS and NRDA. Better still, the trust agreement does not impose restrictions on the trustees' ability to invest the corpus. Indeed, the settlement agreement borrows the generous language from the Platte River trust documents regarding management of the corpus.

Although the GLFT is less concerned about owning or acquiring land than many of the trusts in this volume, its land assets have significantly shaped the trust's organizational priorities. The land is largely undeveloped and includes eighty miles of waterfront. It was valued at the time of the settlement at $7 million.[19] The real property was included in the settlement because it resolved a huge stumbling block in the negotiations: it offered an opportunity to bridge the disparity between plaintiffs' and defendants' estimate of the value of historic fish mortality. The utility companies owned land purchased as far back as the 1930s, which they carried on their books at the acquisition price. If surrendered to the trust, they could be credited for the market value of the property at the time of the settlement.[20] The difference between the acquisition price and the credited value brought the parties' conflicting evaluations of historic fish mortality closer together. It also significantly diminished the cost of the settlement to the utility companies.

TRUST ORGANIZATION AND ACTIVITIES

Trust activities to date have focused on three basic goals: planning and getting organized, dealing with the land in the corpus, and establishing the parameters for developing what will be the trust's main ongoing program, grant giving.

As soon as the settlement was reached, the DNR created a trust coordinator position to assist in start-up activities. However, the DNR was not anxious to maintain a dominant presence in GLFT affairs, given the hostility of the legislature. Acting in his capacity as chair of the GLFT board, the head of the DNR pushed the trustees to assemble the necessary support structure. Taking advantage of the settlement provision that requires the board to meet quarterly, the GLFT made rapid progress in addressing administrative issues, land transactions, and trust programs.

Among the trustees' first steps was to contract with a facilitator to lead them in a year-long strategic planning process. The GLFT began with a flurry of informational meetings and trainings—but interestingly, no public participation or input—that led to a series of well-informed decisions regarding administrative organization. The trustees carefully weighed three options for their structure: depending on constituent organizations, which they rejected due to the legislature's concerns about state participation; establishing an independent staff, which they rejected for reasons of cost; and hiring consultants, which was the route they took. In short order, the trustees had obtained the services of a diverse array of professionals.

The trustees arranged for an administrative services consulting firm to provide basic support at the outset. The firm eventually provided full-time "permanent" staff for the GLFT. In addition, the trustees soon decided to pursue an application for 501(c)(3) status, as contemplated in the trust agreement. They hired an attorney to assist in that tedious effort, in the land transactions, and in a formal effort to understand the nature of the trust's beneficiaries. Although the minutes of subsequent meetings evince a certain amount of "sticker shock" regarding the cost of the attorney, the decision was reviewed and renewed frequently. Rounding out the team, the trustees hired an accounting firm and began planning for management of the corpus. The trustees' salutary but unusual self-education process included contact with a representative of the North Dakota Wetlands Trust, who was invited to attend a meeting to discuss, ironically, trust management.

This emphasis on administrative structure provided an opening for extensive discussion of a special logo for the GLFT. This is an arguably frivolous element of a serious and critical aspect of the shape of the trust. The first goal the trustees identified was to establish a sound organizational structure. That included developing operating policies, a definition of the trust's relationship to the SAT, a strategy for grant making, an approach to fund management, and a process for daily administration and accountability. These goals were achieved within the first year. The planning effort resulted in a sound organization, carefully agreed-to organizational mission and vision statements, a strategic plan, and a financial plan. Basic principles were very much a part of the organization's founding culture. The trustees paid exceptional attention to identifying the beneficiary and to translating that into a trust purpose.

It was more challenging for the GLFT to find a niche. The trust agreement is specific regarding the GLFT's relationship to similar organizations working in the Great Lakes. The document prohibits the trust from using its money, property, or income "as a substitute for traditional sources of funding for the enhancement, propagation, protection, and replacement of Great Lakes fishery resources, but shall supplement" those traditional resources. Drawing sharp lines between the activities of other public and private organizations, with broad mandates and great discretion to interpret them, and what the trust ought to do is not easy. The EVOS public advisory group, as noted in chapter 5, made a significant effort to develop criteria for identifying unique EVOS programs and gave up, relying on the judgment of the trustee council. The GLFT document puts emphasis, helpfully, not on the theoretical reach of the various missions but on what had traditionally been done.

The GLFT trustees made a serious stab at identifying a supplementary niche. Early in the project planning process, the state attorney general's office made a detailed study of other state, private, and federal organizations pursuing goals similar to the GLFT's in the Great Lakes region and began the process of identifying a distinct institutional niche for GLFT activities. Unlike the situation in North Dakota and along the Platte River, the Great Lakes is alive with organizations having missions that overlap entirely with that of the GLFT. They include the U.S. Fish and Wildlife Service; the National Oceanic and Atmospheric Administration and its Environmental Research Lab in Ann Arbor; the State Coastal Zone Management Program and Sea Grant programs at the University of Michigan, also in Ann Arbor; the U.S. Environmental Protection Agency Office of Great Lakes Programs; the Michigan and regional Great Lakes Protection Funds; the Great Lakes Commission; the Great Lakes Fishery Commission; and the several states and tribes and their various agencies. This list does not include the many private organizations operating in the area. The analysis found precious little turf for the trust to claim as its own. A distinctive focus on rivers and their linkages to the Great Lakes; a focus on wetlands restoration (since wetlands management for wildlife can be harmful to fisheries interests); a coherent regionally oriented education program; and, most interesting, a program to acquire fishing rights and thereby reduce the pressure of commercial harvest were among the suggestions proffered.[21]

The good stab failed. The GLFT could not, in such a crowded field, identify a unique or supplementary program. All the bases were covered. The trust has fallen back on an effort to work in close consultation with other funders and researchers in the region.

The SAT is not a "project" or "activity" of the GLFT. Under both the state agreement that established the trust and the FERC settlement that accompanied it, the SAT has independent activities. Most important, perhaps, quite apart from the trust, the SAT approves the model that defines the annual damage payment to GLFT.[22] More troubling, at least potentially, the settlement agreement created a significant potential role for the SAT in GLFT decision making. Specifically, the document provides that trust projects will be "considered and recommended by the Scientific Advisory Team prior to being proposed and considered by the Board of Trustees."[23] In addition, the agreement provides that the SAT will have responsibility for recommending and defining research projects, retaining contractors, selecting technology, implementing projects, and defining protocols and procedures for oversight of projects.

Concern was exacerbated by SAT leadership and funding. Members of the SAT are appointed by twelve organizations, many of which also appoint GLFT trustees. Also appointing SAT members are the defendants in the lawsuit, Consumers Power and Detroit Edison. Indeed, the SAT is cochaired by the appointees from the DNR and a utility company.[24] The agreement gives no guidance for most of the SAT's internal activities, except to provide that disputes will be resolved by the same complex dispute resolution process that applies to interpretation of the settlement as a whole. Although the SAT has considerable responsibilities, the settlement provides only that the power companies will fund its activities, albeit not to exceed $15,000 per year. Most of that money is spent on travel expenses for SAT members not affiliated with public agencies. The SAT does not have staff to perform its sometimes heavy workload.

The trust responded to this potentially divisive situation simply by rolling the SAT into its planning, during which the group defined clear parameters for the SAT panel's participation in GLFT projects. SAT members participated fully in that process and thereafter routinely attended trust meetings. The outcome is a salubrious one—the SAT can make recommendations but not dominate the trust program.

The SAT issue was relatively easily addressed. Dealing with the land was more laborious. Because of the real estate, the GLFT actually created a separate legal entity, the Great Lakes Fishery Trust Land Corporation, to assume ownership of the real property as it was conveyed from the utility companies. The land corporation retained sufficient funds to pay property taxes and other expenses involved in holding the land. As the land was sold, the proceeds were transferred to the trust.

The labor actually began for the DNR before the settlement was final. Prior to accepting the properties included in the settlement, the agency did a rapid assessment.[25] Those parcels with the highest ecological values, particularly those that fell near or within existing state holdings, were simply transferred directly to the DNR and never became part of the trust. The estimated value of those lands is $14 million. The remaining properties became part of the GLFT corpus. After more thorough evaluation, the land was to be sold, although not necessarily to the highest bidder. The settlement provided that, subject to a right of first refusal granted to the Little

River Band of Ottawa,[26] some properties were to be offered to the U.S. Forest Service. Another set of properties was offered to the leaseholders before it was transferred to the trust. The remaining land was to be sold on the open market.

The Forest Service moved to acquire property within the Huron Manistee National Forest, much of it in wild and scenic status along the Ausable and Manistee Rivers. At the agency's recommendation, the transfer was facilitated by the Trust for Public Land (TPL). The TPL purchased the land from the trust at 90 percent of the appraised value and sold it to the Forest Service for the full value. The 10 percent "commission" compensated the TPL for conducting appraisals, assembling information in support of the transactions, and lining up and maintaining congressional support. The GLFT found that it cost 8 to 9 percent of the sale price to market the property through commercial land brokers (excluding the congressional packet) and happily paid the 10 percent. In 1999, Congress appropriated funds to complete Forest Service transactions involving over 6,000 acres.

Environmental protection on the transferred parcels was a bit of a challenge. The settlement agreement specifically required the trustees to make an assessment of the natural and archaeological resources of each property and to protect environmental values on the land before it was sold. To facilitate that effort, the agreement permitted below-market sale of the land.[27] The trustees responded in two different ways. They simply assumed that the Forest Service shared their commitment to environmental and resource protection. The trustees did not take any steps to protect the fishery or archaeological resources on those lands being sold to the Forest Service. Instead, the GLFT executed a nonbinding letter to the Forest Service stating its expectation that the resources would be protected to the full extent of applicable laws and in ways consistent with what the GLFT itself would do. This reliance on the Forest Service's good intentions into the distant future is curious.

The GLFT's approach to the land sold to private parties is only slightly more impressive. In part, the trustees were caught between their obligation to use the land to raise money for the trust and their mandate to protect the environmental value of the parcels. Most of the environmentally sensitive parcels were sold to the Forest Service or transferred to the DNR. On the remaining parcels, the trustees compromised the two priorities by focusing primarily on water resources, which they protected almost exclusively with conservation easements requiring 100-foot buffer strips around sensitive areas.[28] The easements reduced the property values by an estimated 10 percent, which does not seem an unreasonable compromise on fair returns to the trust. Once executed, the easements were transferred from the GLFT Land Corporation to the GLFT. Herein lies the problem: the conservation easements constitute a continuing responsibility for which the trust has not made adequate preparations. The easement device seems particularly ill advised for an organization planning to terminate in less than twenty years. The trust has made no provisions for an easement defense fund and has taken none of the easement protection steps that are routine for the land trusts discussed in Part IV. In all, the inevitable conflict between the mandated environmental protection of settlement properties and the trustees' obligation to maximize the corpus seems poorly resolved in both the Forest Service and the private sales.

The GLFT's financial management program is interesting because it includes a plan not simply for investing the corpus but for spending down the principal as well. This is in apparent conflict with the settlement agreement, which states simply that "this trust shall continue in perpetuity." The agreement also, however, creates some wiggle room by allowing the trustees to determine the expenditure of the funds, including spending down the principal.[29] During the strategic planning process, the trustees decided to terminate the trust in 2020. This decision is revocable, but it is presently the basis of trust activities and planning.

The sunset of the trust is tied, for good reason, to the expiration of the FERC license granted to the Ludington Project. The trust allowed itself a year following the last payment in 2019 to go out of business in an orderly fashion. The trustees concluded that because GLFT funds are to mitigate the damages from the plant operation, they should be spent during the period the plant is licensed to operate. Unspent trust funds suggest that there are resource damages going unmitigated. Any funds remaining after the FERC license expires could complicate discussion of mitigation for the next license period. Trustees from the state agencies also stressed the significant time commitment that the GLFT requires. They acknowledged the state's interest in the trust's existence and operations but argued that an open-ended commitment was not appropriate.

The trustees' decision, perhaps not surprisingly, was not supported by the SAT. A recurring pattern in our explorations is that scientists argue for research funding in perpetuity. At least part of the concern reflects the importance of long-term studies, for which support is notoriously difficult to sustain.

In spite of all its structural and organizational investment, the GLFT decided not to develop projects itself but to disburse its funds through a grant program. Early recipients appear to reflect pressure from the Michigan legislature, emphasizing public uses of fishery resources—specifically, visible improvements clearly directed at public education and improved public access, such as improved shore fishing at Great Lakes piers and breakwaters. The trustees wanted to demonstrate right away to the Michigan public that it was receiving benefit from the GLFT.

The GLFT held its first grant cycle in 1998 and made six awards totaling only $2.5 million. The first cycle was limited so that the trustees and staff could work out the mechanics of soliciting, processing, and choosing funding proposals. The second round of proposals will focus, trustees hope, on funding "themes" with five- to fifteen-year projections. The trust is undertaking several activities to launch this comprehensive plan. In summer 1999, the trust held a strategic planning retreat to establish long-term goals and objectives for the grant programs. The trustees hope that this will guide the development and selection of proposals over the term of the grant program. The GLFT and other foundations and fund grantors in the region are also exploring possibilities for working in partnership. The GLFT has established partnerships with the Great Lakes Fishery Commission, the Michigan Sea Grant Program, the Michigan Great Lakes Protection Fund, and other Michigan-based foundations to evaluate grant proposals and develop funding criteria.

The GLFT has enjoyed mostly smooth sailing, and it is tempting to attribute its success—especially in comparison to the difficulties in North Dakota— to superior trust documents, greater awareness of trust principles in trust operations, and the significant investment in institutional development and support at the outset. All this is arguable, but it is hard to account adequately for the GLFT's more benign environment when making comparisons between the two organizations.

In the end, the dogs that did not bark are perhaps the most interesting. The trust format seems pivotal in the successful marriage between public and private organizations. A potentially horrendous agglomeration of previously incompatible organizations joined easily to establish the trust. It is especially notable that although the trust was receiving compensation for damages to federal interests and resources, the DOI did not insist on an EVOS-type arrangement with CRIS or NRDA, nor did it impose investment restrictions on the trust. Also significant, the framers and trustees seem to have had little difficulty in devising a process that included Native Americans as participants and allowed them to negotiate to protect their own interests. The tribes were involved at the beginning.

We do not want to overstate the importance of a well-drafted document—even the GLFT's careful process created some potential hazards with the SAT and barely avoided an early and fatal encounter with the legislature. However, the process was locally conducted and locally informed and took advantage of rather than falling victim to local peculiarities. Perhaps as important to the GLFT's excellent start is the special attention paid to the trust beneficiaries and obligations.

We do, however, wonder about the trust's activities. The purpose of the trust is clear—to "mitigate for the losses in use and enjoyment of fisheries caused by the power plant," specifically, by funding "enhancement, propagation, protection, and replacement of Great Lakes fishery resources." The GLFT framers made a unique effort to ensure that trust activities would add to existing programs in the region rather than simply displace other investments. It is not clear that the trustees have succeeded. In spite of the imaginative effort, undertaken early in the organizing phase of the trust, to inventory existing programs and identify gaps in programmatic coverage, the GLFT appears to be emphasizing programs that do not clearly mitigate damage to the resource. It is not obvious that improved access for fishing is an offset for fish mortality. One could argue that less fishing or the retirement of extant fishing rights, as suggested by one analyst, would be more appropriate to the trust mission. The risk in insisting on hewing so closely to narrowly defined purposes is that it may strangle an organization's vitality and ability to adapt to changing circumstances. However, the GLFT purposes are broad, and the trustees are responsible for $71 million in public funds. Trust principles allow observers to point to the stated purposes and wonder whether the trust is pursuing them.

PART IV: FAMILY, CHARITABLE, AND LAND TRUSTS

The organizations discussed in Part IV are all "private," meaning that they are formed and supported with private funds and run by private boards. Nevertheless, the main point of our discussion is to underscore how public they are or are becoming. To support that assertion, we look at three organizations: the Phillips Memorial Trust, a charitable trust created as a philanthropy by an extremely wealthy woman, which became the seed for a complex regional conservation effort; a major conservation organization, the Society for the Protection of New Hampshire Forests (SPNHF), which was formed to promote federal acquisition and protection of forests but since the depression has turned increasingly toward private stewardship; and the Napa County Land Trust (NCLT), a local institution whose activities are shaped, directly and indirectly, by the changing land regulation in the region. Along the way, we look at two families that used private trusts to simplify their own joint decision making and then worked with land trusts, using conservation easements, to perpetuate their conservation goals. Although the choices in this chapter are not what most of us would consider governmental, all of them are deeply shaped by public policies and supported by a web of governmental institutions and regulations.

Although it is still our purpose to explore the utility of trust principles in a new era of conservation organizations, neither the NCLT nor the SPNHF is organized as a formal trust. Both can appropriately be described as land trusts. Use of the word *trust* does not, we reiterate, mean that a land trust is structured by the trust principles described in chapter 2. Further, the term *land trust* has no fixed or legal meaning and is applied to a wide array of organizations. We discuss these nontrust trusts along with family and charitable trusts for three reasons. First, the family trusts we studied are frequently so deeply involved with land trusts as to be inseparable from them. Second, even though they are not organized as trusts, the land trusts make extensive use of trust principles and formal trusts in their operations. Finally, because land trusts are clearly the most rapidly pro-liferating of the new conservation organizations and are often presumed to be formal trusts, we should introduce them into this discussion.

The Land Trust Alliance, an umbrella organization of land trusts, keeps data that indicate that only 130 land trusts existed in the United States in the mid-1960s. By 1990, the number had increased to 889, and by 1998 to 1,213. It is common to describe land trusts' explosive growth in terms of environmental awareness, dismay with urban sprawl, and a response to decreasing government willingness to regulate or acquire private property.[1] Our cases suggest that other factors, very much a part of the new ideas about government, are also key to understanding land trust expansion. First, the 1965 changes in the Internal Revenue Code discussed in chap-ter 1 formally defined conservation easements and allowed income tax deductions for conservation easements donated to charitable organiza-tions.[2] Conservation organizations; units of local, state, or federal govern-ment; and nonprofits were designated as "qualified" to accept donations of tax-deductible easements.[3] Second, in 1981, the National Commissioners on Uniform State Laws approved a Uniform Conservation Easement Act, which was adopted in sixteen states and has shaped the evolution of con-servation easements and land trusts in many others.[4] The proliferation of ostensibly private land trusts has been facilitated by a web of public policy choices.

Private conservation, and particularly land trusts, is currently enjoy-ing a period of almost uncritical public adulation as the tool of choice in conservation.[5] Government regulators also seem to believe that they can avoid the political costs of enforcing rules simply by buying easements. Land trusts currently appeal to a broad range of constituencies because they appear to have the flexibility to make decisions and investments more quickly than governmental agencies.[6] Unlike regulations, easements are negotiated with willing sellers or donors and can be tailored to achieve particular conservation goals while accommodating the needs of the indi-vidual landowner.[7] Easements can keep property in private hands and on the tax rolls and are likely to cost less than outright acquisition.[8]

In spite of the current enthusiasm for private land conservation, it is not a new conservation tool. The first relevant effort probably began in South Carolina in 1856, with the formation of a women's group to preserve the buildings and grounds at the home of George Washington.[9] Private organizations that might now be called land trusts existed across the United States from that time forward.[10]

Our cases remind us that in Maine, the federal government's with-drawal from land acquisition is not viewed as a lamentable fall from grace—Maine conservationists have fought federal involvement consistently. The

Rangeley Lakes experience discussed in chapter 9 suggests that piecing together a landscape of small parcels is a challenge that land trusts can meet. The New Hampshire experience suggests that the conservation easement can be used to extend conservation to the less well-heeled and to include families of modest means as stewards of the land.

Our discussion of this stew of trusts and trustlike organizations, of public and private choices, focuses on four topics. The first is accountability. It is simply not true that private organizations need not be accountable to the public. Charitable and family trusts bear a special burden in this area. Private charity clearly gives considerable influence over the definition of community needs to those who control the greatest wealth. Supported by government tax policy, private endowments and charitable trusts are appropriately accountable to the public. The groups in our discussion pursue accountability with mechanisms that are not routinely thought of in those terms. Accordingly, private conservation trusts and nontrusts also have a lot to teach public organizations about little-explored tools for what we know and typically discount as public involvement.

Second, we talk about stitching together landscapes of private property. Will we find ourselves conserving small, isolated parcels, former estates and gardens, interrupted by the donors' retained rights to build homes for their children and grandchildren? Do trusts and land trusts have the resources and the staying power to protect whole landscapes and watersheds, which are now the preferred units of conservation discussion?

Third, how and under what circumstances should private landowners be allowed to perpetuate their management preferences into the distant future? The family trusts we discuss are private rather than charitable. They are subject to the rule against perpetuities, and will likely dissolve in the next several decades. Land trusts play an important role in perpetuating families' conservation goals. The Napa land trust has been particularly creative in using trusts in combination with easements to confuse title to resources that might otherwise be vulnerable if the organization were subject to a large liability judgment or similar reversal. But the question of perpetuating the particular preferences of individual donors and settlors persists. Is the dead hand a serious obstacle to landscape-level management?

Finally, although private conservation has a long history in this country, the current emphasis on easements is a bit of an experiment. Conservation easements are defined in state and federal law, and it is not clear how the relevant statutes will be interpreted several decades hence, when landowners not involved in the original transaction want to use their lands in ways circumscribed by the easement. Will the land trusts be there to enforce the restrictions? Will the courts allow them to do so? At a minimum, it is clear that when the question arises, the voluntary process of the easement transaction will be morphed into a less voluntary one. If all goes well, the land trust will act pretty much in place of the state, enforcing the conservation restrictions agreed on by prior owners or generations.

We are in the halcyon days of private efforts and have generally not encountered many frustrations as yet.[11] Our three case studies give us some clear indications of the strengths and risks of this approach.

CHAPTER NINE

Stephen Phillips Memorial Preserve Trust: Pebbles Causing Ripples

The Stephen Phillips Memorial Preserve Trust is unlike the other family trusts discussed in this part. It does not involve an expanding family seeking a structure to help it make joint decisions about managing family land. Rather, it was established as a philanthropy by Phillips's widow, Betty, specifically to protect public recreation access and scenic values in the Rangeley Lakes area of Maine.

The Phillips trust is important to our inquiry for four reasons. First, we find the dead hand in the Phillips trust legacy. The rule against perpetuities evolved to prevent landowners from binding future generations to their preferences. However, as noted in chapter 2, as a practical matter, charitable trusts are exempted from the rule against perpetuities. The Phillips trust is perpetual and, along with the related conservation easements, reflects Mrs. Phillips's management proclivities. Her preferences are not likely to become a major management issue, but they do make us wonder for how long, and in what detail, trustors should bind future generations to their preferences.

Second, the trust has had an enormous impact on land management in the region. Mrs. Phillips's 400-acre island became the seed for a growing web of land conservation. By the late 1990s, public access had been protected on more than 33,000 acres of the Rangeley Lakes region of Maine,[1] and the area continues to expand. The Phillips trust provided a starting point for joint government and private landscape conservation where ownership is mixed but largely private. Her island is no longer simply a private matter.

Third, the Phillips trust is interesting because it involves numerous organizations. The program includes the Phillips trust, the U.S. Forest Service, the state of Maine, local land trusts, and at times several major corporations as well. Press treatment of the Phillips trust legacy praises the coalition of high-powered players as nothing short of a miracle. However, it is important to be realistic about the potential instability of the management coalition and some of its constituent organizations.

Fourth, it is also important to wonder about the long-term consequences of the approach. Maine's conservationists have been less likely than New Hampshire's (discussed in the next chapter) to view the federal

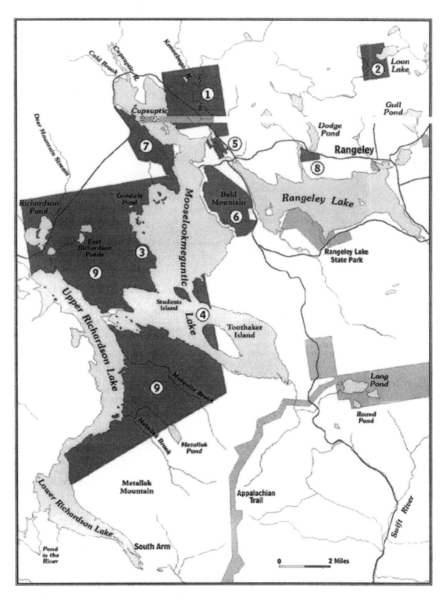

The map shows areas protected by the Phillips trust in close proximity to Rangeley Lakes Heritage Trust (RLHT) easements and other areas acquired by the state of Maine following the public lots controversy. Parcels 1 through 4 are protected with conservation easements donated by Mrs. Stephen Phillips and the Stephen Phillips Memorial Preserve Trust to the RLHT: (1) a 3,092-acre parcel with four miles on both banks of the Kennebago River and over two miles of frontage on Cupsuptic Lake and Cloutman Pond; (2) a 778-acre parcel with 6,000 feet of frontage on Loon Lake; (3) a 2,000-acre parcel on the west shore of Mooselookmeguntic Lake, including eight miles of frontage, ten islands, and Little Mud Pond; and (4) a 687-acre parcel on the east shore of Mooselookmeguntic Lake, including all of Students government as a good choice for ownership of lands to be conserved. In the Rangeley area, we can view the alternatives. In the short term, residential development has been prevented. In the long term, questions may arise regarding the advisability of splicing and dicing ownership of the landscape into so many separate estates. The array of easements, entitlements, and responsibilities promises to complicate management and may, in coming years or decades, look less effective than it now appears.

THE PEBBLE—ESTABLISHING THE TRUST

The Rangeley Lakes region of Maine is a spectacular intersection of natural and cultural forces. Regional historian Herbert P. Shirrefs urges us to "give a cheer" for the millions of years of geological processes, primarily the glaciers that bulldozed the area, leaving "six thousand wonderful inland bodies of water of varying sizes, receiving or discharging five thousand or more equally beautiful rivers, streams, and brooks."[2] Half a dozen or more major interlocked lakes dominate the headwaters of the Androscoggin River in the southwestern part of the state.

This natural bounty remains relatively undeveloped for the simple reason that large timber and water power companies have owned the area in huge parcels since at least the mid-1800s. Not much land has ever been for sale. In the late nineteenth and early twentieth centuries, the region was dotted with sporting camps and public houses. They catered to Gilded Age fishermen who escaped from the commercial centers of Boston and New York for extended periods in the summer. The camps and hotels were built on lands leased by the corporate owners. When the tourist industry came

---

Island and one-third of Toothaker Island, with five miles of shore frontage. Parcels 5 through 9 have been protected through cooperative efforts of conservation organizations, individuals, corporations, and state and federal governments: (5) a 150-acre Rangeley River corridor acquired by the RLHT from the Union Water Power Company, with two miles of river and lake frontage; (6) a 1,953-acre Bald Mountain tract purchased from International Paper by the RLHT and sold with protective covenants to the state of Maine through the Land for Maine's Future Program; (7) a 1,257-acre parcel with 3.4 miles of frontage on Cupsuptic and Mooselookmeguntic Lakes, purchased by the RLHT from Boise Cascade and protected with a conservation easement held by the U.S. Forest Service's Forest Legacy Program; (8) a 100-acre Hunter Cove Wildlife Sanctuary with over 3,000 feet of frontage owned by the Maine Audubon Society and managed by the RLHT; and (9) 22,806 acres of "public lot controversy lands" now owned by the state of Maine and managed by the Bureau of Parks and Lands on Mooselookmeguntic and Upper and Lower Richardson Lakes, including twenty miles of shorefront. (Cartographer: Matt Kania; courtesy U.S. National Park Service)

on hard times around World War I, the lakeshores were not left open for subdivision into private homes and camps.[3]

Interest in the area revived during what is known as the public lots controversy of the early 1970s. Public lots originally arose from a practice, introduced in the 1780s, when Maine was part of Massachusetts, of granting land to townships for the support of schools and the ministry. In the 1850s, the state of Maine put all the public lots under the care of a state land agent who was to manage them, with the proceeds applied to the same purposes. Major timber companies purchased permits to harvest grass and trees on the public lots. Those permits became an issue in the 1970s when, in response to a legislative effort to reorganize management of the lots, the successor corporations asserted that they still had an exclusive right to enter the public lots to harvest timber. A decade of litigation established that, to the contrary, they did not have that right. This evolved into a protracted period during which the timber companies and the state tried to sort out title and locate the long-lost public lots on the ground.[4]

The trust land was marginally involved in the public lots controversy. Mrs. Phillips was, by marriage, a Pingree heir. Largely unfamiliar outside of New England, Pingree heirs occupy an important place in Maine history and land management. Stephen Phillips was a descendant of a nineteenth-century Salem, Massachusetts, merchant and lumber baron whose heirs continue to control vast tracts of land throughout Maine. The Pingree heirs were among the landowners most deeply involved in the public lots controversy. Of the roughly 400,000 acres ultimately recovered by the state in the dispute, about 40,000 came from Pingree holdings. Indeed, the state made a major effort to acquire the Phillips trust lands as well, but Mrs. Phillips was not budging. She did not trust the state to manage the area to the same exacting standards as she envisioned.

Thus, while it is doubtless true that Mrs. Phillips was a frugal, determined, public-spirited woman who personified the classic 'Yankee' virtues that the press loves to dwell on, she was no ordinary widow.[5] She wielded enormous wealth and power. She built the trust holdings with the significant resources at her disposal. A Massachusetts native whose childhood outdoor experience was in the Adirondacks region of New York State, Betty Phillips's interest in Maine was spurred by her husband Stephen's concern.

As a child, Stephen had spent his summers in the Rangeley Lakes area living in primitive camping conditions, and as an adult, he introduced his bride to the area. It has long been a Maine tradition that private holdings are open to public hiking, hunting, camping, and recreation. When Stephen Phillips became aware that the 400-acre Students Island in Lake Mooselookmeguntic was slated for subdivision, he became concerned that the long-established public access would end. He simply purchased the land before the developer could. He planned to continue his acquisition and protection efforts, but his death in 1971 left that task to his widow. She pursued it with zeal, and by her death a quarter of a century later, the Rangeley Lakes land protection effort had become a model of how to parlay a relatively small landholding into an enormous public asset.

Pursuing her husband's wishes, Betty Phillips established a trust, an arrangement that was familiar to her. The trust purposes are clear and articulated at length. The lands conveyed to the trust were to "be maintained insofar as practical in their natural state to the end that the scenic resources constituted by them may be conserved forever." In addition, the trust was to "enhance public opportunities for recreation," and the trustees were authorized to make the lands available for "primitive camping, picnicking, nature study, and like activities" and to make rules and regulations for their use. And because the land was to be "maintained as a sanctuary" for wildlife, hunting and trapping (but not fishing) were forever prohibited "upon and within the premises."[6]

The trust instrument provides for a minimum of five trustees. However, it also gives the group authority to expand to no more than seven, which it did almost immediately. Mrs. Phillips served as president of the board until her death, and all the other trustees have been family members, old friends, or business associates of the Phillips family. The trustees receive no compensation and have no term of office. The trust instrument makes no provision for removing a sitting trustee but does allow for a trustee to resign following adequate notice. Unlike some other trusts in this volume, no outside organization is allowed to appoint a trustee. The remaining trustees are authorized to fill any vacancies that occur.

In the late 1990s, the board still included only individuals who were intimately familiar with Mrs. Phillips and her wishes for management of the trust properties. Board renewal will soon become an important trustee responsibility. This raises for them, as it did for Mrs. Phillips, the issue of what will happen to her preferences about land management when the board is increasingly composed of individuals who were not so personally involved with the trustor. This concern led Mrs. Phillips to overlay the trust document with extensive terms and conditions in perpetual conservation easements granted on what were to become trust properties.

The trustees were given enormous discretion concerning the management of trust lands and the operation of the trust in the original document. The trustees are allowed to amend the provisions of the trust instrument in order to maintain the trust as charitable under the requirements of any relevant jurisdiction. They are required to care for, maintain, and improve the facilities using "funds available in their hands." The trustees are authorized to charge for the use of trust property but forbidden to engage in any business activities or make any investments that would jeopardize the charitable trust status and thus its favorable tax status. They are also authorized to purchase additional land to achieve trust purposes and to engage in a full range of real estate transactions, such as leases and covenants, if doing so is, in their opinion, expedient. Finally, they are granted absolute discretion to invest in a broad range of stocks, bonds, securities, or other financial instruments.

In addition to the words of the trust instrument, the current trustees make much in the press and in interviews of their awareness of Mrs. Phillips's clear ideas about land management and her determination that they should be carried out. Not all her priorities were recorded in the trust instrument. For example, it is apparently well known among the current trustees that Mrs. Phillips did not approve of fire or prescribed burning as a management tool. Although the trustees are dedicated to implementing Mrs. Phillips's wishes in this regard, her unrecorded preferences are not binding on them or future trustees.

In spite of the fact that trustees are not limited in their ability to manage funds to support trust purposes, and although it is perfectly clear that Mrs. Phillips anticipated that the trust would make, spend, and hold money, the trust did not at first contain any money. Until her death, the corpus consisted solely of its original endowment, the 400-acre island and associated onshore property originally purchased by Stephen Phillips in 1971. At the time of her death in 1996, that situation altered significantly.

First, Mrs. Phillips had made a modest endowment for funding the operations of the trust. Second, she added to its corpus approximately 6,400 acres in the Rangeley region that she had been assembling since the trust was founded in 1978. A "marital trust" from her husband included land, but Mrs. Phillips was not permitted to alienate it during her lifetime. She was, however, able to swap those lands for other Pingree land in the area. She vigorously pursued trades and was abetted in this by the Seven Islands Corporation, which manages the Pingree land. Seven Islands was as anxious to reposition its holdings away from the Rangeley area as she was to consolidate there. The 6,400 acres that she assembled were at the penumbra of the Phillips trust, slated to become part of the corpus when her will was probated. During the pendency of that transaction, the trustees of the Phillips trust, including Mrs. Phillips, managed the marital trust properties.

It was also during this period, however, that Mrs. Phillips became concerned about the ability of subsequent trustees to achieve her priorities over the long term. Accordingly, she worked to establish a land trust in the Rangeley region. Then, in a series of transactions, she granted conservation easements first on the Phillips trust lands and then on the marital trust acreage. The easement reiterates the basic conservation purposes of the Phillips trust, but it reserves for the grantor and her heirs the right to maintain and expand an existing residential dwelling, guest facilities, and related buildings on one portion of the property.[7] All the Phillips land is subject to both the terms of the trust and the terms of the conservation easements.

The initial absence of management funds led the trustees to adopt an interesting approach to program funding. At the outset, approximately half of their operating budget came from rentals and camping fees on the trust and related properties. The other half, which the trustees characterize as "nondiscretionary" funds, comes from small contributions. The trustees were concerned that the public would come to view the trust as the private preoccupation of a single, idiosyncratic donor. This could affect the trust's status as charitable. Therefore, they sought to diversify its support beyond Mrs. Phillips's original gift. Aware of this concern, a closely affiliated local civic group, the Mooselookmeguntic Improvement Association (MIA), makes an annual contribution of $1,000 to the trust. In addition, each trustee has made a small personal contribution each year to run the organization and to expand, ever so slightly, its donor base.

A related fear of making too much money has led the trustees to take a very conservative approach to investments. Because Mrs. Phillips added a small endowment for operating expenses just prior to her death, the trust now earns approximately one-third of its annual funds from investment income. The trustees' authority to manage their new financial resources is among the least restricted we have seen. In most of the other trusts we explored, the trustor or concerned government officials have severely constrained the trustees' discretion to invest. Although spared unreasonable restrictions in the trust instrument, the Phillips trustees are nevertheless concerned that they might jeopardize their favorable charitable trust status if they make too much money. Accordingly, they have made no effort to achieve significant returns on the new fund but pursue a small but steady income.

THE RIPPLES

Even as Mrs. Phillips assembled her lands for protection, the Rangeley Lakes region was coming under enormous pressure for residential development. Boise Cascade proposed to subdivide and sell off eighty-acre parcels on the shore of Cupsuptic Lake. Pleasant Island Peninsula was sold to developers, and local residents became alarmed at the flagged property lines that became increasingly apparent to boaters out on Mooselookmeguntic and Cupsuptic Lakes (see map, page 156).

Concerned citizens first activated the nearly moribund MIA and used it as a vehicle to challenge the developments.[8] The proposed change of ownership threatened not only the parcels directly involved but also the long-standing tradition of open public access to lands managed in large blocks for timber and pulp. The developers applied to the state's Land Use Regulation Commission to have the areas along the lake rezoned. The MIA intervened successfully, and the proposal was put on hold.

The larger threat, however, was a comprehensive statewide planning process. The Lakes Concept Study was planning future lakeshore development with the aid of a computer model driven by a kind of triage system. The model rated areas on a number of environmental and public values but, irrespective of the result, tended to consign easily accessible areas to further intense development. Thus the Rangeley Lakes region, which has extremely valuable environmental and recreational attributes, was pushed toward development because it was close to urban areas such as Lewiston and to the Maine Turnpike. The MIA intervened again, arguing that the model had an unfair impact on the Rangeley region and that accessible and undeveloped areas ought to be a priority for protection rather than destruction. The MIA was successful in pressuring the state to reconsider the logic of its planning tool, and it ultimately put the Rangeley area into a special category in the lakes study—despite its proximity to civilization, it would enjoy special protection.

In spite of the problems created initially by the Lakes Concept Study, the challenges of conversion of forested land to residential and second home development were not unique to the Rangeley area or to Maine. By the late 1980s, the sale of industrial forestland in the Northeast had perceptibly destabilized the timber industry. Because 85 percent of the industrial forestlands in the northeast is privately owned, the trend threatened to alter the economy of the entire area radically. When Diamond International offered for sale more than a million acres of land in New York, Maine, New Hampshire, and Vermont, both the U.S. Congress and state governments became concerned. Congress authorized and funded the U.S. Forest Service to study productive private forestlands in the Northeast and recommend strategies for preserving them. The Forest Service study proceeded in cooperation with the Northern Forest Lands Council, which had been established by a regional Governors' task force concerned with the same subject.[9]

In 1990, the joint effort bore fruit, and Congress adopted amendments to the farm bill that created the Forest Legacy Program.[10] The program is a classic example of devolution and dispersion–era legislation. It abjures federal land acquisition and aims to preserve the heritage of private ownership and the productivity of private lands by fostering cooperation. The core of the program directs the secretary of agriculture to work with state, regional, and local governments and private groups to protect important "scenic, cultural, fish, wildlife and recreational resources, riparian areas and other ecological values."

The major instrument for achieving this protection is the purchase of conservation easements. The act provides for a cost-share arrangement among participating entities—all levels of government plus private groups, landowners, corporations, and local nonprofits. The U.S. Forest Service would own easements but could not provide more than 75 percent of a project's funding. Administrative and monitoring responsibilities for legacy areas could be delegated to public or private organizations in the affected region, including local land trusts. Forest management activities, such as timber harvest, that are, in the opinion of the secretary of agriculture, consistent with the purposes of the statute are permitted on legacy lands.

This Forest Legacy Program was evolving as MIA activists were recognizing its weaknesses as an organization. Having achieved gratifying success in shaping the Lake Concept Study, the MIA had failed in its next effort to garner support for land protection programs. The MIA was left with no clear idea of how to proceed. Simultaneously, Mrs. Phillips, worried that the purpose of the Phillips trust needed greater protection and assurances than the trustees could provide, was seeking support for her own efforts. In the process, she encountered Dick Spencer, who had been in the thick of the Lake Concept Study fight. In response to Mrs. Phillips's request, he initiated founding activities for the Rangeley Lakes Heritage Trust (RLHT). Their collaboration began just as the Forest Legacy Program passed through the final rounds in Congress. As Spencer noted, what Betty Phillips and the MIA were trying to accomplish separately "suddenly became part of a much larger effort."[11]

By early 1991, both Mrs. Phillips's desire for a double layer of protection for her lands[12] and the Forest Legacy program's need for a match were unfolding rapidly. But the RLHT was still in the process of being established—setting up a 501(c)(3) organization is an arduous process. Moreover, the RLHT was the new kid on the block, and participants did not have much experience crafting conservation easements. Phillips and Spencer turned for guidance to an established land trust, the Maine Coast Heritage Trust (MCHT). The MCHT helped draft the original easement and agreed to hold it until the Rangeley Lakes trust was completely established. And because the MCHT staff lawyers and Rangeley Lakes founders were following the development of the Forest Legacy Program in Congress closely, they knew that a private match was required to procure federal funds. Assured by drafters of the Forest Legacy Program that a conservation easement could serve as a match only if the easement specifically stated that it was intended for that purpose, the easement on the Phillips trust property was carefully crafted to meet the requirements of the developing federal program.[13]

The easement was also designed to describe Mrs. Phillips's priorities for land management. Having traveled extensively over the properties during her long lifetime, she had detailed knowledge of each parcel. She also had very clear ideas about the level of recreational use, the kind of vegetation management, and the kinds of access that were appropriate.[14] The resulting easements are lengthy for the genre, including what Spencer has characterized as an "incredible level of wording" about her priorities.

The purpose of the easement is similar to that of the Phillips trust: "to conserve forever the scenic, natural, and wildlife habitat values . . . and to enhance public opportunities . . . for outdoor recreation, including primitive camping, picnicking, nature study, and similar uses that are consistent with the preservation of its scenic and natural resources." The length of the document can be attributed in part to the need to condition that basic mandate to allow the continuation of existing uses and buildings, most but not all of which were related to primitive recreational use.

Reflecting the Maine tradition that private lands are open to the public unless posted to the contrary, the easement provides for public access by agreeing to "refrain from posting the Protected Property against trespass." However, Phillips's predilections are reflected in the next phrase, which states that the public access is restricted to "daytime, quiet, non-motorized low impact outdoor recreational uses." Thus, the Phillips trustees may control, limit, or prohibit by posting and other means night use, use of primitive camping areas, open fires, use of motor vehicles, hunting, trapping, and any use that may interfere with or be harmful to other members of the public or that "may have an adverse impact on the conservation values" of the property.[15]

As a result of these overlapping responsibilities, the relationship between the Phillips trust and the RLHT is important to our story. The Phillips trust now holds title to and manages the complete 6,800 acres (the original 400-acre corpus, plus the 6,400 acres from the marital trust). This was supplemented by a small purchase in 1998 by the Phillips trustees for inclusion in the Phillips trust holdings. The Phillips trust maintains the camping sites on the properties, hires and compensates site managers, collects and expends the rents, and invests and expends the small trust endowment. The Phillips trustees proceed under the terms and conditions of both the trust instrument and the easements granted on the marital trust lands. Hence, they exercise the rights reserved to the grantor of the easement.

The Phillips trustees are presently considering the extent of their future role in the region. In spite of the one small purchase, they are as yet unresolved whether the trust should continue, as Mrs. Phillips had envisioned, to make land acquisitions in the area, or whether they should focus their efforts on being simply a nonacquiring catalyst for protection as development pressure continues.

The RLHT monitors the easements that it holds in perpetuity, but it neither owns nor manages the Phillips trust property. The RLHT has run an environmental educational and recreational summer program using an old Boy Scout camp on Phillips trust property.[16] Relations between the two organizations have been extremely cordial but surprisingly limited. Although the RLHT plays a small role in the continuing activities of the Phillips trust, the easements on Mrs. Phillips's marital trust lands began to play an enormous role in the RLHT's program almost as soon as the ink was dry.[17]

The RLHT is fully resolved to pursue an active role as a deal maker and easement holder in the Rangeley Lakes area. Spencer approached the U.S. Forest Service, which was looking for a pilot project in Maine for the Forest Legacy Program. Again he proposed (this time, under the auspices of the RLHT) the acquisition of the Boise Cascade lands on Cupsuptic Lake, so long threatened by development. Well positioned as part of a regional protection effort, the RLHT received the entire Forest Legacy allocation to the state of Maine in the first year of the program. The resulting transaction left the U.S. Forest Service holding an easement on a 1,257-acre parcel, including 3.4 miles of frontage on Cupsuptic and Mooselookmeguntic Lakes. The Rangeley trust subsequently purchased the underlying fee title.

Emboldened, the RLHT went back to Land for Maine's Future, this time with a proposal to protect Bald Mountain, a parcel owned by International Paper. Again working with the Maine Coast Heritage Trust, the RLHT brokered the deal, buying Bald Mountain. The trust then sold it to the state of Maine, which used funds from the Land for Maine's Future Program for the acquisition.[18] The RLHT has also acquired a 150-acre parcel from Union Water Power Company, with two miles of river and lake frontage, and it manages a 100-acre wildlife sanctuary for the Maine Audubon Society.

All those involved in the Rangeley Lakes effort are ecstatic about the Phillips trust and its role in precipitating regional cooperation to support land protection and public access. Success stories like the Phillips and Rangeley trusts' are so praised in the press and academia that the cautions that ought to accompany this relatively new approach to land protection are insufficiently discussed. We use the Phillips trust to do so.

One of the dominant themes of any press report on the Phillips trust is that Betty Phillips was a determined woman who knew what she wanted and pursued it with skill and persistence. She was greatly concerned that her wishes regarding management of the land be respected after her death. Nothing that she insisted on is particularly objectionable or radical. It is the inclusion of her preferences in perpetual trust documents and easements that suggests the problem that the dead hand entails. This provides a different perspective on the EVOS trust's science-dominated discussions of how long the organization should stay in business and the GLFT's decision to sunset in spite of the trust document's explicit provision to the contrary. Dead-hand issues explore for how long Betty Phillips's particular approaches to management should be felt on the landscape.

Mrs. Phillips's priorities create a familiar conflict: she wanted the lands preserved in a wild state, yet she wanted to protect public recreational access. Yet she evinced considerable flexibility as a decision maker when these two priorities came into conflict. For example, the *Maine Times* reports admiringly that although she did not want to allow motorized access to trust campsites, she did not openly forbid it. She simply "moved the boat launch down the beach and over a flight of stairs."[19] Similarly, although she sought to proscribe motorized vehicles on trust land, associates note that when confronted with the fact of already existing snowmobile trails, Mrs. Phillips agreed to allow them to remain.

During her lifetime, Mrs. Phillips was willing and able to bend the black-letter commands of the trust instrument and easement documents. Conversely, other preferences not expressed in the same documents are very clear to current trustees as restrictions. Specifically, Mrs. Phillips consistently impressed on the Phillips trustees that she did not consider fire to be a tolerable element of a natural landscape. She permitted no prescribed burning on trust lands and would not approve a "let-burn" approach to naturally occurring fires. Regarding the issue of fire, the trustees appear to feel bound by her wishes, in spite of recent ecological studies that conclude that fire is natural and necessary to a healthy ecosystem. Mrs. Phillips's flexibility as a manager seems to have been withheld from future trustees.

In the case of the Phillips trust, the trustor was distinctive but basically a reasonable and effective manager. The restrictions she insisted on do not seem particularly problematic. The point is, of course, that other trustors may be less reasonable. Further, what may not seem a problem today may emerge as highly undesirable in future circumstances, with a different set of public preferences and a different base of ecological knowledge. The fire issue is a good illustration. Had the trust been written in the 1940s or even the early 1970s, it is likely that Mrs. Phillips's understanding of fire management would have been written into the trust documents as a binding constraint rather than being a mere personal obligation that the trustees recognize and abide by but could easily loosen or ignore.

In extreme cases, as noted in chapter 2, the law allows trust documents to be adapted to meet evolving public policy. Trust provisions are ultimately enforced in the courts, and the trustees can petition the courts for a change in rules. Moreover, the courts can modify or nullify trust provisions that are "contrary to public policy." This is a limited power and could not be used to strike down a provision that is merely silly, undesirable, or inefficient. However, the tenacity with which Mrs. Phillips sought perpetual protection of her own priorities ought to be a warning flag: it is possible to create enormous problems for future trustees with trust provisions that are overly specific, detailed, or personalized.

The most conspicuous success of the Phillips trust is its role in precipitating a landscapewide effort to conserve and protect ecological and recreational resources. Although each individual parcel is important, the whole is greater than the sum of its parts. The value of any protected parcel is enhanced by the proximity of another. In a region where private landownership is the norm, it is particularly important to anchor regional approaches. Yet potential dead-hand problems are magnified in an environment that features diverse settlors, donors, and organizations.

The key element to stitching the Rangeley landscape together was the cluster of institutions—public and private—that formed to undertake the task. The diverse partnership that came together to protect the more than 33,000 acres in the Rangeley Lakes area is astounding and in many ways a model of what is possible when people work together toward a common goal. However, it is important not to lose sight of the possibility that such diverse and complex collaborations may be unstable. Potential problems seem to be of two types: day-to-day management, and institutional sustainability. The management issues can be suggested by envisioning a trail that passes from a Phillips parcel to a Forest Service easement on a Boise Cascade parcel to an RLHT parcel. In the first and last legs of the journey, hunting is forbidden; on the middle leg, it is encouraged. On the first, motorized access is forbidden, but not on the last two. The trail signs could become mighty complex, and enforcement difficult.

Many management problems could be resolved, but it is not clear that the institutions involved have sufficient stability to make the agreements last. Although the newcomer RLHT might appear the most likely candidate for shaking up or folding, Forest Service priorities are buffeted by both political winds and simple personnel changes that could make it the least reliable partner.

We find it ironic that title and responsibility for managing landscapes could reasonably be viewed as fragmenting by this landscape-level coalition. Almost every parcel that we discussed is fragmented—not into the surface and subsurface ownerships that so confound Westerners in many regions, but among different rights holders. One party has development rights, another the right to plan and manage timber, another the right to enforce rules of access, another the fee ownership and the right to rental returns on boating and camping.

Land protection in the Rangeley Lakes area is on a roll. The Pingree heirs are, as we write, looking for a buyer for conservation easements on much of the land that surrounds Phillips trust efforts. Conservationists, although concerned about raising the $35 million presently being discussed, are understandably pleased. However, even as it provides a wonderful model of the possibilities for devolution and dispersion of authority over conservation, the Rangeley experience hints at some of the risks and potential pitfalls. Betty Phillips and her trust put into motion an auspicious start that merits continuing attention.

CHAPTER TEN

Society for the Protection
of New Hampshire Forests

Founded in 1901, the Society for the Protection of New Hampshire Forests (SPNHF) is among the oldest conservation organizations in the United States. The Society, as it is affectionately referred to, strives to protect land by using it well. Its programs are diverse and numerous, and a reasonable way to approach the range of Society activities is to begin with the assertion, familiar to biologists, that ontology recapitulates phylogeny: the development of the individual mirrors the evolution of the species. The Society has been a consistent innovator in the conservation field, and it provides a useful lens for viewing the development of conservation organizations in this country.[1] Its focus on government land management was intense and epochal, but brief. It has grown, elaborated, and diversified, both leading and reflecting the nation's shift in emphasis from land and resource conservation to environmental protection. Twenty-five percent of its land is preserved in unmanaged natural areas. Nevertheless, the Society has remained fundamentally true to its roots as a forestry association, working to improve stewardship and support sustainable economic use of the state's forest resources.

The Society is not primarily a land trust. Nor is it a trust as described in chapter 2. It is organized as a 501(c)(3) nonprofit corporation. Nevertheless, trust principles are apparent in many aspects of Society activities. Our discussion of the SPNHF focuses on those trust and trustlike aspects of the Society, providing perspective on the utility of trust principles even when institutional designers have no interest in founding a trust per se. We highlight three areas of Society activity that rely more or less on trust principles—planned giving, endowment management, and mitigation banking—and we emphasize a fourth, the interplay between family trusts and conservation easements.

EVOLUTION OF SPNHF PROGRAMS

Concern about devastating harvest practices and subsequent flooding and fires led to the Society's founding. Its first focus was the growing movement to establish national forests in the East. This effort led to the passage of the Weeks Act in 1911 and to the authorization of the White Mountain National

Forest shortly thereafter.[2] Continuing in that vein, the SPNHF was among the first U.S. organizations fostering conservation of scenic and recreational resources by purchasing them and donating them for management as national forests, state parks, or town forests (a New Hampshire tradition). Throughout the depression, the Society spearheaded state- and regionwide campaigns to acquire forestland faced with development or ill-conceived logging.

The Society has continued to work in close partnership with the state on a broad variety of conservation and environmental initiatives. However, it soon de-emphasized its fund-raise, purchase, and donate approach and began its own system of reserves to conserve land and to demonstrate sustainable forest management practices.[3] The limitations inherent in turning land over to the government for conservation are manifest in the Society's current efforts to force the state of New Hampshire to remove a 180-foot communications tower built on the top of Mount Kearsarge in Wilmot, New Hampshire. The Society donated the 521-acre site to the state in 1949 as a memorial to the Society's founder, a former governor of New Hampshire. The deed was specifically conditioned to require that the state maintain the parcel as a "forestry and recreation reservation for public use and benefit." Noting that the tower violated the deed restrictions, Society president Jane Difley regretted the lawsuit but underscored that the organization takes its role as a protector of both open space and the tools for conserving them quite seriously.

A focus on private stewardship is the most durable element of Society programs. The Society works on the assumption that private owners are or can be encouraged to become excellent stewards of the land. In support of that proposition, it embraces, sometimes unfashionably, the idea of economically productive private management of forest resources. This primary commitment is reflected in its emergence as a major conservation advocacy group. Although its support for the Weeks Act bore fruit in a mere decade, its active efforts to convince New Hampshire to adopt taxing policies on timberlands that would encourage stewardship rather than rapid liquidation of forest resources took half a century. Along the way, the Society ran a nursery to make seeds and seedlings available to private landowners for reforestation (1902), successfully advocated the appointment of a state forester to regulate forest management practices and control fire (1909), opposed destructive forest harvest practices and purchased many scenic parcels threatened with unregulated logging, and initiated a summer nature camp for public school teachers in the state (1932). In the late 1940s, the Society sponsored the Tree Farm program in New Hampshire, a certification program for forest landowners who manage at least ten acres for multiple values.[4] In the 1990s, the Society worked assiduously to cultivate green certification for forest products. The timber harvested from its own land is SmartWood certified.

This historic commitment to private land stewardship has positioned the SPNHF comfortably in today's changing conservation climate. Private

The 180-foot communications tower built on top of Mount Kearsarge dwarfs a fire lookout long established on the site. (Courtesy Society for the Protection of New Hampshire Forests)

ownership, sustainable management, and public-private partnerships that are emerging as central in national conservation circles have long been the heart of Society conservation programs. Particularly important to the emergence of land trusts in New Hampshire was the Society's 1960s campaign to amend the New Hampshire constitution to allow undeveloped land to be taxed at low rates. A ten-acre minimum for what is called a current use assessment allows small landholders to participate in preserving open space, and a development penalty allows towns to recoup lost revenues.[5] Beginning in the early 1970s, the SPNHF was among the aggressive national leaders in defining and developing the concept of the conservation easement. At present, the Society holds around 400 easements covering more than 58,000 acres of land.

The Society's cooperative relationships with other land trusts in the state and region are a crucial element of its land protection activities. With land trusts forming throughout many regions of the United States, questions about duplication of effort, dissipation of social capital, and fragmentation of the landscape become important. The Society is one of almost forty organizations in New Hampshire described as land trusts.[6] Is this institutional density desirable? Unexpectedly, perhaps, the SPNHF has actively worked to found many of those organizations in order to ensure the protection of small, locally important parcels. Many of the organizations own and manage easements that the Society collaborates in monitoring and enforcing. In addition, the Society organized and anchored the Trust for New Hampshire Lands, a collaborative state-private effort that raised more than $50 million to protect lands at a scale beyond even the Society's resources.[7] Finally, the Society frequently develops programs with similar state and national organizations. For example, the Society has worked with the Nature Conservancy and the Audubon Society of New Hampshire[8] on a program supported by a grant from the U.S. Environmental Protection Agency in the Ossipee region of the state. The division of labor for the project suggests how the organizations focus their programs to support rather than compete with one another: the Nature Conservancy focuses on rare and endangered species, Audubon concentrates on wetlands and wildlife travel corridors, and the SPNHF concentrates on key watersheds and productive upland forests.[9]

The Society, like many other large, charitable nonprofits, depends on donors and members to support much of its activity. Accordingly, it encourages potential donors to consider including the organization in a variety of financial arrangements that are collectively referred to as planned giving. Many of these arrangements are private or charitable trusts, which can be structured to produce federal income tax deductions and reduced estate taxes while allowing the donor to provide income for her own lifetime or the lifetime of her heirs. The Society provides an attractive, albeit standard, brochure describing a number of trust options that potential donors can adapt to their financial planning needs. Most of the trusts are variants on a standard charitable remainder unitrust. The basic format is that a donor establishes a trust, identifying resources that will pay income to a specified beneficiary (the donor or another) until she dies, at which time the trust corpus becomes the property of the Society. The trust format is attractive because it allows the donor to enjoy income tax benefits at the time the trust is established, during her lifetime.

Planned giving turns out, however, to be a bit of a misnomer. The donor plans, to be sure, but the Society, which ultimately benefits from the trust arrangement, is frequently pleasantly surprised. Although such trusts provide a substantial portion of Society funding—bequests account for approximately 30 percent of the Society's $7.5 million annual support and revenues—they are frequently unknown to the Society until the beneficiary dies and the Society receives the corpus of the trust. This is because the arrangement of the trust is undertaken by the donor, typically in consultation with an attorney or accountant, and the tax benefits are achieved when the donor files her income tax returns. The Society is not necessarily "in the loop" when all this takes place.[10] Some donors do inform the Society that they have included the organization in a trust arrangement, but many do not. It is therefore not possible for the Society's director of planned giving to estimate the resources that are likely to come the Society's way, in total or in any given year, as a result of these planned giving trust arrangements. The director is also well aware that trust and other bequest arrangements are a two-edged sword. Although it is possible to configure a trust so that the Society receives an annual donation, that is not the typical format. Hence, bequests may come in lieu of an individual's annual contributions. To the extent that the Society can plan for this trust-based giving, it focuses recruitment on donors who have given all the annual donations that they are likely to, and those who will continue to make them in spite of having included the Society in a trust arrangement.

Anticipated or not, the proceeds from planned giving sooner or later wind up in the Society's endowment fund. Management of just over $12.2 million produces approximately $1 million annually, or 14.3 percent of the Society's total support and revenues. Management and utilization of the endowment are directed by three factors, none of which specifically mentions trust principles: the investment policies established by the SPNHF board and financial committee, the organization's status as a 501(c)(3) corporation, and the recently promulgated Financial Accounting Standards Board (FASB) requirements for nonprofit corporations' recording and reporting of financial contributions. Although trust principles are not specifically mentioned anywhere, they are clearly in evidence.

Basically, the endowment is a pot of money that the Society manages and expends to accomplish its organizational goals. Most of the principal is donated to the organization, and some is dedicated to specific purposes. It is not unlike a sum that our hypothetical grandmother would give to a bank to manage and make available for her heirs' education. The funds are held under a strict set of guidelines that embody the same elements of prudence, accountability, and undivided loyalty to the settlor's intent that characterize the grandmother's trust. The Society board of directors and its financial committee prudently mandate relatively conservative investment of endowment funds; the organization does not take large risks with its donors' money.

Expenditures are also tightly defined. As a 501(c)(3) nonprofit, the Society is required to spend its endowment on charitable purposes identified in the federal tax code and further specified in the documents filed by the Society with the IRS when it filed for nonprofit status. In addition, board policies restrict the organization to a very conservative spending policy: every year it can spend from the endowment no more than 5 percent of a three-year rolling average of the endowment's value. Notice that this spending policy is, in current financial markets, more conservative than a restriction limiting spending to annual interest only. The Society's managed funds are currently earning closer to 12 percent; thus, the policy covers inflation and presently has the effect of plowing some investment earnings back into the endowment.

Finally, the Society is obliged to record and report on contributions under rules promulgated in 1993 by the FASB. FASB standards define three classes of assets contained in the Society's endowment: permanently restricted, temporarily restricted, and unrestricted. The difference among these three types of assets turns entirely on the intent of the donor. Permanently restricted funds are limited by "donor-imposed stipulations that neither expire by passage of time nor can be fulfilled or otherwise removed" by action of the organization. Donor-imposed stipulations on temporarily restricted assets can either expire or be removed when the organization accomplishes stipulated undertakings. Use of unrestricted funds is limited only by the nature of the organization and the purposes specified in its articles of incorporation, bylaws, and similar documents.[11]

The Society does not describe its endowment as a trust, and there is no reason that it must. Nevertheless, the endowment is a special brand of trust, and board, FASB, and IRS restrictions reflect basic trust principles. The Society must manage donated funds prudently and spend them with undivided loyalty to the donor's intent and the stated purpose of the organization.

A small Society sortie in the mitigation banking arena puts an interesting spin on its trustlike activities, especially when compared to the relatively complex organizations required in similar situations discussed in this volume. We characterized the Dade County Wetlands Trust as a minimalist approach to organizing accountability for mitigation funds, which would make the Society's role in holding and managing funds to mitigate a small hydroelectric dam an invisible trust. Perhaps that is appropriate—all the trust basics were in place, but it was never necessary to mention any of them.

In the mid-1980s, a private developer moved under the Public Utility Regulatory Policies Act of 1978 (PURPA)[12] to redevelop a small hydroelectric plant on land near Dummer, New Hampshire. PURPA was so intent on encouraging hydropower that it specifically allowed investors to develop facilities on land that did not belong to them. The proposed plant was designed to divert most of the flow of the Androscoggin River, effectively dewatering a section along New Hampshire Route 16, including lands that had been donated to the state for conservation purposes. That section had become a popular white-water canoeing area. The Society became involved because it has an enormous interest in protecting the integrity of land restrictions even when it was not the donee, and because the impact on the fishery and recreational resources was significant. It joined with the Appalachian Mountain Club (AMC) and sued to halt the development.

The legal challenge was eventually settled when the developer agreed to major revisions in dam operation that would provide increased flows to protect downstream fish and water releases for boating. In addition, the settlement required the developer to make annual contributions to a mitigation fund. Payments were to cease in 1998, and any unexpended funds were to be returned to the developer. The money was to be spent by a committee made up of representatives of the state Department of Environmental Services, sportsmen's groups, the AMC, and the developer.

The Society simply acted as the fiscal agent for the operation, holding and investing the funds until they were expended or returned. The arrangement raises important questions about the role of the developer in spending mitigation funds. Unfortunately, in this case, after the committee authorized a small study of fisheries in the area, the developer hired an attorney to block further expenditures by arguing that whatever activities were proposed did not meet the terms of the agreement.

While the committee haggled, deposits and interest accrued until the Pontook Mitigation Fund contained a tidy sum. With time running out, the committee was finally able to purchase fifty acres along the river and develop it as a cartop canoe launch. The state Fish and Game Department will manage the land. The purchase absorbed about half of the fund, and the rest was returned to the developer.[13] This Tinkerbell of mitigation trusts barely came into existence and then simply disappeared. Nevertheless, trust principles silently underwrote the whole operation.

Much of the flash and glamour in both current and historic conservation programs has attached to large parcels with undeniable scenic or habitat value. It would therefore be easy to underestimate the importance of the family homesteads, small woodlots, and family trusts discussed in this section. None of the properties were acquired, as were those in the Phillips trust, primarily for their conservation value. It is difficult to imagine bumper stickers demanding action to Save Highland Farm or Bois de Brodeur. The conservation easements do not, in fact, suggest that the parcels will even be "saved" from logging—their maintenance depends on continued forest harvest, and several of them already include a home and related buildings.

Why, then, is this story important? Family homes, second homes, woodlots, and farms have long been a major focus of the Society's operations, but the effort to conserve working landscapes, to use them gently and well, is just forming as a central element of the environmental agenda. Although it is no Yosemite Valley, Bois de Brodeur is not a housing development either. Parcels like it constitute a significant portion of the national landscape and must be part of any conservation effort that does not rely on government land acquisition and eviction of the inhabitants. Using such properties well, and developing tools to support conservation-oriented family management, provides an opportunity for individuals and families to take responsibility for conservation in their own lives and to see themselves as having a role in the future of the land they inhabit.

From the perspective of a student of trust principles and their role in conservation, the Society's experience with conservation easements on family trusts teaches us two particularly important lessons. First, the trust–conservation easement combination simplifies family decision making and provides some ground rules for allocating both the resources and the responsibilities for managing them. The trust emerges, in general, as a tool for maintaining peace in families trying to stabilize their collective connection with the land over two and three generations. It provides an instructive window into the joys and challenges of maintaining a family property for conservation purposes.

Second, these experiences hint at the kinds of institutional support required to make family decisions work. Trust principles are themselves an ancient institutional form in which enormous social capital has been invested. The easement-holding organizations are modern variants of that basic model, but they do not stand alone. The Society's experience illustrates both the importance of a product mix in the land trust field and the importance of a web of supporting state and local regulation. The complex infrastructure underlying families' ability to choose a trust structure for conserving their land is worth exploring.

BOIS DE BRODEUR

A large, attractive sign proclaiming "Bois de Brodeur" identifies a thirty-three-acre woodlot in East Concord, New Hampshire.[14] Felix Brodeur, a practical and hardworking man of modest means, purchased the land in 1940. During World War II, the property was heavily logged to support the war effort. Thereafter, it was managed to provide lumber to build and cord wood to heat the Brodeur family home. Forty years of careful management restored the forest for recreation and wildlife. By the early 1980s, the senior Brodeur had come increasingly to see his woodlot as a conservation resource. Before he died in 1983, he had refused several lucrative opportunities to sell the property to developers. Instead, he deeded the land in common to his five children, who immediately established a trust to provide a structure for joint decision making concerning the property. In 1990, with disagreement growing among the next generation regarding the fate of the land, the beneficiaries of the trust voted to donate a conservation easement to a local land trust just starting operations.

The sibling trustors were also to be the beneficiaries of the trust. They drew the trust purposes from a statement their father had written in 1978, when he was obliged to explain to the board of assessors why he had failed to renew his "current use" tax status on the parcel:

Three generations of Brodeurs—Arthur, his daughter Theresa Le Bel (far left), and her children Christine (left center) and Robert (far right)—admire the sign designating their family property, crafted and placed there by Arthur in May 1990. (Courtesy Rose Freeman)

I, Felix Brodeur, age 88 years, did not realize that application for current use had to be applied for each year. As sole owner of the land, I wish to keep it for my family to use for forestland, environmental conservation, and as a source of energy, such as firewood.

The trust establishes a simple management regime for the woodlot. The trustee is the oldest lineal descendant younger than seventy-five years of age living in the area. The trustee consults with the other beneficiaries but has broad discretion to pursue trust goals. Amendments to the trust require the concurrence of 75 percent of the beneficiaries. This informal arrangement has provided a simple means for identifying an individual to assume the modest record-keeping, form-signing, and management requirements of the parcel.[15] Felix's eldest child served as trustee for almost ten years. In 1990, she passed the task to the youngest, the three middle siblings having declined to serve. In 1999, the family was preparing to pass the responsibility to the next generation.

Maintenance and management expenses are met by funds generated by occasional timber sales planned by a consulting forester. Receipts are deposited in a simple passbook savings account until needed for trust expenses. Property taxes are paid by whichever members of the family have harvested cordwood during the year. When no one has cut any firewood, some members of the older generation have simply chipped in to pay the taxes. The beneficiaries meet from time to time to name a new trustee, to discuss the purposes and general business of the trust, and to renew their joint relationship to the land.

The original trustee successfully applied for Tree Farm status for the parcel. Tree Farm status requires a forest management plan for the area and encourages recreational use of the property. The family is happy to have the property open for limited public use.[16] Unlike the situation in Napa County, California (see chapter 11), the trustees are not concerned about liability and do not carry liability insurance. Under New Hampshire law, none is necessary. The state encourages landowners to open their property to recreational use by ensuring that cooperative landowners will not be held liable for accidents on their property unless they are caused by landowner negligence.[17]

The family has hit only one major snag in the informal operation of the trust. In 1988, the five siblings first considered the idea of donating the parcel to the Society. The idea was not popular with several members of the next generation. The dispute led to an interpretation of the trust that surprised the five trustor-beneficiaries: an attorney concluded that the trust document included all lineal descendants of Felix Brodeur at least twenty-one years of age, not just his five children, as voting beneficiaries. Thus, the move to donate the land would require approval of 75 percent of the first and second generations combined. By 1988, that included the five original trustor-beneficiaries plus thirty more. Rather than seek a second legal opinion regarding who was and was not a qualified beneficiary-voter, the original five acknowledged that the reinterpretation provided a way to include members of the next generation in trust management. They put their proposal to a vote of the larger group, and the donation just barely failed to attract the necessary 75 percent approval.

The issue of what to do with the woodlot gained renewed urgency two years later during a statewide property reassessment. With the land evaluated for use as house lots, the taxes soared beyond the means of the Brodeur heirs. The trustee requested the town to reconsider the tax because the lot mistakenly had not been assessed under the "current use" program. Town officials acted to prevent skyrocketing tax bills from forcing development throughout their jurisdiction.

In this context, a conservation easement appeared to be an attractive option. It provided a middle ground between those beneficiaries who wanted to sell the property for house lots and those who wanted to donate it to the Society. The family could maintain ownership and access for firewood while lowering their property taxes and creating a conservation legacy that would have pleased Felix Brodeur. The Society declined the offered easement because of the property's small size. However, the newly established Concord Conservation Trust (CCT) accepted an easement. The requisite 75 percent of the trust beneficiaries twenty-one years of age and older agreed to an amendment to the family trust to allow for the easement, which was donated in April 1990.

The easement on Bois de Brodeur was the first easement owned by the CCT, whose primary focus is land protection through donated conservation easements. Presently, the CCT holds easements on about 100 acres; it has a membership of around 200 people, an annual budget of approximately $8,000, and a board of ten to fourteen people from Concord or neighboring towns.[18] The five siblings granted an executory interest in the easement to the SPNHF. This executory interest means that although the property interest in the easement is held by the Concord group, the Society assists in monitoring easement compliance and will enforce the easement if it is violated and the Concord trust does not respond.

Retiring from her post, founding trustee Rose Brodeur Freeman admonished her heirs and future trustees of Bois de Brodeur:

> Respect the land, maintain it in its living-green condition, compromise on differences of opinion with the focus on the wishes of the primary donor. Be proud of the conservation efforts of the past; especially of the original family owner, your father, grandfather or great-grandfather.

More we could not ask from or for a thirty-three-acre woodlot just east of Concord.

HIGHLAND FARM

Highland Farm is also a family trust that is protected by a conservation easement on which the Society holds an executory interest. However, the property contains the Burgess family home, which is still in regular, continuous use as a residence for some and as a ski lodge and vacation home for others. The farm's conservation value is enhanced by the fact that it is one of a number of protected areas in the neighborhood of the White Mountain National Forest.

The Burgess family is only the second owner of the property. In 1908, Abby Bullock, soon to be Abby Burgess, purchased Highland Farm from heirs of the French Huguenot family that had originally cleared the land in the eighteenth century. She paid $10 per acre for 120 acres, and the sellers threw in the house and barn at no charge. In the early 1970s, the family purchased an additional parcel when they learned that road construction was contemplated up the mountain across the road from their house. The new parcel was described in an ancient deed as containing fifty acres. However, when it was surveyed at the time of the sale, it turned out to contain approximately eighty acres. The sellers, a family named Trickey, stuck with the original deal, and Highland Farm presently contains about 190 acres. Pleased with their real estate coup, the family continues to refer to the more recently acquired area and themselves as the "Trickey Lot."

When Mrs. Burgess was in her seventies, she deeded the farm to her four children, who held it in common. Their attorney recommended that they establish a trust to codify their intentions regarding the property and simplify family decision making. Working with the Society in the late 1970s, the four siblings first placed a conservation easement on the original parcel and then established the trust. In 1993, the trustees granted a conservation easement on the Trickey Lot as well.

In 1977, the trustees donated a conservation easement to the town of Jackson. New Hampshire towns are, of course, authorized to own land or interests in land, and the town meeting had voted to support a conservation easement program in Jackson.[19] The donation allowed the four siblings to take an income tax deduction. Because the deduction was larger than any of the donors could use, given their incomes for a single year, each of them took advantage of provisions in the tax code that allowed them to roll the remaining portion of their charitable donation forward as a deduction for five additional years. The family members, a former trustee notes, were paid for doing what they wanted to do anyway.

The first easement was simple—it requires the owner to pay the taxes on the property and to maintain the property open, undivided, and undeveloped forever, with no new structures or commercial, industrial, or mining activities. The easement allows the family to maintain its residential use of the property. It also permits them to cooperate with and provide access to the Jackson Ski Touring Foundation, a community-based nonprofit organization that maintains about 160 miles of trails in and around the town and runs a series of ski events, classes, and facilities during the ski season. Officials from the town of Jackson walk the property once a year to ensure that the conditions of the easement are being met. The Society holds an executory easement, as it does on Bois de Brodeur.

A year after granting the easement, the family created a trust that reflects the same conservation purposes as the easement and establishes a light decision-making structure for the family. The trust purpose is twofold: to maintain the property undivided for the residential and recreational use of the Burgess family, and to exclude commercial use or development of any kind. Many family members are Quaker, and trust business proceeds largely by following "the sense of the meeting," or the consensus of the beneficiaries. There is an occasional selection of a new trustee, who is responsible for routine decisions and paperwork and for keeping track of the growing number of beneficiaries and their addresses. The declaration gives the trustee enormous discretion to manage the trust property—to borrow, mortgage, lease, sell, construct, demolish, and, in general, "do all other acts or things which an owner of real property can do." Mostly, the trustee maintains a long-term forest management plan, in consultation with the Society and other resource professionals, and pays expenses and banks any profits from sales in a simple passbook account maintained to pay taxes and maintenance expenses on the family home. The property is managed, as is permitted by the conservation easement, to produce timber.

The family has formally altered the trust document only once, when questions arose about how to allocate interest in the trust when the original 25 percent shares allotted to the original beneficiaries passed to the next generation. Would the offspring of each of the four siblings divide their own parent's 25 percent share among themselves without regard to their number,[20] or would all members of the second generation share the property equally, as had the first? Eventually, the first four amended the trust to allow for equal shares among all second-generation beneficiaries. Such equality irks those in the first generation with few children, but it simplifies relationships, voting, and decision making for the second generation.

Nevertheless, not all of the eligible offspring have elected to become participants in the trust. One cousin, for example, lives outside the area and did not accept his share of the trust when his father passed his interest on. That decision had the effect of increasing the beneficial interest of all the other second-generation participants in the trust. Being a beneficiary does entail responsibility for paying an annual assessment for maintenance of the property. Because the house was built in 1812, it requires considerable attention. Those in permanent residence bear much of the burden, but each beneficiary is assessed approximately $250 per year to cover expenses. This is about half the assessment of a decade ago, when there were lower costs but fewer beneficiaries.

The trust document provides elaborately for trust termination. Fifty percent of the beneficiaries can vote to terminate the trust. Alternatively, the trust will expire without a vote (following the rule against perpetuities in private trusts discussed in chapter 2) twenty years after the last of the original beneficiaries dies. In either event, the trust property is slated to be divided among the interest holders. Because the easement precludes subdividing the land itself, this requires that the property be sold with the easement still in place, and the proceeds divided among the interest holders. However, the beneficiaries might decide to devise another trust or similar structure to maintain joint ownership.

The second easement accomplishes the same things as the first, but the process for achieving an easement has become much more elaborate and imposes some modest costs and inconveniences on the donor.[21] In 1993, Highland Farm was caught in the same tax reappraisal that affected Bois de Brodeur. The property was reassessed at about $2 million. This led the trustee to donate a second conservation easement, this time on Trickey Lot, to the town of Jackson. Again, the Society holds an executory interest. Because the land was already held by a trust that generated only a small annual income, this donation produced no income tax benefits for the heirs. However, following appeals from both the town of Jackson and the family, the easement did lower the assessed value, and thus the property taxes, on the farm.

The easement has been changed once, to accommodate a neighbor's error. When building a home on an adjoining parcel, the neighbor failed to leave a sufficient setback from the Burgess property. To prevent trouble with the local zoning body, the Burgess trustee offered to swap a small strip of trust land next to the offending house for a similar strip of the neighbor's. The swap involved taking the first strip out of the easement and replacing it with the second. The action required the approval of both the Conservation Commission of the town of Jackson and the Society. Both reviewed the trade to ensure that it did not create a private gain on resources that had already been donated (which could have concerned the IRS) and to ensure that it had no impact on the conservation values protected by the easement.

The Society began by organizing to encourage the federal government to acquire and conserve resources. Soon it pulled back from reliance on government ownership and worked to create an environment in which private landowners, including the Society itself, could be educated and encouraged to conserve the land. Although the Society continues to lobby at the state and federal levels, it no longer emphasizes government acquisition of land but prefers to encourage private stewardship and gentle use of working landscapes.

The Society is not merely a land trust, nor is it a trust. However, trust principles pervade its fund-raising and management and play a significant role in its conservation easement programs. They are particularly important in the complex process of conserving family lands. The Society's efforts to do so have involved creating and supporting numerous local and private organizations and lobbying for a diverse array of tax and other programs. And the Society itself plays an important public role as the guarantor of last resort for many easements that it does not own.

CHAPTER ELEVEN

Napa County Land Trust

The word *Napa* conjures up visions of small, country roads skirting rolling fields of grapes ripening in the warm summer sun until being meticulously crafted into world-famous wines. The deep green vines throw the gold, drying grasses of the surrounding cattle pastures into sharp relief.[1] Napa is that place, but the vision may need a slight edit: the vineyards are increasingly owned by large corporations, the little back road is now Highway 29, and the towns are more and more oriented toward a growing local biotech economy[2] and capturing the 5.5 million tourists who come each year in search of a pleasant weekend in wine country. Napa is one of nine Bay Area counties, just over an hour from San Francisco, providing city dwellers with an easy drive to a rural escape. Many who visit come back to stay, and the population growth rate in Napa County is approximately 2 percent per year.[3]

The Napa County Land Trust (NCLT) is not a trust as described in chapter 2 but rather a tax-exempt, nonprofit corporation with over 1,000 dues-paying members. However, in many facets of its institutional organization, the NCLT draws on formal trusts and the basic idea of a fiduciary relationship to direct its practices. It is those aspects of the NCLT that most interest us in this volume. This chapter describes three aspects of the NCLT—endowment funds, land held in trust, and the culture of the organization—to explore how trusts and trustlike tools are used in conservation and land protection. Our discussion highlights the NCLT's emphasis on a clear purpose and its particular focus on stability and continuity in pursuing that purpose. These features emerge as the core of the NCLT's approach to accountability. The trust has invested heavily in defining, projecting, and maintaining an image of rectitude and coherence in order to convince both Napa residents and potential donors that it can be trusted to manage perpetual easements over the long term. In the process of recruiting donors and members (who, it is hoped, will ripen into active participants in organizational activities), the NCLT becomes accountable to its public.

We are also interested in the NCLT's relationship to the changing economic and regulatory environment in Napa County. The NCLT's organizational priorities have evolved in part in response to the changing context of land protection in the county. At present, Napa County government is looking for private partners in its intensifying land regulation effort. The NCLT organization has explored and until now rejected that route for institutional development, continuing its established emphasis on donated easements. However, it is not clear for how long private organizations like the NCLT can accurately be viewed as "private," or what that will mean in a period of increasing dispersion of government authority.

FOUNDING CONTEXT

Napa County has had an off-again, on-again commitment to growth control and land use planning during the last third of the twentieth century. Earth Day–era efforts resulted in the designation of the entire floor of the Napa Valley as an Agricultural Preserve Zone, which permits current use assessments for agricultural lands under the state's Williamson Act.[4] The subsequent election of slow and no-growth county commissioners led to the adoption of a forty-acre minimum lot size for the rapidly urbanizing area. In a 1976 backlash against the imposition of land use controls, the conservationists lost a pivotal seat on the County Commission, and the minimum lot size was halved.[5] The NCLT was formed that same year by county residents who were committed to maintaining Napa as a unique rural region of California. The battle over land use in Napa heated up and did not stabilize until the early 1990s.

At the same time that urban growth and sprawl issues became particularly contentious in Napa County and elsewhere, conservationists throughout the nation were increasingly drawn to conservation easements and land trusts to address them. Local land trusts such as the Napa organization proliferated rapidly, aided by a long-standing commitment of the larger, better-established organizations to spin off and catalyze the formation of smaller, local ones. The NCLT's development can be linked to the availability of external institutional support. The Trust for Public Land (TPL) ran a program in the late 1970s that was intended to foment the growth of local land trusts in the San Francisco Bay Area. TPL personnel believe that this program was instrumental in the emergence of the NCLT and two others in adjacent counties, the Sonoma Land Trust and the Marin Agricultural Land Trust, all between 1976 and 1980.

The Napa group was established to preserve three things—natural resources, wildlife areas, and historic sites—from the development pressures that threaten Napa County. The organization accepts donations of land or conservation easements, enters into conservation agreements, and monitors the lands that it has committed to protect. The land trust also works with governmental agencies at the local, state, and national levels to aid in the acquisition of land for open spaces, parks, and wildlife refuges. However, the NCLT founders' conservation priorities reflect the fact that the land in Napa County is held in predominantly private ownership and is likely to stay that way. The land use decisions of private owners have an enormous impact on the form and future of Napa County's environment and on the lifestyles of Napa residents. With this in mind, the NCLT works with willing landowners to protect lands permanently.

As befits a small organization operating on a shoestring, the NCLT grew slowly. By 1979, it had received two property donations, a 600-acre botanical preserve on Mount George that it continues to manage, and a 38-acre marshland property that it conveyed to the state to be managed as a state wildlife area. The trust secured its first donation of a conservation easement on a ranch, a 635-acre property in Pope Valley, in 1980. In 1988, twelve years after its founding, the NCLT established its first conservation easement on a vineyard property, on a 24-acre section of the 980-acre Green Valley Ranch.

Currently, the trust has protected approximately 15,000 acres in over sixty properties. It owns four permanent preserves (2,083 acres) that are open to the public by appointment and holds conservation easements that protect another 9,349 acres. And the NCLT has acquired and transferred the ownership of 1,874 acres to state and local agencies that manage the lands as parks or wildlife areas, holding them open to public access.[6] In addition, the NCLT has been active in supporting the conservation efforts of other individuals and organizations within Napa County—assisting individuals who agree to put conservation restrictions on valuable parcels of lands that would otherwise be sold for development and helping to start another land conservancy focused on acquiring lands for a research preserve.[7] Although the NCLT has participated in a wide range of land protection activities, accepting and monitoring conservation easements is the activity to which it has committed its organizational resources.

ENDOWMENT MANAGEMENT

Like the Society for the Protection of New Hampshire Forests, the NCLT holds most of its financial resources in restricted endowment funds, that is, in what could be considered a formal trust. Income from the funds provides a significant portion of the organization's annual operating budget of $360,000. The Napa organization's approach to managing the endowment is interesting, however, because it is not treated as one common pool. The endowment is divided into many separate funds, including an Easement Management Fund, four Permanent Preserve Funds, a Land Preservation Fund, a Reserve Fund, and an Easement Defense Fund. Each is prudently managed, as any trust should be, to achieve maximum income

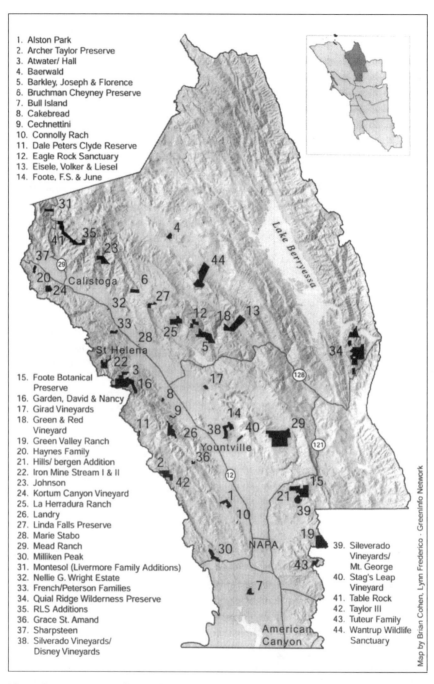

1. Alston Park
2. Archer Taylor Preserve
3. Atwater/ Hall
4. Baerwald
5. Barkley, Joseph & Florence
6. Bruchman Cheyney Preserve
7. Bull Island
8. Cakebread
9. Cechnettini
10. Connolly Rach
11. Dale Peters Clyde Reserve
12. Eagle Rock Sanctuary
13. Eisele, Volker & Liesel
14. Foote, F.S. & June

15. Foote Botanical Preserve
16. Garden, David & Nancy
17. Girad Vineyards
18. Green & Red Vineyard
19. Green Valley Ranch
20. Haynes Family
21. Hills/ bergen Addition
22. Iron Mine Stream I & II
23. Johnson
24. Kortum Canyon Vineyard
25. La Herradura Ranch
26. Landry
27. Linda Falls Preserve
28. Marie Stabo
29. Mead Ranch
30. Milliken Peak
31. Montesol (Livermore Family Additions)
32. Nellie G. Wright Estate
33. French/Peterson Families
34. Quial Ridge Wilderness Preserve
35. RLS Additions
36. Grace St. Amand
37. Sharpsteen
38. Silverado Vineyards/ Disney Vineyards

39. Sileverado Vineyards/ Mt. George
40. Stag's Leap Vineyard
41. Table Rock
42. Taylor III
43. Tuteur Family
44. Wantrup Wildlife Sanctuary

Map by Brian Cohen, Lynn Frederico - GreenInfo Network

Napa County is one of nine Bay Area counties within easy tourist and commuting distance of San Francisco. The NCLT protects or holds interests in 15,000 acres in sixty different properties. (Cartographer: Bryan Cohen, Green Info Network) consistent with the preservation of capital. However, the investment goals for the funds are adjusted to meet the restrictions on their use and the anticipated needs to be served by the funds.

The restrictions have been imposed either by donors, who have requested that gifts be dedicated to a particular purpose, or by the land trust's board of trustees. A donor might request that a donation be applied, for example, to the upkeep of a permanent preserve. Board-restricted funds are, in theory, somewhat more flexible; the money can be moved from fund to fund or used for diverse purposes if the board makes a formal decision to alter its status. Board-restricted funds include the assets in the Easement Monitoring Fund and the Land Preservation Fund.

Investment guidelines and spending policies for the various funds differ according to the use of the fund. The Easement Management Fund, Permanent Preserve Funds, Land Preservation Fund, and Reserve Fund are all managed to emphasize current income. The Easement Monitoring Fund supports baseline documentation on new conservation easement properties and annual monitoring efforts on all the properties that the NCLT holds easements on or owns in fee. The Permanent Preserve Funds are each committed to the management and operation of one of the organization's permanent preserves. Only the income from these funds is available for expenditure.

The Land Preservation Fund and the Reserve Fund are also managed to emphasize current income, but the board is permitted to spend the principal as well as the income. The Land Preservation Fund is dedicated to purchasing "sensitive and threatened resource lands on an emergency or opportunity basis."[8] The theory is that this fund must be flexible and readily available for an opportunity that suddenly becomes available. Invasion of the principal is, however, intended to be temporary. The NCLT is committed to replenishing the Preservation Fund. The Reserve Fund is intended to address any unforeseen expenditures that might arise during a fiscal year. The fund is also available in its entirety for NCLT expenditures, if necessary.

The NCLT requires a landowner to make a donation to the Easement Defense Fund when it accepts a conservation easement on the private owner's property.[9] The NCLT believes that the second and third owners of a parcel with a perpetual easement are less likely to have a commitment to the terms of easement and that enforcement is more likely to be necessary in the future.[10] Therefore, the Easement Defense Fund is managed not to maximize current income but to maximize long-term growth and future returns. As in the Land Preservation and Reserve Funds, the board is authorized to invade principal to meet the goals of the fund. Investing for long-term growth in the Defense Fund is intended to maximize the funds available to defend the easements in ten, fifteen, twenty, fifty years—as the property owners of easement parcels are further and further removed from the actual negotiation of the easement. The board is hopeful that the existence of the fund may act as a deterrent to easement challenges.

The NCLT manages each of the funds a little differently, fitting the investment and spending restrictions to both donor or board restrictions and the use of the fund. The organization has also considered putting each of the endowments into separate formal trusts. The goal would be to complicate title to the funds sufficiently to render them unattractive to creditors should the NCLT confront a large liability. Doing so would arguably provide an extra margin of protection for the funds beyond the liability insurance the trust maintains. However, the board has not taken that step. It is not clear whether the NCLT would have to file separate income tax returns for each fund under a separate trust arrangement. Doing so, or even employing an attorney to decipher whether doing so is necessary, would be costly. There is a limit, one board member notes, to the expense and nuisance one should endure to protect against relatively remote risks. The board has concluded that although the extra margin of safety would be desirable, the costs outweigh any potential benefits.

LAND HELD IN TRUST

The NCLT has used trust principles in a second, direct way: it holds one of its major preserves in trust. The owners of the Archer Taylor Preserve, a redwood forest in southwest Napa County, are donating the land over time. The process began with an 80-acre gift in 1993. Eventually, the NCLT will hold the entire 380-acre parcel in trust. In the meantime, the land trust operates the entire property under a lease from the owners. However, the trust's relationship to the Archer Taylor Preserve is even more confusing than the similar arrangement between the Phillips trust and the Rangeley Lakes Heritage Trust discussed in chapter 9.

The NCLT's original plan for the preserve was to take title to the property and donate a conservation easement on it to another land trust. The reason for so doing was twofold. First, the easement holder would be in a position to keep an eye on the NCLT, should the Napa organization be tempted to use the land in ways not intended by the donor. In this, the NCLT's plan resembles Betty Phillips's trust-easement arrangement and the overlapping easements on EVOS trust lands.

The other reason for putting an easement on land already owned by a conservation organization was to reduce its attractiveness to a judgment creditor. If the NCLT should encounter a liability that outstrips its insur-

Although Napa County is best known for its vineyards, some of the NCLT's most spectacular protected properties are in the hills in the southeastern part of the county. The Archer Taylor Preserve is held by the NCLT in a formal trust. (Photo: Parry Mgad; courtesy Napa County Land Trust)

ance, the land could be used to satisfy the judgment against it. If the NCLT did not own the development rights, that is, if the land had an easement on it, the NCLT could not lose them in a judgment. Thus, the land would not be subject to development even if it were lost to a judgment creditor or the like. At bottom, the goal of the intended easement was no different from the goal of any other easement. It is unusual, however, for a land trust to grant an easement on its own land to another land trust.

Unfortunately, the plan did not work out. Surprising, the NCLT could not find a land trust willing to accept an easement without charging what appeared to the board as an exorbitant easement defense fee. The fallback was to put the preserve in trust. But the NCLT had by then already taken title to the first parcel of the preserve. Therefore, when the NCLT put the first parcel into a trust, it was putting its own assets in trust and was therefore the settlor of the trust. In addition, the NCLT selected itself as trustee.[11] The NCLT is also one of the beneficiaries, as the trust is established for the benefit of "the Napa County Land Trust and all the residents of the County of Napa, California."

All but the first parcel has been or will be donated to the NCLT in trust. The arrangement allows the donor to put restrictions on the use of the land. In addition, the NCLT hopes that the trust and the multiplicity of beneficiaries, in combination with the deed restrictions, will sufficiently confuse title to the preserve and thus protect it from development in case of an unfortunate liability. However, the potential benefit of separating lands held in trust from the NCLT's corporate assets is just a theory and has not yet been tested in court.

INSTITUTIONAL STRUCTURE

The NCLT has grown substantially since its founding. Like many local land trusts, it was initially an entirely volunteer organization and operated on a minuscule budget. The first full-time staff member was hired in 1988, and the office had expanded to six full-time employees by the end of 1999. Although the NCLT now has a permanent office and a degree of regularity in its professional staff, the heart of the organizational culture remains with its volunteers—the members, the board, and the web of committees that play a crucial role in organizational accountability and outreach. Much of the organization is defined in the process of recruiting and orienting a pool of volunteers from which most board members are ultimately drawn. Although not a trust, the NCLT reflects and specifically incorporates basic trust and fiduciary concepts in defining board responsibilities and in creating an organizational culture.

Board of Directors

The organization's most visible volunteers are those who hold seats on the NCLT's board of trustees. The Board members are also the official "members" of the 501(c)(3) tax-exempt corporation that is the land trust, and all corporate powers of the organization are exercised by and under the authority of the board. The NCLT calls its board members "trustees" or "directors" interchangeably, and it describes their obligations in trust terminology that ought to be familiar to readers:

> First, Board members must satisfy the *reasonably prudent person test* which requires that they fulfill their duties as a reasonably prudent person would do and thereby avoid mismanagement, non-management and self-dealing or conflict of interest.[12]

Until 1997, there was no limit on the length of time an individual could serve on the NCLT board. Several board members had helped form the organization in the 1970s, and their constant presence on the board and dedication to its initial mission contributed to the NCLT's stability. In 1997, however, the board voted to limit themselves to two three-year terms. After one year off the board, former members are eligible to return, although that has not happened. This change was made to prevent staleness and to ensure vitality, new ideas, and enthusiasm in the organization. Even with this new diversification, however, board culture is relatively constant. The fifteen-member group is self-perpetuating, which means that vacancies are filled by the board, not by any outside appointing body. Moreover, the terms are staggered; new members enter an established board one or two at a time, allowing them to adapt to the established culture of the board.

The NCLT's shift to limited board terms was accompanied by the development of a manual to introduce members to established NCLT activities and priorities. Created in 1997, it is carefully maintained and updated. The *Board Member Policy Manual* draws heavily on trust principles to describe the trustees' responsibilities to the organization and its beneficiaries:

> Morally and ethically, members of the Board of Trustees are also accountable to the community generally and to donors to the NCLT. Board members must understand that they can be held personally liable for compensatory and punitive damages if they fail in their fiduciary and other obligations to the NCLT by failing to exercise reasonable oversight of the organization and its activities.[13]

Interestingly, the trustees are asked to demonstrate undivided loyalty not directly to the beneficiaries, as they would be in a trust relationship described in chapter 2, but to the clear purpose of the NCLT organization. However, the NCLT presents itself as being directly accountable to the "community." Although the exact mechanisms through which the organization communicates with the public are not explicit in the guiding documents, the manual is clear in establishing that the land trust has a responsibility to the public.

Continuity arises as well from the fact that most new board members have participated in the network of volunteer committees involved in most of the NCLT's programs. An individual typically attains a seat on the board after spending a significant amount of time working closely with program staff to design and implement board policies. The new member is ceremoniously presented with a binder that includes the policy manual, minutes of twelve previous board meetings, and all recent NCLT publications. The process continues during a formal orientation, in which officers and staff work to teach new members how the organization functions and to clarify the roles and responsibilities the new member has accepted. This process ensures that board members begin from a shared understanding of their obligations as trustees and are particularly conscious of the NCLT's clear sense of purpose.

Mission

The organizational culture emphasizes a clear mission. The policy manual is emphatic that the organization has a well-defined purpose and must stick to it. "Whatever the NCLT does must be designed to further its goals and mission statement and must be measured against those goals," the manual states. "By virtue of its Articles of Incorporation, the NCLT's goal is fixed and not open to alteration without fundamental change in the organization."[14]

The NCLT's stated mission is to "acquire and preserve natural resources and wildlife areas for the use and enjoyment of present and future generations, to preserve and protect historic sites, to educate the public about the wise use of natural resources, and to work with other organizations with similar objectives."[15] Acquisition includes both conservation easements and title in fee simple. Although nothing in the bylaws specifically prohibits the trustees from accepting easements outside of Napa County, they discourage such commitments,[16] and the NCLT's resources are devoted to land protection within the county. Direct, focused, and stable, the NCLT's purpose serves as a reference point for decision making about policies and projects.

Perpetuity

Everything about the NCLT signals its commitment to a perpetual mission. The board is particularly aware that a conservation easement is a permanent restriction that is noted in county records and encumbers the property on which it applies. The manual is clear that land and easements held by the land trust are to be protected for the "use and enjoyment of present and future generations."[17] Once the NCLT accepts an easement, it has a responsibility to monitor and enforce the deed restrictions in perpetuity. Knowing that its commitments are enduring and expensive, the trust does not accept every easement offered. It carefully assesses the relative costs and benefits of each proposed project to determine what commitments of time and energy the property will require from its limited resources. The factors considered include parcel size, distance from existing preserves and other easements, special conservation values, visibility from a highway (which is important in terms of a parcel's value as a view shed), urgency of development threat or potential for residential development, number of parcels extinguished, and difficulty of monitoring the property.[18]

Accountability

The NCLT's approach to accountability grows out of its long-term commitment to trustlike easement stewardship. Accountability quickly merges into the question of how the NCLT can build and maintain a reputation as a reliable and trustworthy guardian of conservation easements. In this particular institutional setting, prudent management is as much about politics and public relations as it is about endowment investment strategies. Similarly, thinking in terms of public involvement in planning or public comment on organizational activities does not make sense, given NCLT goals and organizational culture. Formal processes of public accountability may be more appropriate for a public agency that has the power to impose its will on dissenting landowners. The NCLT depends on the goodwill of Napa citizens and landowners and requires their willing donations and support in order to take any action. Accordingly, both board and staff express a clear concern about what they call "public credibility," and the NCLT devotes careful attention to maintaining the organization's credibility and integrity in the eyes of the public. The NCLT views itself as responsible to three overlapping groups: the general public, its members, and potential easement donors.

The NCLT communicates openly to the broader Napa community about its actions, recognizing the importance of "full communication of relevant information on the NCLT and its activities."[19] It publishes a quarterly newsletter that is mailed to members and is freely available at the county library. It also guides a series of annual local hikes on permanent preserves, and one of the permanent preserves is managed specifically to achieve educational outreach. Connolly Ranch, a twelve-acre demonstration farm and ranch in Napa City, is dedicated to educating young people about environmentally sound agricultural land use and runs programs in conjunction with local 4-H groups, Americorps, and the Napa city schools.

The NCLT is also accountable to its membership. Members are recruited through word of mouth and through the same public communications process the NCLT uses to communicate with the general public. The Connolly Ranch environmental education center is a particularly important point of contact. Members pay a small sum in annual dues—$30 for individuals and $50 for families—although many donate beyond the minimum. Technically, the members of the corporation are those on the board of trustees. The 1,200 people who join the organization to support its activities have no voting rights and do not, for example, participate in the selection of trustees.[20]

This does not mean, however, that the members have no role in NCLT governance. The members become active in the organization through a web of committees that work to support the organization. Most NCLT organizational decisions go through at least one committee made up of both board members and general members before being brought to the full board for a final assessment. Finance, Project, Monitoring, Volunteer, Membership, Major Donor and Planned Giving, Leadership Development, Publicity/Outreach, Risk Management, and Special Events are just some of the important committees. These committees provide an arena in which NCLT members influence board decisions and help to encourage a responsive board by maintaining board contact with some of the more attentive beneficiaries. Finally, the committee structure serves as a forum for leadership development, encouraging individuals to not just pay their dues but also become actively involved in the organization and consider becoming board members in the future.

Finally, the NCLT is accountable to Napa landowners. The organization believes that its success or failure depends on how Napa's diverse landowners react to the NCLT's projects and politics. "Willing" landowners of all stripes and beliefs must trust the NCLT sufficiently to donate conservation agreements. The NCLT believes that in a relatively small community, every action of the trust may be precedent setting. This possibility requires the trust to make sure that it has carefully examined all the implications of any proposed NCLT action. For instance, although the NCLT has pursued a range of projects, its primary focus is on accepting donated conservation easements. Accordingly, it has not purchased any easements and does not anticipate doing so. To buy even one easement, the trustees reason, would decrease the likelihood that other landowners would be willing to make a donation of an easement on their property.[21]

Another significant component of this relationship between the organization and the diverse local landowners is the NCLT's political neutrality. This neutrality is a matter of institutional policy, as described in the policy manual:

> The NCLT will not support, oppose or become otherwise involved in politically sensitive or controversial issues that could cause members, supporters or the general public to consider whether or not they should continue to support the organization, its programs and its goals.[22]

Becoming embroiled in a political debate could jeopardize the NCLT's position as both an effective negotiator of conservation easements and the honest and fair agent of easement monitoring and enforcement. Given the deep divisions among Napa's landowners regarding land use issues, NCLT activities must appeal to a broad spectrum of potential donors. A rabid environmental group is unlikely to appeal to landowners interested in continuing agricultural use on the property or retaining some subset of development rights.

Essentially, the NCLT must maintain the confidence of Napa County residents in order to achieve its land protection goals. Here, accountability emphasizes not the standard realm of public participation in administrative decisions but gaining the confidence of the community. Twenty-five years after its founding, the NCLT believes that it has had considerable success in creating this public image. Its records indicate an increasing number of easement donations with every year of its existence.

A ROLE FOR THE FUTURE: PUBLIC AND PRIVATE LAND PROTECTION IN NAPA

The NCLT has built a web of relationships with the public, its members, and Napa landowners in an institutional culture emphasizing continuity and commitment to its focused purpose. It defines itself as an organization that accepts voluntary donations of conservation easements from willing landowners. However, it is not obvious that it can maintain that clearly defined role. The regulatory and economic environment in which it pursues its organizational goals has changed dramatically in the last quarter century. The NCLT may be pressed into assuming the higher political profile that it has long abjured.

The question was first raised in 1986. A developer entered Napa County intending to purchase a 3,000-acre ranch, develop 1,000 acres of the property, and donate an easement on the other 2,000 acres to the NCLT. The developer hoped that the NCLT's participation in the project would be beneficial to his efforts to obtain the necessary permits. The land trust was not, however, willing to be seen as supporting the project or guaranteeing to the county that the project was environmentally and socially sound. The president of the NCLT issued a press release saying that the NCLT would negotiate with the developer about a conservation easement only *after* the proposed project had been approved by the county.

Political purity was not, in this particular instance, costly. Two different developers have subsequently failed to bring a proposal to fruition. However, the NCLT is concerned that should it continue to decline this type of invitation, another organization with less experience and dependability in easement monitoring could be drawn into the process. Because NCLT programs depend on the credibility and efficacy of easements in the region, no matter who is responsible for them, the result could be problematic.

More recently, the county asked the NCLT to play a similar role as a partner in its permitting program. As part of the process, developers may "donate" easements on some of their land in order to receive the county's permission to develop other portions. In part, this is tempting. The NCLT is clearly the local organization most qualified to monitor and enforce easements in Napa County. It has over twenty years of experience developing the institutional capacities to do exactly that. Moreover, it is highly likely that the required easements would have significant conservation value and that the land trust could protect substantial quantities of land by agreeing to hold, monitor, and enforce those easements. However, they are not donated voluntarily. If the NCLT accepts regulatory easements,[23] the organization may become associated with local government or be seen as facilitating development projects in ways that will damage both the environment and the NCLT's carefully cultivated image as a politically neutral land conservation organization.

The NCLT is currently struggling with how to address this question— whether to maintain its culture as an organization that accepts voluntary donations while simultaneously working as a partner in the county's development approval process. The fact that the NCLT would be moved to join the county in this way only to ensure that easements are carefully managed, monitored, and enforced does not make the change of posture any less troubling for the NCLT. It is mulling these fundamental issues of institutional culture and purpose at an awkward time. Both the political and the economic environments in which it operates have evolved rapidly since it was formed a quarter of a century ago. It is not clear that the NCLT's chosen niche has an important future in Napa.[24]

The NCLT's changing institutional environment reflects the forces of hollowing out and contracting out in government. The issue of institutional proliferation may be a special problem in the land trust field. The pattern of a larger land trust aiding in the establishment and organizational development of other land trusts organized on a smaller geographical scale is widespread in the land trust arena. As noted earlier, the NCLT has been both aided by national groups and involved in the birthing of a smaller land trust in the county. The number of land protection organizations alone raises significant questions about potential competition among local, regional, and national land trusts for financial support, constituencies, and conservation easements themselves. Of particular relevance to the NCLT is the formation, in 1979, of an organization called Napa Landmarks, because historic preservation was an element of the NCLT's original mission. The diversification of organizations in the conservation arena continues, and the NCLT will have to adapt to its changing niche among private organizations.

The county's invitation to partner with the NCLT suggests another important element of this changing environment. Since the 1976 dispute that eroded early land use planning requirements, Napa has been moving slowly in the direction of more stringent land protection. The forty-acre minimum lot sizes on the valley floor were restored, and the hillsides that drain into the valley's agricultural land preserve are designated as agricultural watershed and open space. Lot sizes in that zone are restricted to 160-acre minimums. Strict restrictions also curtail development on the hillsides themselves, protecting conservation values and ridgeline view sheds. Napa citizens eventually grew tired of the back-and-forth on policies regarding subdivisions and housing developments and passed an initiative that restricts the county commissioners' ability to alter the designation of agricultural lands in the county's land use plan. In 1990, county voters adopted Measure J, which prohibits any changes in agricultural designations until the year 2020. This has removed at least some of the urgency for land protection in the region.

Finally, the NCLT has sought donated easements in an increasingly tough economic environment. A major motivation driving landowner donations is that, as noted in chapter 1, they are viewed by the IRS as charitable gifts and are therefore deductible from the donor's income taxes. For a number of years in the early 1990s, this was not a reliable impetus to charity in Napa County. Many vineyard owners spent most of that decade replacing vines damaged by the phylloxera outbreak. Replanting is a significant expense, and many potential donors among Napa's vineyard owners have not experienced the excesses in annual taxable income that would inspire a quest for tax deductions. Hence, a deductible donation is less attractive than it was in the 1980s. As the vineyards recover and require less intense investment, the NCLT is hopeful that the charitable deduction will become a significant motivating force once again.

The NCLT is moving to fill what board members view as an institutional gap in the protection of agricultural lands in the county. Although the NCLT has had success in preserving lands on the hillside above the

Napa Valley floor, it holds few easements in the center of the valley, the heart of the county's prime viticultural land. The trustees see the present strict county regulations as providing a small window—until 2020—during which those lands can be protected. It is not clear what will happen to the lands when Measure J expires. Accordingly, in 1998, the NCLT began a major campaign to recruit growers located in the Napa County agricultural preserve as conservation easement donors. It is hoping to ensure that by 2020 as much of Napa's agricultural land as possible will be permanently protected, even if land use regulations change.

The NCLT believes that its goals may be abetted by the demographics of vineyard property owners in the valley. Many of the independent family owners of the noncorporate vineyards have reached the age when they are beginning to consider passing their lands on to the next generation. The early years of the twenty-first century will provide a crucial opportunity to encourage landowners in the agricultural preserve to donate conservation easements on their highly regulated agricultural lands. The issue of estate taxes is likely to become increasingly important within the valley. Conservation easements provide an attractive way of reducing estate taxes for landowners who want to keep the vineyard land in agricultural production. The NCLT hopes that the inheritance tax benefits will encourage landowners to negotiate easements.

The NCLT's present deliberations over its future role in county programs underscore the difficulties private groups encounter in trying to remain private in the current political climate, where governments are seeking private partners to ease the financial and regulatory burdens of public programs. Nevertheless, the NCLT has, to a greater extent than any other organization in this volume, utilized the fiduciary relationship and trust principles and mechanisms to structure its organization and activities. Its efforts to multiply protection for its funds and preserves through a blending of trusts and conservation easements merit consideration by other similarly situated groups.

Finally, the NCLT suggests that accountability is not entirely made up of keeping tabs on funds, enforcing rules, and holding accountable. Accountability is achieved in the process of seeking the public cooperation that a private entity requires to survive. The NCLT's approach to accountability ought to suggest alternatives for public organizations. The fundamentals are quite simple: instead of obliging tax payments and seeking comments on its programs, the trust conducts itself scrupulously in order to elicit private contributions of land and cash and seeks participants who will join and run its programs.

CHAPTER TWELVE

Conclusion

The evolution of the Society for the Protection of New Hampshire Forests reflects the past century's changing assumptions about land and institutional arrangements for conserving it. The Society was founded in 1901 to lobby for federal acquisition and protection of eastern forests. After many decades of supporting the U.S. Forest Service, the Society now owns and manages its own reserves and is laboring to develop alternatives to federal management of the White Mountain National Forest. The institutions of land conservation are changing, and the Society is now pursuing the land protection it was founded to urge the federal government to undertake.

This is in part because the nature of what we are trying to conserve is also changing. Our notion of land as parcels has given way to a more complex notion of landscapes of interconnected natural systems and mixed ownership. The Society encourages private, sustainable land stewardship. It underwrites the enforcement of easements held by private and local government organizations that the Society worked to establish. These programs view privately owned and managed lands both as protected and as integral parts of the ecological landscape.

Although the SPNHF's story is far from unique, land and resource management in the United States is peculiar in the extent to which the standard model of relying on government has dominated the narrative. The changing complexion of government institutions clearly observable in other policy arenas has perhaps been slightly masked in the land and resource conservation field. However, the organizations discussed in the preceding chapters are clear indicators that the devolution and dispersion of government authority long observable in education, health and human services, and other policy areas have come to land and resource management. Our case studies also make clear that trusts and trust concepts have an important and instructive role to play in programs that are increasingly concerned with issues of shared authority and institutional design.

In this final chapter, we summarize what we have learned about trusts under three broad headings. The first focuses on what the trusts teach us about the devolution and dispersion of government. We conclude that the shifting authority observed in our stories is appropriately described in terms of a blending of public and private institutions. The second section discusses how key trust elements—clarity, undivided loyalty, and perpetuity—address problems of democratic governance inherent in that blending. The final section focuses briefly at a less theoretical level, emphasizing some nuts and bolts of trusts operating in land conservation. We highlight key insights gleaned from our trust stories and provide several thoughts about how trust principles might be usefully applied to land conservation.

TRUST PRINCIPLES AND THE DEVOLUTION AND DISPERSION OF GOVERNMENT AUTHORITY

All the organizations we studied—whether they are formal trusts or they simply adapt trustlike principles to some aspect of their operations—have in common one major thread: the trust provides a framework in which a pot of money is dedicated to a specific purpose. Occasionally land is included as part of the pot, but the basic element is money. Moreover, many of the trusts examined in this volume, especially those in Parts II and III, have been set up more or less specifically to avoid normal government operations. The framers define the purposes, and the trustees manage and allocate the funds outside of standard legislative channels for goal setting, appropriations, and accountability.

This avoidance is important, because without exception, the funds and resources involved are appropriately viewed as *public* and the trusts and trustlike adaptations as instruments of *public policy*. The resources are frequently made available in contemplation of, as compensation for, or to mitigate some kind of resource destruction. In one example, the federal and state governments established, in a sloppy and ill-conceived process stretching over half a century, a trust intended to provide both land and money to rehabilitate native Hawaiians crushed by American annexation. More typically, the destruction results from an oil spill, a power plant, or construction in a wetlands. Because of the public's interest in the damaged resource, the funds are appropriately regarded as public, even if Exxon, a developer, or a power company actually signs the check.

Even when private resources are the kernel that gives rise to a conservation trust, as in the case of Bois de Brodeur or Betty Phillips's trust honoring her husband, the public makes significant contributions in the form of relief from income, property, or inheritance taxes. These tax policy tools appeal to many, as noted in chapter 1, because such government "expenditures" are off budget—the money does not show up as public income or outgo. This arrangement gives those with private wealth substantial—one might argue inappropriate—control over the achievement of public policy objectives. Nevertheless, these tools have become, especially in the land trusts we discussed, a central element of government activity in the land conservation field. Of course, the land trust format has also given families of more modest means, such as the Brodeurs and the Burgesses, an opportunity to dedicate their family lands to conservation as well. The trusts we studied are an instructive component of the dispersion and devolution of government authority outlined in chapter 1.

Although laws embodying trust principles are fairly consistent throughout the United States, the organizations that we lumped under the heading *conservation trust* are very different from one another. But as we have seen, a fiduciary relationship is adaptable to many different needs and settings. The government trusts discussed in Part II—Dade County, the EVOS Trustee Council, and the DHHL—facilitate joint decision making and sharing of authority among federal agencies, between federal and state agencies, and among field professionals from all three levels of government. Hence, they generally encourage devolution of government authority from the federal government to states and localities.

These trust-based models of authority sharing among levels of government are not the perfect embodiment of a Sagebrush Rebel's dreams. The federal lands have not been "returned" or turned over to the states. Nevertheless, trust principles provide a convenient mechanism for describing and sharing decision-making authority. They constitute a starting point for a different approach to achieving Rebels' and many others' aspirations for sharing power and for putting decision making closer to home, where it is more subject to local control. Similarly, when the family and private organizations we observed use public funds or tax-exempt donations to achieve government priorities, authority is dispersed. In most of the cases we studied, the governments providing tax relief have no further direct participation in the program.

However, we have also seen that continuing indirect involvement of the state is frequently mandatory to the success of these private organizations. The private and family trusts covered in Part IV—the Phillips and Rangeley Lakes group, the SPNHF, and the Napa County Land Trust— rely heavily on federal, state, and local policies that support and facilitate their programs. Many organizations have worked hard to create a web of regulations and policies that underwrite their activities. Many states have, for example, recognized land trusts and legislated extensively to define easements, who can hold them, and under what terms. The SPNHF is a grandmother of invention in this field.

Moreover, all three levels of government appear to be taking increasingly active partner roles in many of these nonprofit organizations. A major component of the Rangeley Lakes Heritage Trust, for example, is to commandeer federal and state funds and to direct federal programs such as Forest Legacy to serve its own conservation priorities. The same private organizations also manage properties and easements acquired by state and federal agencies, and they frequently cost-share with public agencies on acquisition of the lands, further commingling public and private funds. Our conservation trusts demonstrate that it is inadequate to think only in terms of private organizations edging into areas and authorities inscribed as governmental in the Progressive Era model. The opposite is also true—governmental agencies are increasingly inclined to pursue their missions under cover of or on the terrain of private ones.

Power is also dispersed when conservation trusts are used to allow public and private decision makers to share authority in quasi-governmental organizations. In several of our cases, representatives of environmental advocacy groups share power with representatives of power companies and with public agency professionals in the expenditure of public funds. The Platte River, North Dakota, and Great Lakes trusts were all established to settle contentious public debates, and some or all of the protagonists—both public and private—were included as trustees managing the expenditure of public funds. In the Platte River and North Dakota cases, public funds have been used, quite intentionally, to form conservation organizations in regions where federal and private organizations had both previously failed.

At the end of this volume, we are more willing to think in terms of the blending of public and private, and of federal, state, and local, than we were at the beginning. We have found that in the lumpy and complex soup of dispersing and devolving governmental authority over land and resource management, it is increasingly difficult to locate clear boundaries between governmental and nongovernmental organizations. The Napa County Land Trust, for example, was formed to provide private leadership during a period of intense public controversy over local land use regulation. It is presently consider_____ ____ and cons of becoming the holder and enforcer of easemen_____ ____te developers during the county permitting proce_____ ____ly associated with government, it also _____ ____icated organization will assume that rol_____

Even if the_____ the county's invitation, it is still, in effec_____ ____nctioned land use regulations when it _____ ____econd and third landowner removed from the _____ ____imilarly, when the ostensibly private SPNHF becomes __ _____ _ last resort on conservation easements owned and monitored by u__ ____icord Conservation Trust, an organization established as part of a local government, the boundary between public and private is blurred. It appears that as government agencies look for partners, it may become difficult for private organizations to remain completely private for long.

BLENDED DEMOCRATIC GOVERNANCE AND
TRUST PRINCIPLES: CLARITY, ACCOUNTABILITY,
AND PERPETUITY

With this devolution, dispersion, and blending of government authority has come a raft of problems in democratic governance. Three seem paramount in our cases. The most important is accountability. Once a conservation trust is established to put public funds and purposes outside of the normal government channels, how does an interested citizen or public official keep tabs on it? Some legislatures have been understandably hostile to trusts on their turf. A more difficult question is, once many trusts have been established, how can anyone ensure that they will, as a group, achieve landscape conservation goals in a region? In other words, how do we monitor the sum of the parts as well as the individual organizations?

The second issue is clarity, itself an important element of accountability. How can one define a purpose that is sufficiently clear to ensure that trustees will have useful guidelines for programmatic choices without binding them so tightly as to prevent them from working effectively in a fluid political environment and adapting to altered circumstances and new knowledge? To ask this question from a different direction, we might wonder what trust principles add to our understanding of administrative discretion—long discussed as allowing public agencies flexibility while ensuring adequately defined delegation of congressional authority.

Perpetuity is the final concern. The conservationists' traditional emphasis on forever—the slogan what is gone is gone forever, what is saved must be saved forever, comes to mind—runs into equally powerful notions of intergenerational equity. The law against perpetuities and the dead hand in trust law underscore a cornerstone of American property law: that no set of property owners should bind future generations. It also runs quietly into the experience of several of our trusts. Exploring these issues in the organizations we profiled provides insight into the utility of trusts and trust principles in the changing institutional array of land and resource conservation.

Issues of accountability, clarity, and perpetuity are not, of course, unique to the conservation trusts in this volume. Ted Lowi's critical analysis of the growing participation of private interest groups in the exercise of public authority was noted earlier. Describing what he viewed as an undesirable dilution of public authority as the "end of liberalism," Lowi sought in clear legislative mandates and close judicial enforcement of those mandates a route back from the dilution of government authority. Other reformers have sought to achieve accountability through greater fiscal control of government agencies. Many reformers of the new resource economics school, most notably Randal O'Toole, have focused for a decade or more on reforming the Forest Service by introducing businesslike incentives into agency operations.[1]

Trusts and notions of trusts seem to fit rather well with both Lowi's classic critique of early phases of the hollowing out of government and the economists' priorities for facilitating it. This odd juxtaposition is itself thought-provoking. Trusts are businesslike, requiring trustees to evince prudence and to engage in a thorough assessment of risks and returns, balanced always in favor of meeting trust goals. More interesting, the trust's particular emphasis on clarity fits well with Lowi's insistence on greater specificity in authorizing legislation. Similarly, the courts' central role in trust enforcement might appeal to Lowi's quest for "juridical democracy," enhanced judicial oversight of the exercise of public authority.

But trusts are not merely single-minded businesses, and conservation trusts are not merely an appealing middle ground halfway between government's and private business's approaches to organization. The fiduciary relationship at the core of a trust is dominated by the notion of the trustee's undivided loyalty to a specific beneficiary. This basic obligation is attenuated somewhat in the charitable trusts that occupied most of our attention in this volume, because the public benefits from the birds, the wetlands, the fishery, and even the rehabilitation of native Hawaiians. Therefore, the public and not the birds or the native Hawaiians is technically viewed as the beneficiary of the trust. Nevertheless, in the trusts that paid serious attention to it, the undivided loyalty obligation has operated as a stabilizing factor in the face of political pressure.

The core idea of undivided loyalty requires that the framers be clear about the purpose of the trust, so that the trustees can pursue that goal with undivided loyalty to the beneficiary and none other. Clarity of purpose appears in our cases to be facilitated by the relative ease with which a trust is established, and it can be compared to legislation that recasts and redefines a public agency's mandate throughout its existence. Trust flexibility arises not from changing and amending the trust but from interpreting and applying the clear purpose within the context of undivided loyalty.

The particulars of trust management are broadly familiar. Almost every law student in the country has taken a course in the subject. As we have seen, lawyers can pull the basic principles off the shelf to structure decision making about a pool of money in diverse contexts. Whatever trust framers forget to mention, trust principles will frequently provide. In part because it is relatively simple to establish a trust, it is possible to give an organization based on trust principles a clear mandate. Similarly, it is relatively difficult to change trust purposes; once set, they are likely to remain in place unless altered by the courts.

What is striking is that North Dakota's problems appear to be quite unusual—they arise from uniquely unfortunate trust documents. Most of the trust purposes we studied are clear, brief, and not overlaid with myriad other priorities to confuse decision making. In the North Dakota case, we saw what can happen when trust purposes are not clear. Forced to balance prairie pothole conservation with responsiveness to and cooperation with farmers, the trustees have found it difficult to move agricultural operations in the direction of wetlands protection without simply subsidizing them.

Several of our conservation trusts have experienced problems with the trust's undivided loyalty mandate not because of a murky or compromised purpose but because of a poorly planned structure. Again, the North Dakota trust has had the worst problems, but the EVOS trust also had difficulties at the start.

The most common structural problem is the expectation that trustees will act simultaneously as representatives of the appointing authority and as trustees. Given the context in which many of our trusts were established, this may be unavoidable. However, many potential problems could be avoided by applying organizational tools that are probably even more familiar than trust principles. For example, terms of office protect trustees from arbitrary removal; staggered terms of office protect the board as a whole from radical upheavals. A diversity of appointers is also wise. It is particularly disruptive that the North Dakota governor appoints all three of the state's representatives—half of the board—at his pleasure.

This is not to say that involvement of elected officials is inappropriate. However, there are other approaches that are far less destructive of basic trust elements. The Great Lakes model—in which the Conservation Commission appoints the head of the Department of Natural Resources, who then becomes chair of the board of trustees—depends of the relationship between the governor and the commission and cannot be replicated everywhere. However, the notion of ex-officio appointments has been effectively applied elsewhere. The Dade County trust is made up exclusively of ex-officio professionals, and when one moves or retires, his or her replacement joins the board. Ex-officio political appointees serving as trustees provide stability while still allowing a governor significant influence in the choice of trustees. The nonprofit norm of a self-sustaining board also has appeal. Once an organization is on its feet and the dust from any precipitating dispute has at least partially settled, the issue of representation can be softened by allowing the sitting trustees to select future ones.

But trust framers do not make all the crucial decisions about structure. There is a tendency among the trusts we studied to view staffing as an unnecessary luxury. Even the EVOS trust, for which adequate funding has never been an issue, began by scrimping on administrative support to save money. Our cases suggest that investment in staff is not necessarily a misallocation of trust resources. Especially when forces surrounding the trustees tend to erode undivided loyalty, professional staff may be able to provide clarity, institutional memory, and a consistent public face. These benefits are quite apart, of course, from staff contributions to programmatic development and implementation.

The peculiar notion of undivided loyalty potentiates the clarity of a trust purpose. It requires decisions that differentiate between appropriate activities and subsidies to established interests. The DHHL, for example, was intended to serve native Hawaiians, not cane growers. By making that clear, the undivided loyalty concept can afford the trustees some protective cover when pursuing politically unpopular trust purposes. This combination provides a test for thinking about when it is appropriate to establish a trust. If the framers do not want to achieve the clearly stated goal, they probably should not establish a trust.

We are surprised at how little reference many of our conservation trusts make to the trust and trust principles. This does not mean, we hasten to underscore, that they are violating the trust, although in the instance of the DHHL, it is quite clear that the trust has been violated for decades. Rather, we mean that most of the trusts we studied are not taking full advantage of trust principles.

Undivided loyalty is not, however, an unmitigated good. It may complicate trust accountability. The basic accountability issues are easily stated: to whom should the trust be accountable, and for what? Accountability is not always a problem for trust managers. When a grandmother dedicates funds to her heirs' education, accountability is a relatively simple matter. To the grandmother and her heirs, the trustee is accountable for money. When trustees enter the public arena, they become more directly involved in public policy implementation. However, they encounter more difficult issues of programmatic and public accountability. Trust principles do not address these accountability issues very well and may be viewed as a barrier to their achievement.

The core idea of a trust traditionally involves money, and the most fully evolved trust rules about accountability concern financial accounting. This is frequently viewed as a problem for trusts aimed at protecting environmental values. When the goal is improved habitat or wetlands protection, there is no equivalent of dollars and cents to count, and indicators of success in achieving trust goals are not well defined. Conservation advocates are particularly inclined to underplay the importance of fiscal accounting, preferring to talk in terms of "priceless resources" or to seek indicators of environmental quality or ecosystem health. They view the trust's emphasis on financial issues as an institutional flaw.

We are not unsympathetic to this view, but we conclude that it is considerably overstated. Without money, there are no programs. Before one can protect the birds, their habitat, and their health, one has to pay for the truck, the scientist, and, in many instances, the farmer's lost use of fields.

Even if we had perfect measures of bird health and ecosystem health, we would still argue that financial accountability is an important element of conservation.[2] What did you do with the public's money is always an important question of accountability.

Because we believe that fiscal accountability is central to the achievement of ecological purposes, we are surprised at how inconsistently our trusts perform on financial disclosure, the simplest and most straightforward element of accountability. Some are above reproach, a river of information about where the money came from and where it has gone. Some publish their financial doings on the Web, others in glossy annual reports, and some in monthly or quarterly balance sheets that are readily available and easily interpretable. Others do not appear to prepare any financial information that is routinely available for outside review, reflecting a puzzling disregard for trust requirements. This omission is particularly unfortunate in trusts involving government agencies. As in the EVOS trust example, the bracing experience of an external audit is an opportunity for agencies unaccustomed to accounting for appropriated funds to see that it can be done. The learning experience should not be overlooked. Financial accounting is an important element of accountability, and the omission is simple to remedy.

Public agencies could also learn from the trust element of prudence when approaching programmatic accountability. Prudence requires a careful analysis, balancing the risks and benefits of any decision. It also requires careful monitoring of resources and decisions and use of the best available tools both for tracking those decisions and for changing them when errors are perceived. This strikes us as very different from public agencies' current approach to analysis and monitoring.

Although the framework for this programmatic accountability is a key element of trust requirements, we note that the trusts we studied pay even less attention to programmatic accountability than they do to financial accountability. Many engage in extensive, detailed planning processes, but few return later to ask whether trust activities are actually meeting trust goals. This may occur because current ecological tools and concepts are not adequate to the task.

It is important to observe that this pattern does not arise from trust principles but in spite of them. Closer scrutiny of the trustee's obligations in prudent decision making would produce a different result. However, few of our trusts have tried very hard to tie their activities to specific ecological outcomes. This disconnect is not prudent. Our conservation trusts will have more difficulty remedying this accountability problem than the financial disclosure one, but pursuing it is obligatory.

The most useful model of what trust-based programmatic accountability might look like is land trusts' emphasis on easement monitoring. The

Concord Conservation Trust annually walks Bois de Brodeur. The SPNHF has an annual aerial monitoring program for all its easements. First, the criteria are clear and simple—no subdivisions, no motorized access, no pesticides—whatever the parties have agreed to. Although the purposes are broad, the easement translates them into goals that can be accounted for in currently available, easily measured terms. Second, funding to support monitoring and enforcement, if necessary, is an important element of the program. It is still necessary to evaluate whether the exclusion of development, motor traffic, and pesticides is creating the intended benefit for migratory birds, for example. Trust principles do not add to or detract from that problem. What they can contribute is an insistence on prudence in defining, implementing, and evaluating the program.

The most difficult problems arise in the context of public accountability. A trust is clearly not the appropriate vehicle for maximizing this goal. Undivided loyalty to a specific beneficiary is not, as we saw in the DHHL case, synonymous with political responsiveness. This is true even when the beneficiary is the general public. Trust principles can, however, provide some ground rules for striking a balance between accountability goals and trust purposes. If a trust or trustlike principles are being applied to truncate normal legislative routes to public accountability, serious thought must be given to what is going to operate in place of legislative oversight. That reflection must proceed in clear awareness that the normal mechanisms for trust accountability—reliance on a vigilant beneficiary to sue an errant trustee—do not work particularly well in most of the instances we explored. The DHHL is particularly distressing.

The situation is not much better, however, in the charitable trust context, wherein beneficiaries and trust purposes depend for enforcement on the attorney general. The Platte River trust's experience suggests that attorneys general may become most interested in trust affairs for political reasons. The more likely outcome is that trust enforcement rarely becomes sufficiently visible to attract an attorney general's attention, and enforcement issues are not always raised when they ought to be.

The conservation trust's virtue in the public accountability arena may be that most of them have not been caught in the public accountability experiment begun in the 1960s, with direct public involvement in agency deliberations and planning. Public agencies have been struggling, with more or less enthusiasm, to supplement the standard election-based model of accountability with public involvement. Numerous variations on the standard notice-and-comment format have been tried. Our conservation trusts demonstrate, first, that there is much to be done to improve notice-and-comment programs, which are basically moribund as practiced by most public agencies, and second, that there are diverse other routes to public accountability yet to be tried and adapted to this period of changing thought about government and land.

The EVOS trust approach to public comment demonstrates that much can be done to refurbish the tedious format of public involvement in government decision making and science. While grateful for *anything* that would improve current practice, we find some of the best routes to accountability in the nonprofits. The Napa County Land Trust's approach to maintaining public support is particularly instructive. The organization works assiduously to maintain a clear public face precisely to appeal to potential donors. This is politically prudent, but it is also a form of public accountability. It conjures the familiar bumper sticker wondering what would happen if the Defense Department were forced to hold bake sales and the schools were fully funded. It also echoes the free-market economists' yearning for fees for services and similarly "efficient" modes of allocation.

Even more suggestive are the elements of accountability inherent in Napa's committee structure and board recruitment. Its approach emphasizes accountability not as an element of enforcement but as an essential part of organizational operations and maintenance. Although this approach could be viewed as a variant on the agency's notice-and-comment procedures, the difference is that the NCLT does not simply ask folks to come to a hearing and comment. Instead, it asks them to come and stay and work to design programs and then help implement them. What is normally called public participation is really only public comment. The NCLT is actually pursuing public *participation*. It offers not merely a chance to be heard but also a process for working up from committee service to ultimately serving on the board. Its process of organizational maintenance and decision making is essentially a public accountability strategy.

Conservation trusts provide several different perspectives on perpetuity. The conservationists' preference for the long term has been noted. In the preceding chapters, we saw some of the costs. Some are encapsulated in thinking about the dead hand. The idea that one generation should not irrevocably commit subsequent generations to a particular land use is not likely to be convincing to conservationists attempting, with limited success, to prevent such apparently irreversible resource commitments as species extinction, pesticides in breast milk, PCB accumulation in whale fat, and urban sprawl. Our cases suggest that it is appropriate to separate the notion of perpetual conservation from perpetuating either the peculiar proclivities of a conservation donor or a specific organization. The Great Lakes trust, in spite of a clear mandate to the contrary, is planning to terminate in 2020. The trustees' thinking has two elements, both of which are instructive. First, the trustees view perpetuation of the trust, beyond the term of the FERC license that it accompanies, as a potentially complicating element in future discussions of license renewal. If there is money lying around after the permit period, perhaps further remediation is not necessary. Similar logic is reflected in the trustees' second conclusion: that resource damage in the present ought to be mitigated in the present. Trading present damage for long-term benefits is not, they concluded, in the best interests of the resource. The EVOS trust's early decision to set aside a significant proportion of funds intended to restore damaged resources raises the same questions: if there is $150 million left over to fund research unrelated to the fading impacts of the oil spill, it seems fair to conclude either that Exxon paid too much or that there are still uncompensated damages that the EVOS trust ought to have addressed.

Science as an alternative to politics, or, more precisely, emphasizing science as a way of avoiding political controversy, is not unique to our conservation trusts, but it characterizes several of them. This constitutes an interesting element of the old Progressive Era model of government programs and legitimacy that appears to be carrying forward into the twenty-first century. It is encouraged, we observe, by scientists. We confess to a bias against scientists who seek to fund long-term basic research with restoration funds. And we attribute some of the push for perpetuity, particularly in the EVOS trust, to an ascendance of "big science." Perpetuity for research while resource damage goes unaddressed does not strike us as a good deal for the damaged resources.

The basic provisions for dealing with the assets of nonprofits may provide a useful approach for thinking about both perpetuity and consolidation of proliferating organizations. If a nonprofit becomes inoperable for any reason, it terminates activity but must pass on its resources to another similarly situated organization. This, when added to the trust notion of cy pres, which would allow the courts to enter the discussion of whether a trust was inoperable, might provide a starting point for backing off slightly from this commitment to perpetual organizations.

GUIDANCE

We are emboldened by several years of thinking about these organizations and their experiences to draw together some of the more useful lessons for those who are less interested in issues of governance and more interested in action.

First, it seems incredible that the North Dakota framers included extensive protections against potential shortfalls in federal funding of the Garrison diversion but failed to ensure that the state would meet its commitment to the trust. However, the North Dakota trust has paid, in cash and in frustration, for an important lesson for everybody else on this path.

Framers must begin by identifying means to ensure that those required to put up money for the corpus will do so.

Second, and only slightly less obvious, those entering into partnerships with the federal government should proceed with caution. We see a real difference between involving federal professionals at the local level in a group effort, such as the Dade County Wetlands Trust, and dealing with Washington-based department-level officials. It is the latter that concerns us most. The uninitiated should not allow federal lawyers to slip in a vague reference to fund management "the way it is always done" through CRIS and NRDA if they can possibly avoid it. If it cannot be avoided, the costs should be calculated up front and compensated. Similarly, practitioners should heed North Dakota's unfortunate experience with the Departments of Justice, Commerce, and the Interior and work diligently to avoid their involvement in defining restrictions on corpus investment. Several of the trusts in this volume have worked successfully with federal agencies and have not been forced to deal with the myriad problems that the North Dakota and EVOS trusts have encountered.

Third, and in the same general vein, we are quite impressed by the notion of overlapping easements developed by the EVOS Trustee Council. The state government holds conservation easements on lands acquired with EVOS trust funds by federal agencies, and vice versa. This step has less to do with the assumption that some of the agencies are perfidious than with the recognition that they are all subject to changing political winds. The Great Lakes reliance on a nonbinding letter to guarantee the Forest Service's continued adherence to conservation priorities strikes us as imprudent. The SPNHF's experience with a communications tower on Mount Kearsarge and the pendency of federal legislation that would return many of the EVOS land purchases to native corporations suggest reasons for extreme caution.

We expand that point further in light of the Phillips trust and NCLT experience. Private organizations with limited resources and significant liability exposure—or simply an abiding concern for perpetual protection— ought to consider granting conservation easements to another organization on the preserves they own. Overlapping easements strike us as a fruitful approach to myriad long-term institutional problems. Restraint is necessary to avoid the kind of potentially confounding restrictions we encountered in the Phillips trust. However, restrictions to ensure against judgment creditors and the vagaries of institutional drift are worth discussing.

Fourth, we reiterate our concern about setting public resources outside of standard routines of accountability and then effectively shutting off the trust's judicial enforcement mechanism. Much of the promise of the trust can be lost if there is no possibility that well-established expectations will be adhered to. The gaps in financial disclosure and programmatic accountability suggest that further experimentation is necessary. We believe, for example, that framers might fruitfully explore a special kind of public advisory or scientific advisory group, one that would go beyond the EVOS and Great Lakes examples, to identify circumstances under which an outside group would be authorized to receive and review financial accounts and programmatic evaluations and ultimately to sue to enforce the trust.

Fifth, and far more important than enforcement, is education for trustees in the basics of their obligations and the peculiar strengths and requirements of trust principles. Trust principles and trustlike formats can be useful in any setting. However, the advantages of a trust are lost if the trustees do not understand their obligations or do not know how a trust differs from other organizational forms. When an organization is set up to be a trust, that ought to become an important element of how it defines and evaluates its options, establishes priorities, and presents itself to the world. Our cases have demonstrated that there are enormous advantages in doing so, for the organization and for resource protection and management.

Finally, we observe an unexpected reticence, especially in the environmental community, to think beyond familiar modes of "direct" conservation. In the Platte and North Dakota trusts, for example, environmental directors have all but halted expenditures for education, in contexts where it strikes us that education is the key to conservation. This reticence is compounded, in other cases, by a focus on land acquisition when that may not be the most appropriate way to achieve trust goals. We do not accuse the EVOS Trustee Council of a lack of effort, but perhaps a lack of imagination. Perhaps buying all that land was less important to the trust's restoration purposes than developing a program for purchasing fishing rights in Prince William Sound. Similarly, the Great Lakes Fishery Trust is, in the name of restoring the fishery, supporting public access and similar projects that arguably increase fishing pressure. In this case, the idea of purchasing and retiring fishing rights was suggested but not pursued. We think that this is unfortunate. The trust puts resources outside the normal chain of command. Ideally, it also ought to put them outside the normal routines of conservation, to define and develop new ideas and approaches that might not initially attract direct-mail donors or legislative appropriations. Our conservation trusts have not uniformly exploited this opportunity.

The conservation trusts and trustlike organizations we described reflect changing thought about government and about land. The model of centralized scientific planning and management of the public domain that became controlling during the Progressive Era of Theodore Roosevelt and Gifford Pinchot has not been adequate to meet changing public expectations regarding resource conservation in the closing decades of the twentieth century.[3] Reliance on government landownership and regulation is being replaced by an amazing spectrum of organizations sharing authority to manage mixed ownership landscapes to achieve a variety of public goals—from habitat and biodiversity protection to the economic sustainability of agriculture, forestry, and rural communities. Conservation trusts are an instructive and potentially useful element of that emerging institutional array.

Appendix

ABBREVIATIONS

AMC	Appalachian Mountain Club
ANCSA	Alaska Native Claims Settlement Act
BLM	Bureau of Land Management
CAW	Create-a-Wetland [program]
CCT	Concord Conservation Trust
CNR	College of Natural Resources
CRIS	Court Registry Investment System
CRP	City and Regional Planning
DEP	Department of Environmental Protection (Florida)
DERM	Department of Environment Resources Management (Dade County, Florida)
DHHL	Department of Hawaiian Home Lands
DNR	Department of Natural Resources (Michigan)
DOI	Department of the Interior (U.S.)
EPA	Environmental Protection Agency
ESA	Endangered Species Act
EVOS	*Exxon Valdez* Oil Spill [Trustee Council]
FASB	Financial Accounting Standards Board
FERC	Federal Energy Regulatory Commission
FWS	Fish and Wildlife Service (U.S.)
GEM	Gulf ecosystem monitoring
GLFT	Great Lakes Fishery Trust
HHC	Hawaiian Homes Commission
HHCA	Hawaiian Homes Commission Act
HIT	held in trust
IRS	Internal Revenue Service
LTA	Land Trust Alliance
LWCF	Land and Water Conservation Fund
MBPP	Missouri Basin Power Project
MIA	Mooselookmeguntic Improvement Association
MOA	memorandum of agreement
MOU	memorandum of understanding
NCLT	Napa County Land Trust
NDWT	North Dakota Wetlands Trust
NEPA	National Environmental Policy Act

NOAA   National Oceanic and Atmospheric Administration
NPS   National Park Service
NRDA   Natural Resources Damage Assessment and Restoration Fund
NWF   National Wildlife Federation
ORRRC   Outdoor Recreation Resources Review Commission
PAG   public advisory group
PL   Public Law
PRT   Platte River [Whooping Crane Critical Habitat Maintenance]
            Trust
RLHT   Rangeley Lakes Heritage Trust
SAMP   special area management plan
SAT   scientific advisory team
SCORP   state comprehensive outdoor recreation plan
SPNHF   Society for the Protection of New Hampshire Forests
TPL   Trust for Public Land
TVA   Tennessee Valley Authority
UDB   urban development boundary

Notes

CHAPTER 1. A NEW ERA IN LAND
AND RESOURCE CONSERVATION

1. We build, therefore, on previous efforts to introduce a specific but extremely widespread application of trust principles to land management: the school and institutional lands granted by the federal government to the states when they joined the Union. Approximately 150 million acres in twenty-two western states are managed under trust principles to support common schools and similar public institutions. The state trust lands provide enormous insight into the tools and management philosophies of public organizations managing public resources similar to those managed by the U.S. Forest Service and the Bureau of Land Management. The states do approximately the same things as the more familiar federal multiple-use agencies, but they do them in significantly different ways. See Jon A. Souder and Sally K. Fairfax, *State Trust Lands: History, Management, and Sustainable Use* (1996).

2. The information problem generally is discussed in National Research Council (NRC), National Academy of Sciences (NAS), *Setting Priorities for Land Conservation: Report of the Committee on Scientific and Technical Criteria for Federal Acquisition of Lands for Conservation* (1993), 24–25.

3. The rise of the now-crumbling normal model is traced in the land and resources context by Leigh Raymond and Sally K. Fairfax, "Fragmentation of Public Domain Law and Policy: An Alternative to the 'Shift-to-Retention' Thesis," 39 *Natural Resources Law Journal* 1 (1999).

4. See, for example, Gregg Easterbrook, *A Moment on Earth: The Coming Age of Environmental Optimism* (1995).

5. A good place to start is Lester M. Salamon, ed., *Beyond Privatization: The Tools of Government Action* (1989), especially chap. 1. See also Helen Ingram and Steven Rathgeb Smith, *Public Policy for Democracy* (1993), and Anne Larason Schneider and Helen Ingram, *Policy Design for Democracy* (1997). The community movement also focuses on the virtues of local democracy. See, for example, Daniel Kemmis, *Community and the Politics of Place* (1990).

6. See Sally K. Fairfax, et al., "The Federal Forests Are Not What They Seem: Formal and Informal Claims to Federal Lands," 25 *Ecology Law Quarterly* 630 (1999).

7. Lester M. Salamon, *Partners in Public Service: Government–Non-Profit Relations in the Modern Welfare State* (1995), 21.

8. For a discussion of the political science literature relevant to natural resources, see Sally K. Fairfax, "Old Recipes for New Federalism," 12 *Environmental Law* 945 (1982).

9. Discussed in Samuel T. Dana and Sally K. Fairfax, *Forest and Range Policy: Its Development in the United States* (1979), 208-12. It is well known that the ORRRC precipitated institution building at the federal level as well, but with less durable impact. The federal Bureau of Outdoor Recreation, formed at the ORRRC's behest, was ill conceived, easily eliminated by Secretary of the Interior James Watt, and forgotten at little cost.

10. The federal agencies' problems in real estate transactions have been widely discussed. See, for example, NRC, NAS, *Setting Priorities.*

11. The deductible nature of a conservation easement is discussed in almost every guide to the subject, which are numerous. Its legal history is discussed in Burnett R. Maybank III, "Tax Implications of Conservation Easements in South Carolina," 7 *South Carolina Environmental Law Journal* 1 (1998). See also Janet Diehl and Thomas S. Barrett, *The Conservation Easement Handbook: Managing Land Conservation and Historic Preservation Easement Programs* (1998), and Stephen J. Small, *Preserving Family Lands: Book I: Essential Tax Strategies for the Landowner* (1998) and *Book II: More Planning Strategies for the Future* (1997).

12. Salamon, *Beyond Privatization*, 18.

13. See, for example, Lowi's classic *The End of Liberalism* (1969).

14. David Farrier, "Conserving Biodiversity on Private Land: Incentives for Management or Compensation for Lost Expectations," 19 *Harvard Environmental Law Review* 303 (1995), chronicles the growing political importance of biodiversity. Biodiversity, which he describes as the "'fourth horseman' of the environmental apocalypse," runs counter to traditional perceptions of conservation and is redefining them (303).

15. See, for example, Charles Geisler, "Property Pluralism," in Charles Geisler et al., eds., *Property and Values* (1999), and Fairfax et al., "The Federal Forests Are Not What They Seem."

16. See Eric Freyfogle, "The Owning and Taking of Sensitive Lands," 43 *UCLA Law Review* 77 (1995), for a particularly useful recapitulation of the tension between landscape theory and private property rights in the context of wetlands protection.

17. This discussion is based on Gary Musolf, "The Government-Corporation Tool: Permutations and Possibilities," in Salamon, *Beyond Privatization*, 231 ff. See also National Academy of Public Administration, *Report on Government Corporations: A Report Based on a Study by a Panel of the National Academy of Public Administration for the Office of Management and Budget* (1981).

18. Musolf, "Government-Corporation Tool," 232–33.

19. This section is intended to provide a basis for limited comparisons between a trust and a nonprofit and does not constitute legal advice on incorporating a nonprofit. For background on nonprofits, see William Powell, *The Nonprofit Sector: A Research Handbook* (1987); Lester Salamon, *America's Nonprofit Sector: A Primer* (1992). Nonprofits constitute a huge and important element of American life, including half of all hospitals, colleges, and universities; 60 percent of social services organizations; and almost all civic organizations and symphony orchestras. See Lester Salamon, *Holding the Center: America's Nonprofit Sector at a Crossroads* (1997), 5. Much of this discussion is adapted from Anthony Mancuso and Barbara Kate Repa, *The California Nonprofit Corporation Handbook*, 6th ed. (1991), chap. 1.

20. Mancuso and Repa, *California Handbook*, chap. 1, p. 2.

21. Ibid. Another way of phrasing this is that a nonprofit observes the "nondistribution constraint," that is, it cannot distribute financial surpluses to those in control. Discussed in Council on Foundations, *Grantmaking Basics* (1992), 8.

22. Mancuso and Repa, *California Handbook*, chap. 1, p. 3.

23. Ibid., p. 7. For exceptions to this personal liability rule, see chap. 1, p. 8.

24. Michael O'Neill, *The Third America: The Emergence of the Nonprofit Sector in the United States* (1989), 16–17.

25. Salamon's *Partners in Public Service* is probably the best place to start.

26. See Elizabeth T. Boris and C. Eugene Steuerle, eds., *Nonprofits and Government: Collaboration and Conflict* (1999), and Nancy J. Knauer, "Reinventing Government: The Promise of Institutional Choice and Government Created Charitable Organizations," 41 *New York University Law Review* 945 (1997).

27. Elizabeth Boris notes in *Philanthropic Foundations in the United States: An Introduction* (1991) that charity usually means giving money to someone directly in need, while philanthropy generally involves giving money to organizations that help people in need (18–20).

28. Joseph Sax's pivotal article, "The Public Trust Doctrine in Natural Resources: Effective Judicial Intervention," 68 *Michigan Law Review* 417 (1970), is among the most frequently cited law review articles in history. At a January 1998 American Association of Law Schools panel honoring Sax's work, Yale law professor Carol Rose suggested, only half in jest, that Sax had chosen the ancient notion of public trust for his vehicle even though there were many concepts in water law that would have better served his aims precisely because of the public-spirited ring of the term public *trust*.

29. The historic public trust purpose was clearly to allow for commercial activities such as ports and commerce, wharves, fishing, repair of sails and nets, and the like. See Jan Stevens, "The Public Trust: A Sovereign's Ancient Prerogative Becomes the People's Environmental Right," 14 *U.C. Davis Law Review* 195 (1980).

30. The "domestic dependent nations" phrase is found in *Cherokee Nation v Georgia*, 30 U.S. (5Pet.) 1 (1831), 561–62. See also *Worcester v Georgia*, 31 U.S. (6Pet.) 515 (1832), and *Johnson v McIntosh*, 21 U.S. (8Wheat.) 543 (1823).

31. See, for example, Geisler, "Property Pluralism."

32. Discussed briefly in Sally K. Fairfax and Carolyn Yale, *Federal Lands: A Guide to Planning, Management, and State Revenues* (1987), 151–58.

33. See 16 U.S.C. §460bb. See also U.S. Department of the Interior, *Creating a Park for the 21st Century—From Military Post to National Park—Final General Management Plan Amendment, Presidio of San Francisco, Golden Gate National Recreation Area* (July 1994), and *The Presidio of San Francisco: Work in Progress* (1996).

34. Some organizations that consider themselves land trusts do not include the phrase in their titles. Notable examples are the Save the Redwoods League and the Brandywine Conservancy.

35. Land Trust Alliance, *1998 National Directory of Conservation Land Trusts* (1998). Membership in the LTA is voluntary, and not every land trust elects to join. Of the organizations discussed in this volume, the Platte River and North Dakota trusts are included in the directory, as well as the Society for the Protection of New Hampshire Forests, the Napa County Land Trust, and the Rangeley Lakes Heritage Trust.

36. A few have slipped by unnoticed, such as the Holly Trust. However, Michigan land protection professionals and attorneys generally avoid using the word *trust*.

CHAPTER 2. THE TRUST AS A FRAMEWORK
FOR INSTITUTIONAL DESIGN

1. Because conservation trusts are frequently formed in the process of drafting legislation or settling litigation, we frequently refer to a framer rather than a settlor to indicate that the person or persons establishing the trust terms are not the same as those providing the trust corpus.

2. For a longer discussion of these themes, see Jon A. Souder, Sally K. Fairfax, and Larry Ruth, "Sustainable Resources Management and State School Lands: The Quest for Guiding Principles," 34 *Natural Resources Journal* 271 (1994).

3. See, for example, Norton Long, "Power and Administration," 9 *Public Administration Review* 257 (autumn 1949), discussed in Paul L. Posner, "Accountability and Management Challenges Posed by Third Party Governance Tools" (draft manuscript, 1999).

4. 16 U.S.C. §§531-4(a). Discussed in Souder and Fairfax, *State Trust Lands,* 348, n. 74.

5. The term *perverse incentives* is generally associated with the work of Randal O'Toole; see *Reforming the Forest Service* (1988). Others writing in this vein include Karl Hess, *Rocky Times in Rocky Mountain National Park* (1993).

6. See Souder and Fairfax, *State Trust Lands,* 294.

7. Discussed in G. T. Bogert, *Trusts* (1987), 348–49.

8. This requirement is sometimes incorporated into the state constitution or a statute, but the rules of equity in most states also require it. In a few states, the power may rest with a county law officer as well as with the state. See Bogert, *Trusts,* 554.

9. Frequently, the process of weighing the pros and cons of a trustee's decision takes on the appearance of familiar agency procedures for demonstrating that a decision was not arbitrary and capricious. However, the focus of the analysis and the standard of review are quite different. For a full comparison of the prudence standard as opposed to the arbitrary and capricious standard, see Jon A. Souder and Sally K. Fairfax, "Arbitrary Administrators, Capricious Bureaucrats, and Prudent Trustees: Does It Matter in the Review of Timber Salvage Sales?" 18 *Public Land and Resources Law Review* 165 (1997).

10. This question applies mainly to the purposes of charitable trusts. Basically, the court can be called on to alter administrative provisions of a *private* trust when, due to circumstances that the settlor could not or did not anticipate or due to his or her lack of skill or wisdom, the settlor made an unwise or inconvenient administrative choice. Similarly, the court can change administrative provisions of a *charitable* trust when the settlor's directions hinder the trustee in accomplishing trust purposes.

11. Bogert, *Trusts,* 525–26, discussing *Jackson v Phillips,* 14 Allen, Mass. 539 and *El v Attorney General,* 202 Mass. 545, 89 N.E. 166.

CHAPTER 3. PLATTE RIVER WHOOPING CRANE
MAINTENANCE TRUST: A CLASSIC TRUST

1. According to interviews, the FWS toured the farmland near the river and told landowners that their land would be condemned to create a wildlife refuge. One farmer was reportedly told, "We'll put the headquarters right there, where your house is now." Currently, the FWS pursues research in the area, exercises limited regulatory responsibilities, and does not attempt to acquire land.

2. The environmental groups included two associations of Wyoming ranchers who were concerned about the de-watering of the Laramie River.

3. Memorandum of Decision, *State of Nebraska v Rural Electrification Administration,* CV76-L-242, and *State of Nebraska v Ray,* CV78-L-90 (1978).

4. *Tennessee Valley Authority v Hill,* 437 U.S. 153 (1978).

5. Endangered Species Committee, Application for Exemption for Grayrocks Dam and Reservoir (and Order), February 7, 1979.

6. We call the PRT document classic because it follows the contours outlined in chapter 2. It has also been a model for other organizations founded in similar settings. The PRT declaration has been adopted, sometimes almost verbatim, by framers of the Kodiak Brown Bear Trust and the Great Lakes Fishery Trust; the framers of the North Dakota Wetlands Trust drew on PRT experience as well.

7. Trust Declaration, amended, §II, p. 2.

8. Trust Declaration, §II, p. 2.

9. The trust declaration does not specify the distance on either side of the river in which the PRT can undertake activities. This ambiguity is compounded by the braided nature of the Platte River. Trustees and staff understand the area in which they operate as the "riparian" area of the river, roughly one mile on either side of the outer banks. However, the trust declaration authorizes the trustees to monitor additional areas frequented by sandhill and whooping cranes, near Lewellen and Sutherland, Nebraska. See Trust Declaration, §IV(A)1, p. 5.

10. The principal grows primarily by adding certain investment proceeds to principal and not considering them to be income. For example, capital gains dividends from mutual funds are added back into principal.

11. Trust Declaration, §IV(B), p. 7.

12. Appointments are actually made by the general manager of Basin, the governor of Nebraska, and the president of the NWF.

13. In one instance, the governor was upset with the trust's decision to involve itself in water rights litigation. In another, the newly elected governor of a different party from that of his predecessor exercised his option to appoint a new trustee. However, unlike in the North Dakota trust discussed in chapter 7, the Nebraska governor appoints only one of three trustees. Several long-term observers report that the state appointment is hotly contested and is becoming more so. Explanations differ. For example, one observer thought that it was not primarily party politics involved in the state appointments but whether environmentalists were satisfied with the appointment. Another observer noted that the state's irrigation interests have long attempted to get one of their own appointed as trustee. Others are certain that new appointments come along whenever the governor disagrees with a PRT decision.

14. Trust Declaration, §IV(C)1 and 5, pp. 7–8, 10.

15. Trust Declaration, §IV(C)2, pp. 8–9.

16. Trust Declaration, §IV(A) I, p. 3.

17. Trust Declaration, amended, §IV(A) (1), p. 3.

18. Trust Declaration, §IV(A)1, pp. 4–5.

19. Trust Declaration, §IV(C)4, p. 9.

20. For a more complete discussion, see Guenzler, "Use of a Charitable Trust," 102.

21. One arguable exception is that Basin is required to provide an annual report to the Department of the Interior acknowledging that the conditions for its exemption from the Endangered Species Act are in place.

22. *State of Nebraska v Rural Electrification Association* and *State of Nebraska v Ray*, Memorandum and Order on Petition for Interpretation and Enforcement of Agreement of Settlement and Compromise, U.S. District Court, District of Nebraska, March 23, 1993, p. 5.

23. The PRT does earn returns from one quasi-consulting contract. The FWS entered into a ten-year contract with private landowners to have their riparian

areas cleared of vegetation by the PRT. Thus, the program is both a demonstration project and a fund-raiser.

24. Paul J. Currier, Gary R. Lingle, and John G. VanDerwalker, *Migratory Bird Habitat on the Platte and North Platte Rivers in Nebraska* (1985).

25. The PRT does not charge for this; it is considered part of protecting Platte River habitat.

26. Minutes of the Meeting of Trustees, Platte River Whooping Crane Critical Habitat Maintenance Trust, May 24, 1985, p. 6.

CHAPTER 4. DADE COUNTY WETLANDS TRUST: TRUST LIGHT

1. The official name of the organization is the Freshwater Wetlands Mitigation Trust Fund. See memorandum of understanding between the Florida Department of Environmental Regulation and Metropolitan Dade County Department of Environmental Resources Management, April 27, 1993, p. 5. The Park Service has established a separate trust known as the Everglades National Park Freshwater Wetlands Mitigation Trust Fund; it is an integral part of the project and is administered by the National Park Foundation. See Memorandum of Agreement MA 5280-3-9006 between the U.S. Department of the Interior, Everglades National Park, and the National Park Foundation, February 14, 1995.

2. Originally, Code of Metropolitan Dade County, Florida, section 24-59.21, July 1, 1992; currently, Code of Metropolitan Dade County, Florida, section 24-58.22, September 29, 1997.

3. Those involved have estimated that the trust will last approximately twenty years and receive $60 million (in 1994 dollars) during that time. The actual figures are dependent on the character and pace of development, but only a relatively small unbuilt area still exists in Dade. Obviously, Everglades National Park is the ultimate barrier to Miami's westward expansion.

4. Everglades National Park was authorized during the depression and established in 1947. This is discussed in Sarah Connick and Sally K. Fairfax, "Federal Land Acquisition for Conservation: A Policy History" (draft on file with authors).

5. Lest our discussion give the misimpression that the park is an oasis of protection in a sea of development, it is worth noting that protecting the park has been a challenge ever since it was established. The major problem is water diversions, interruptions, and pollution, but Everglades has also survived numerous proposals for development near or within the park, including most spectacularly a jet port in Big Cypress Swamp and an oil refinery in lower Biscayne Bay. See Polly Kaufman, *National Parks and the Woman's Voice* (1998), emphasizing the work of Marjorie Stoneman Douglas, famous Everglades crusader and author of the classic *The Everglades: River of Grass* (1947).

6. The following discussion draws heavily on Metropolitan Dade County, Florida, Special Area Management Plan for the Bird Drive Everglades Basin, June 1995, pp. I.1–6.

7. The products of a SAMP process should include standards and criteria and implementation mechanisms that address natural resource and development problems within a specific geographic area. In addition, the process should result in both "local and State approval and a Corps General permit for acceptable development activities in designated situations" and "a local/State restriction or an Environmental Protection Agency 404(c) restriction (preferably both) for undesirable activities" (ibid., p. I.2).

8. Ibid., p. I.12.

9. The wellfield was proposed by the Miami Dade Water and Sewer Authority Department. It was expected to provide 80 million to 140 million gallons a day of additional water to the county water supply. Department of Environmental Resources Management, "Bird Drive Everglades Basin Special Area Management Plan: Baseline Studies and Resource Evaluation," Metropolitan Dade County, Florida, DERM Technical Report 90-6, p. 12.

10. Most of the facts in this paragraph come from R. F. Doren, L. D. Whiteaker, G. Molnar, and D. Sylvia, "Restoration of Former Wetlands Within the Hole-in-the-Donut in Everglades National Park," in F. J. Webb, ed., *Proceedings of the Seventh Annual Conference on Wetlands Restoration and Creation* (1990), 17–19.

11. Land developers are not forced into the trust system. Once it is determined that a project will destroy or impact wetlands and how many acres of mitigation are necessary, the landowner has two choices. He or she can work personally or hire a mitigation specialist to work with the relevant agencies to protect or create substitute wetlands, or he or she can choose the trust option and pay Dade County to accomplish the mitigation. County officials have found that most landowners prefer the trust option because it is a much easier and faster process.

12. Memorandum, Frank Bernardino to SAMP Committee Members, "Update on BDEB SAMP," June 11, 1996, p. 1.

13. Metropolitan Dade County Investment Policy, Resolution R-1178-95, adopted September 14, 1995.

14. Hole in the Donut: Interest Revenue 10/93–08/97, attachment to memo of September 17, 1997, to SAMP Implementation Committee Members from the Dade County Department of Environmental Resources Management.

15. Among the more mischievous potential problems for the trust is the opposition of what might be called the "mitigation industry." Not unique to Florida, this group of entrepreneurs is particularly well developed there and could cause problems for the trust. When wetlands mitigation became a prerequisite to development in areas such as Dade County, a new service industry was born. Consultants and similar entities provide developers with wetlands mitigation services. Unfortunately, the track record of such independent mitigation is not encouraging—only 15 percent of the projects permitted by the Corps and 6 percent of those permitted by the state were in complete compliance with the requirements imposed by the permit. As a result, SAMP members rejected reliance on "entities with little or no natural resource management experience to construct and properly maintain . . . isolated mitigation areas surrounded by intense land uses such as those proposed in the BDEB" (SAMP for the Bird Drive Everglades Basin, 4-1). Of course, the entire mitigation idea is questionable and is fairly criticized as an uncontrolled experiment designed to allow developers to destroy existing wetlands and similar resources without any real assurance that the mitigation will work. Be that as it may, it is enshrined in many laws, and the trust's insistence on giving a questionable practice the best possible chance of success is worth the effort. The mitigation industry was hostile to the trust because the costs of the trust's mitigation efforts are calculated based on activities on land already publicly owned and do not include a land cost. Hence, the trust's rates are cheaper than those the private mitigation industry could provide. Further, the trust can project relatively inexpensive future maintenance and monitoring due to the presence of the park and the National Park Service commitment to the project. Thus, trust projects were considerably cheaper and more attractive to developers than were those proffered by the mitigation industry.

CHAPTER 5. *EXXON VALDEZ* OIL SPILL TRUSTEE COUNCIL

1. It is worth noting that the Exxon Corporation has begun a campaign to rename the disaster the "Valdez incident." Residents of Valdez are reportedly not amused.

2. Here we refer to the public trust discussed in chapter 1.

3. The pertinent statutes are section 311(f) of the Clean Water Act, 33 U.S.C. §1321(f), and Comprehensive Environmental Response, Compensation, and Liability Act (CERCLA) section 107, 42 U.S.C. §9607. See also the National Contingency Plan, 40 C.F.R. §300.615(a), and the Natural Resource Damage Assessment Regulations, 43 C.F.R. §11.32(a)(1)(ii).

4. State officials were criticized at the time for settling for what many believed was too small an amount. Subsequent events suggest the wisdom of their haste. Ten years after the spill, private claims are still tied up on appeal, and private and tribal plaintiffs have received nothing of the much-discussed $5 billion private settlement. Moreover, as natural recovery continues, it is increasingly difficult to justify huge sums to compensate for what some now view as temporary damage.

5. Congress rewrote the key section of the Clean Water Act soon after the Exxon settlement to limit carriers' future liability in similar incidents.

6. The civil settlement is accompanied by a criminal settlement. The EVOS Trustee Council manages *only* the funds arising from the *civil* settlement. However, criminal fines are expended in part in the same area and for many of the same purposes as the EVOS trust.

7. In addition, the settlement includes a reopener—a five-year period after Exxon's last payment (September 1, 2002, through September 1, 2006)—during which government plaintiffs may demand an additional $100 million for restoration of damages not known at the time of the settlement, but only if the cost of the restoration is not "grossly disproportionate to the magnitude of the benefits anticipated from the restoration" (Consent Decree, 18–19).

8. MOA, 8–11, emphasis added.

9. At the outset, however, the council considered proposals from the federal agencies to acquire bird habitat in California and elsewhere as part of the restoration effort.

10. After the spill, the Environmental Protection Agency tried to insinuate itself into the proceedings as the EVOS czar. The effort failed, and the EPA disappeared from the documents soon after the settlement.

11. This response is less than satisfactory, given the fact that Exxon was offered a place on the council, which it declined. Apparently having a claim against Exxon is not the decisive factor in determining who can be a trustee.

12. See minutes, EVOS Trustee Council meeting, December 5, 1991, 4.

13. One public advisory group member suggested that early EVOS trust money simply "gold-plated" existing agency programs: pre-EVOS, agency personnel might arrive at a remote research site in a skiff; post-EVOS, they might arrive in a helicopter.

14. See minutes, EVOS Trustee Council meeting, August 25, 1995, 1.

15. The plan also notes that EVOS funds could be used to "enhance or establish alternate subsistence resources, or provide information about the safety and availability of subsistence resources, or even to provide facilities such as a shelter cabin that provides for easier access to alternate resources" (Restoration Plan, 4–5, 19).

16. The exception to this enthusiasm was concentrated in the villages. For example, six of the seven brochures returned from Chignik Lagoon and Perryville said that "habitat protection should not be part of the plan" (Plan Comments, 17).

17. Criteria for selecting target parcels are described in the restoration plan at pp. 22–23 and include "potential benefits that purchase and protection would provide to injured resources and services; . . . support of multiple species and ecologically linked groups of species, . . . providing access to public land, . . . [or] provide critical benefits to a single resource or service." See also EVOS Trustee Council, "Comprehensive Habitat Protection and Acquisition Process: Large Parcel Evaluation and Ranking" (November 1993).

18. Critics of the EVOS program note that the council does not take no for an answer. The target parcels have been identified, and if a seller says no, the trust does not go away; it rethinks and restructures its offer and tries again. Some observers are critical of the pressure that this creates for local villages. The village of Port Graham was emphatic in assuring EVOS trust staff that it was not interested in selling land, but staff members continued to check in from time to time to see whether village leaders had changed their minds.

19. Restoration Plan, 17.

20. This does not mean, however, that the issue of trust funds subsidizing agency programs was wholly resolved. In 1996, the public advisory group asked the staff to draft guidelines for identifying agency activities, as opposed to trust programs. After much discussion, participants concluded that the line between the two was not bright and abandoned the idea.

21. Although the agencies involved certainly do have condemnation authority, the council decided not to use it in the context of EVOS trust acquisitions.

22. Because many of the large parcels are remote and their value somewhat speculative, they tend to appraise for far less than the owners would require for selling them, especially when the gorilla with the millions is known to be in a buying mood.

23. A full exploration of the Alaska Native Claims Settlement Act is beyond the scope of this chapter, and we are not experts. The literature is enormous. Useful starting points that we relied on include Robert D. Arnold, *Alaska Native Land Claims* (1976, 1978); Thomas R. Berger, *Village Journey, the Report of the Alaska Native Review Commission* (1985); David S. Case, *Alaska Natives and American Laws* (1984); and Jerry Mander, *In the Absence of the Sacred* (1991).

24. This was not, it is worth noting, a negotiated settlement between equal parties. Congress legislated the amount and terms of the payment, while the Alaskan Native landowners participated on the same terms as, but with far less experience than, any other affected interest group.

25. Case, *Alaska Natives and American Laws*, 447.

26. See, particularly, Berger, *Village Journey.*

27. The requirement for a vote is not an artifact of ANCSA but rather reflects law applicable in most states to all corporations. A vote is required whenever a corporation disposes of a large proportion of its assets. The Koniag transaction, for example, involved a small portion of corporate assets and did not require a vote. Most of the sales have required votes and were approved by 75 to 85 percent of the stockholders in the corporations involved.

28. Not all that money can be described as expenditures for "science," because general restoration includes pollution prevention, management of human use to protect sensitive areas, and related activities. This estimate does not include

any continued monitoring or inquiry that may accompany the establishment of a post-trust endowment or invocation of the reopener clause.

29. Marguerite Holloway, "Sounding Out Science," *Scientific American* 275 (October 1996): 106. Predictably, perhaps, much of the criticism of damage and recovery assessment comes from Exxon scientists. Unfortunately, they are not always clear about their affiliation. See, for example, John A. Wiens, "Oil, Seabirds, and Science: The Effects of the *Exxon Valdez* Oil Spill," *Bioscience* 40 (October 1996): 587. Perhaps because of the reopener in the settlement and the protracted pendency of $5 billion worth of private damage claims against the corporation, Exxon has paid close attention to the scientific uncertainty in both attributing damages to the spill and assessing recovery. See *Alaska Geographic*, Oil Spill issue.

30. Holloway, "Sounding Out Science," 110–12.

31. Interestingly, the MOA specifies that the funds will be held in the Registry of the U.S. District Court of Alaska. However, the funds are managed by the District Court of Houston, Texas, which manages funds for all CRIS deposits.

32. Elgee, Rehfeld & Funk, Certified Public Accountants, Exxon Valdez Oil Spill Trustee Council Trust Funds Financial Statements and Supplementary Restoration Projects Information, Fiscal Year Ended September 30, 1995, Together with Independent Auditors Report, January 26, 1996, 9–10.

33. In spring 1999, after nearly six years of protest by EVOS trust staff, CRIS officials noted that an error had been made; due to the size of the settlement, the charge should have been only 5 percent of earnings. Thus, starting in March 1999, the fee was halved. CRIS has not, however, been responsive to requests for reimbursement for the overcharge.

34. Early EVOS trust projections underestimated the amount of interest that would be earned by about one-third. Actual investment returns on CRIS-held funds have been about $20 million, on which CRIS has charged approximately $2.1 million in fees.

35. Observers agree, for example, that the Department of Justice is not enthusiastic about programs that support cultural revitalization in villages, even those that respond to interrupted subsistence activities. Therefore, activities such as spirit camps are generally paid for by the state's funds from the criminal settlement.

36. PL 102-277, section 207. All this is discussed in considerable detail in the *Exxon Valdez* Oil Spill Trustee Council Procedures, adopted August 29, 1996.

37. See Elgee, Rehfeld & Funk, Internal Control and Operating Comments, for example, at 13, 14, 18, 19, 27, 28.

38. One staffer who works closely with CRIS is understandably irked that above and beyond the 10 percent CRIS takes for virtually nonexistent CRIS costs, it charges 50 cents per page for the periodic financial reports prepared by the Texas Commerce Bank. A few dollars is not going to break the budget, but it is not a positive element of working with the federal government either.

39. Restoration Plan, 27.

40. The pattern among those that did comment on structure is interesting: those within the oil spill region wanted to discontinue both the public advisory group and the current council; those outside the spill area supported continuing both.

41. During the 1999 legislative session, this draft was known as S. 711.

42. "Preliminary Draft Conceptual Plan: Gulf Ecosystem Monitoring (GEM) Program, July 11, 1999," 8, 31, 7.

43. There are some indications that public attention is waning. In 1993, public comment on the restoration plan was extensive—approximately 2,000 people gave

written or oral comment at twenty-two meetings, 799 returned questionnaires, and 792 wrote letters. Regarding the restoration reserve five years later, 249 people attended twenty-two public meetings, and 1,361 returned questionnaires or wrote letters.

CHAPTER 6. HAWAIIAN HOME LANDS: THE BAD NEWS–GOOD NEWS TRUST

1. For purposes of this chapter, we refer to the trust created by the Hawaiian Homes Commission Act as the Hawaiian Home Lands trust. It is one of three major trusts benefiting native Hawaiians. The Kamehameha Schools Bernice Pauahi Bishop Estate, created in 1884 by a descendant of King Kamehameha I, set more than 434,000 acres of royal lands aside in trust for the education of Hawaiian children. It has recently been the focus of intense public controversy. We ignore the Bishop Estate but keep the ceded or public land trust in view.

2. The Hawaiian Homes Commission Act defines native Hawaiians as those having 50 percent "blood quantum" of those inhabiting the islands when Captain Cook arrived. This definition is presently being challenged as an unconstitutional classification. See Stuart Benjamin, "Equal Protection and the Special Relationship: The Case of Native Hawaiians," 106 *Yale Law Journal* 537 (1996), as discussed in Philip Frickey, "Adjudication and Its Discontents: Coherence and Conciliation in Federal Indian Law," 110 *Harvard Law Review* 1754 (1997). This discussion is more than a scholarly debate—a lawsuit including variants on Benjamin's position presently challenges the whole concept of the trust. See *Rice v Cayetano*, 146 F.3d 1075 (1998), cert. granted, 119 S. Ct. (1999).

3. On sovereignty, see H. Trask, *From a Native Daughter* (1993), and N. Kahanu and J. Van Dyke, "Native Hawaiian Entitlement to Sovereignty: An Overview," 17 *Hawaii Law Review* 427 (1995).

4. A brief introduction to these terms is found in chapter 1.

5. A good place to start on land in Hawaii is Jon J. Chinen, *The Great Mahele: Hawaii's Land Division of 1848* (1958). Maivan Clech Lam, "The Kuleana Act Revisited: The Survival of Traditional Hawaiian Commoner Rights in Land," 64 *Washington Law Review* 233 (1989), is also useful. General histories include Michael Dougherty, *To Steal a Kingdom* (1992); Gavin Daws, *Shoal of Time* (1968); and Linda S. Parker, *Native American Estate: The Struggle over Indian and Hawaiian Lands* (1989). See also Melody Kapilialoha MacKenzie, *Native Hawaiian Rights Handbook* (1991). Our discussion is drawn from these sources.

6. It is argued that the Kuleana Act did not relinquish tenants' rights in the other 99 percent of the kingdom's lands; rather, such rights were diminished by subsequent court decisions. For further discussion on commoners' rights in land, see Lam, "Kuleana Act."

7. Michael M. McPherson, "*Trustees of Hawaiian Affairs v Yamasaki* and the Native Hawaiian Claim: Too Much of Nothing," 21 *Environmental Law* 454 (1991).

8. Lesley Karen Friedman, "Native Hawaiians, Self-Determination and the Inadequacy of the State Land Trust," 14 *Hawaii Law Review* 519, 532 (1992).

9. Joint Resolution of Annexation, 30 Stat. 750 (1898) (J. Res. No. 55). For a historical summary, see S. J. Resolution 19, November 23, 1993, the apology issued on the hundredth anniversary of the overthrow of the Hawaiian kingdom.

10. See Jon A. Souder and Sally K. Fairfax, *State Trust Lands* (1996), for a discussion of the school land trusts.

11. 22 Op. Att'y Gen. 574 (1899), as discussed in *Trustees of the Office Hawaiian Affairs v Yamasaki*, 737 P.2d 446 (1987), 449.

12. These diverse uses ultimately consumed about one-quarter of the ceded lands. At statehood, 287,078 acres of ceded land had been set aside for federal government use, 227,972 of them for national parks.

13. Joint Resolution, 30 Stat. 750 (1898).

14. Organic Act, ch. 339, 31 Stat. 141 (1900).

15. The HHCA purported to set aside 203,500 acres, more or less, as available lands. Inventories of the Home Lands indicate that the true acreage has historically been closer to 188,000, leading to claims of missing lands. Several factors contribute to the discrepancy. The act did not specify Home Land boundaries but rather identified *ahupuaas*, the key unit of Hawaiian land use, and districts by name, with approximations of acreage. Furthermore, inconsistency in whether statutory exclusions were considered in the congressional estimates, lack of maps provided by Congress, and outdated surveys contributed to the difference. For further discussion on the discrepancy, see Appendix 15 of Federal State Task Force on the Hawaiian Homes Commission Act, *Report to U.S. Secretary of the Interior and the Governor of the State of Hawaii* (1983).

16. For more on the creation of the Hawaiian Home Lands trust, see Marylyn M. Vause, "The Hawaiian Homes Commission Act, 1920 History and Analysis" (master's thesis, University of Hawaii, 1962). Lane's quote is from U.S. Congress, House of Representatives, Hearings, 1920, at 121, cited in Vause, "Hawaiian Homes Commission Act," 45–46.

17. See Vause, "Hawaiian Homes Commission Act," chap. 2, esp. 17–20.

18. Three of the commissioners were to be native Hawaiians. Today, four members must have at least one-quarter blood of the races inhabiting the islands prior to 1778. The governor served as the chair of the commission until 1934, when the structure was changed to avoid conflicts of interest. The commission was reconstituted first as a seven-member board and in 1989 as a nine-member board. Board members are appointed by the governor and confirmed by the state senate. Eight seats are allocated geographically; the ninth is the full-time chair.

19. The Home Lands not used for homesteading purposes were managed by the commissioner of public lands, the forerunner of the present Department of Land and Natural Resources. The DHHL was established shortly after statehood and given full authority to manage its lands in 1965.

20. The initial cap was raised in 1928 to $2 million, but this limit was reached in 1933. No additional revenue was received until 1943, when biennial caps were instituted. The caps were eliminated by the state's 1978 Constitutional Convention. See U.S. General Accounting Office, *Hawaiian Home Lands: Hawaii's Efforts to Address Land Use Issues*, GAO/RCED 94-24 (May 1994), 9.

21. From 1970 to 1977, the federal government paid an average rental for homelands of 45 cents per acre, the state of Hawaii paid an average of 12 cents per acre, and the counties paid an average of $3.10 per acre (Hawaii Advisory Committee on Civil Rights, *Breach of Trust? Native Hawaiian Homelands: A Summary of the Proceedings of a Public Forum Sponsored by the Hawaii Advisory Committee to the U.S. Commission on Civil Rights*, ([1980] 16). Political and economic leaders in Hawaii have received leases of Home Lands for less than $10 an acre, with some being leased for $2.50 per acre. See Susan Faludi, "How Everyone Got Hawaiians' Homelands Except the Hawaiians." *Wall Street Journal*, September 9, 1991, western ed., A1.

22. In 1986, the Federal Housing Authority began financing some DHHL homesteads.

23. It is worth remembering that the territorial government was a creature of the federal government and is not appropriately understood as synonymous with "the state," which was still forty years in the future.

24. Auditor, State of Hawaii, *Management and Financial Audit of the Department of the Hawaiian Home Lands: A Report to the Governor and the Legislature of the State of Hawaii*, Report 93-22 (December 1993), 10–12.

25. Major investigations include Hawaii Advisory Committee on Civil Rights, *Breach of Trust;* Federal State Task Force, *Report to U.S. Secretary;* Hawaii Advisory Committee on Civil Rights, *A Broken Trust—The Hawaiian Home Lands Program: Seventy Years of Failure of the Federal and State Governments to Protect the Civil Rights of Native Hawaiians, a Report to the United States Commission on Civil Rights* (December 1991).

26. See *Breach of Trust*, 10, and DHHL Annual Report, 1979–80, 7–8. As it is possible for lessees to have more than one lease but only one residence, the number of leases is not equal to the number of beneficiaries awarded leases. The vast majority of lessees, however, have only one lease.

27. SMS, *Department of Hawaiian Home Lands Beneficiary Needs Study*, prepared for DHHL (1995). It is estimated that at least 25 percent of the applicants had deferred an award at least once. The structure of the list allows applicants to defer awards while retaining their positions on the list. Thus, some applicants who have been on the list for over ten years may have been offered awards in the past. In addition, as applicants can be on multiple lists and lessees can have additional applications pending, the length of the waiting list is not an accurate representation of the number of persons awaiting a homestead.

28. *Keaukaha-Panaewa Community Association v Hawaiian Homes Commission*, 588 F.2d 1216 (1978), 1220 (hereafter *Keaukaha I*).

29. *Keaukaha-Panaewa Community Association v Hawaiian Homes Commission*, 739 F. 2d 1467 (1984) (hereafter *Keaukaha II*).

30. See Eric Yamamoto, "Courts and the Cultural Performance: Native Hawaiian's Uncertain Federal and State Rights to Sue," 16 *Hawaii Law Review* 1 (1994), 37. See also *Price v Hawaii*, 764 F.2d 623 (1985).

31. See Frederick N. Ferguson, Deputy Acting Solicitor, Department of the Interior, to Philip Montez, Director, Western Regional Office, U.S. Commission on Civil Rights, August 27, 1979.

32. Thomas L. Sansonetti, "The Scope of Federal Responsibility for Native Hawaiians Under the Hawaiian Homes Commission Act," M-36978, January 19, 1993. The opinion in *Keaukaha I* (1224) supports that claim.

33. U.S. Department of Interior, Solicitor's Opinion, M-36978, November 15, 1993.

34. *Han v Barr and Price*, 824 F. Supp. 1480 (1993), 1487.

35. Board of Land and Natural Resources, "Conveyance of Land from the Department of Land and Natural Resources to the Department of Hawaiian Home Lands at Various Sites Statewide," October 28, 1994. See also Office of State Planning, *Federal Breaches of the Hawaiian Home Lands Trust* (1992), 38. Incredibly, the task force did not initially include an independent representative of the beneficiaries. In *Kaaiai v Drake* (Case No. 92-3642), the Native Hawaiian Legal Corporation inspired the legislature to add a representative to the group. For discussion, see Yamamoto, "Courts and Cultural Performance."

36. For a good summary of the events discussed in this paragraph, see the findings section of Act 14, Special Session, 1995, §1.

37. The state was not, at least in theory, absolved from making future appropriations to the trust. Act 14 provided that "payments made under this Act shall not diminish funds that the department is entitled to under article XII section 1, of the Constitution of the State of Hawaii."

38. It is worth noting that the resolution was defined and imposed by the state, the entity that had breached the trust in the first place.

39. Act of July 2, 1991, 1991 Sess. Laws 997, HRS 674.

40. *APA v Cayetano*, Civil No. 97-4641 (1998).

41. Discussed in Pat Omandam, "Hawaiians Rip Veto Blocking Land Claims," *Honolulu Star-Bulletin*, June 17, 1999, http://starbulletin.com. The 1991 legislation establishing the panel allowed claimants dissatisfied with the legislature's action on their claims to appeal to the circuit court. However, because most of the claims were never reviewed by the legislature, it is not clear that the court can or will do anything with the complaints it is likely to receive.

42. Hawaiian Home Lands Recovery Act, PL No. 104-42, 109 Stat. 353 (1995).

43. *Lost use* is defined as the value of land during the period when beneficiaries were unable to use lands after statehood (August 21, 1959).

44. This includes licenses on nearly 24,000 acres of land, which produce about $250,000.

45. Although some of this land is planned for future homesteading, the location and topographical features of other parcels make development difficult or infeasible.

46. DHHL, Annual Report 1996–97, 7.

47. Auditor, *Management and Financial Audit of the DHHL*, 11–12.

48. The DHHL's official response is included in ibid., 29–46.

49. Although efforts to open federal housing funds to the DHHL are in the interest of the beneficiary, plans must be developed for the poorest beneficiaries without the assumption that congressional assistance will be forthcoming.

50. In 1993, the governor noted that activities lack a "clear philosophical basis," and he "questioned whether the DHHL was a welfare program or a trust for Hawaiians." Auditor, *Management and Financial Audit of the DHHL*, 11.

51. As applicants can be on more than one waiting list and lessees can remain on waiting lists for other types of homesteads, the number of applications does not necessarily equal the number of applicants.

52. See DHHL, Annual Report 1990–91, 11.

53. See DHHL, Annual Report 1996, 17; Annual Report 1997, 18.

54. DHHL, Annual Report 1997–98, 10.

55. One of the ironies of the DHHL story is that the trust may be declared unconstitutional before it has a chance to operate as a trust. *Rice v Cayetano*, 146 F.3d 1075 (1998), on appeal to the Supreme Court, challenges the continued existence of both the ceded land trust and the Hawaiian Home Lands trust. A white resident of Hawaii who was denied the opportunity to vote in an informal plebiscite concerning native Hawaiian trust affairs brought the case. Although the appeals court held that it was not called on to determine the constitutionality of the racial classification, the case raises Fourteenth Amendment issues and the question of whether the existence of the Home Lands and ceded land trust impermissibly singles out a particular racial group for government largesse.

CHAPTER 7. NORTH DAKOTA WETLANDS TRUST:
WHAT'S TRUST GOT TO DO WITH IT?

1. For an excellent account of wetlands issues, see Eric Freyfogle, "The Owning and Taking of Sensitive Lands," 43 *UCLA Law Review* 77 (1995).

2. Most of our information about the potholes comes from Mark S. Dennison and James F. Berry, *Wetlands: Guide to Science, Law, and Technology* (1993), esp. 118 ff.

3. Pam Dryer, Wetlands Trust Area Concepts Proposal to Board of Directors, January 29, 1992, 1.

4. For a discussion, see Ross H. Espeseth, "North Dakota's Corporate Farming Statute: An Analysis of the Recent Change in the Law," 58 *North Dakota Law Review* 311 (1982).

5. In the Pick-Sloan Missouri Basin program planning, Congress authorized the Bureau of Reclamation to plan and build a series of reservoirs on the Missouri River and a system of canals and other structures to deliver water in a multistate area. The water would be used chiefly for irrigation but secondarily for municipal and rural water supplies. Garrison was the project for North Dakota. Pick-Sloan was first authorized in the Flood Control Act of December 22, 1944 (58 Stat. 891), section 9.

6. The Act of August 5, 1965 (PL No. 89-108, 79 Stat. 433).

7. The 1990 reauthorization of Swampbuster can be found at 16 U.S.C. §§ 3821–24 (Supp. 1991). For a brief overview of Swampbuster, see Paul Thompson and Karen Tyler, *A Guide to Agricultural Wetlands Protection* (1991).

8. U.S. Prairie Pothole Joint Venture, U.S. Prairie Pothole Joint Venture Implementation Plan (April 1989), 15–16.

9. In this case, the Interior Department worked with the Departments of Justice and the Treasury.

10. Statement of Principles to Support the Agreement for Reformulation of the Garrison Diversion Unit, April 14, 1986, 1. The document was signed by the governor of North Dakota, the chairman of the Garrison Diversion Conservancy District, the president of the North Dakota Water Users Association, the president of the National Audubon Society, the president of the North Dakota chapter of the Wildlife Society, the executive vice president of the National Wildlife Federation, and the president of the North Dakota Wildlife Federation.

11. The law did not become effective for two years. Thus, one effect of its passage was to dramatically increase wetlands drainage during the grace period. It was repealed in 1995, ostensibly so that North Dakota would not have a stricter wetlands law than the newly elected Republican Congress was likely to pass but did not. The parties that had been involved in the Garrison negotiations opposed repeal of the law.

12. NDWT Grant Agreement, section A, 1–2.

13. NDWT Strategic Plans 1994–1997, 2, and 1997–2000, 2.

14. In addition, during negotiations to induce the state to make the payments to the trust corpus it had agreed on, the directors agreed to allow the state Fish and Game Department a nonvoting seat on the board. The department had made one payment when a new director ceased the payments but retained the seat.

15. Questioned about the disjunction between the vision and the organization, the Garrison negotiators said that the enthusiasm of the new cooperative spirit they had achieved during the legislative process made such details seem trivial. They assumed that the cooperative spirit and personal goodwill

would endure and so failed to equip the NDWT to advance trust purposes after the honeymoon.

16. When the average terms are broken into charter directors and post-1993 directors, the result is 7.5 years and 2.5 years, respectively.

17. Although the framers were careless about many aspects of the trust, they were meticulous and creative in ensuring that it would not go forward if the Garrison diversion did not. After its first deposit, Interior payments were based on a percentage of the annual Garrison appropriation. If the project were jeopardized, federal payments would be reduced or eliminated.

18. The NDWT was established about six years before the EVOS trust was established. Because the NDWT was not based on payment for civil damages, its funds stayed out of the CRIS morass that has so confounded EVOS trust staffers.

19. It is difficult to avoid speculating that the environmental organizations may have exacerbated problems by appointing not in-state notables sympathetic to environmental protection but out-of-staters to the board.

20. Minutes of the NDWT, January 1987, 3. There is one significant exception to this openness. It is not possible to obtain data on total trust earnings since the NDWT was established. Although the NDWT publishes an annual financial statement, its financial reporting can only be regarded as minimal.

21. This was not an easy process, and views differ on what was actually happening. Gubernatorial directors say that the environmental directors were eventually won over to the cooperative approach and would vote for a project after some rhetoric opposing it. Environmental directors report that they would argue against a project, but if the vote was against them, they would choose not to make an issue of it and vote in the affirmative.

22. We refer to them as directors as well.

23. NDWT Board of Directors, "North Dakota Wetland Trust Guidelines," adopted July 10, 1987, with revised versions issued July 19, 1988, and January 17, 1990.

24. BlueStem, Inc., An Evaluation of the Create a Wetland Program, June 1996, 1.

25. CAW was first applied in Bottineau County. Participants in subsequent counties did not receive the flooded acre fee (BlueStem, Inc., 2). The program has continued to grow slowly.

26. A no-till drill is an expensive piece of farming equipment that plants seeds without turning over, uprooting, or disturbing the existing cover. This aids wetlands protection by reducing soil erosion.

27. NDWT Strategic Plan, August 17, 1991.

28. Dryer, Wetlands Proposal. The report continues, "These practices will either improve agricultural productivity or the Trust will compensate landowners for loss of productivity" (3).

29. The Kenner Slough was purchased and restored by the NDWT and was featured in a video about wetlands restoration and agriculture.

30. Corporate or Limited Liability Company Farming, North Dakota Century Code 10-06.1-10.

31. The Corporate and Limited Liability Farming Law appears ripe for attack on a number of constitutional points. We lose some of our scholarly detachment when we ponder why environmentalist groups criticize the North Dakota trust for apparent inadequacies that they tolerate in organizations enjoying much more supportive environments while simultaneously remaining unwilling to challenge the statute. It would be a significant service to conservation efforts

in North Dakota if some group or individual would take on that fairly obvious task.

32. When questioned about this stunning blunder, one Garrison veteran observed that if they had thought of it, they could have exempted the trust from state laws, because the trust involved federal money and a federal project. But it just did not occur to them. Even if they had thought of it, it strikes us as highly unlikely that the governor's representatives in the negotiations would have accepted such a provision.

33. The NDWT presents a plan to the state agriculture commissioner, who convenes a committee consisting of the director of the Parks and Recreation Department, the state engineer, the commissioner of agriculture, the state forester, the director of the Game and Fish Department, and the presidents of both the Farmer's Union and the Farm Bureau. Also, if the proposed acquisition falls within the Garrison Diversion Conservancy District area, the manager of the district is included. The committee consults appropriate county commissioners, holds a public hearing, and makes recommendations to the governor, who can reject the acquisition in whole or in part. Corporate or Limited Liability Company Farming, North Dakota Century Code 10-06.1-10.

34. Terms of office are designed, in part, to prevent such wholesale losses of institutional memory and momentum.

35. NDWT Strategic Plan 1994–1997, 1.

36. Ibid., 4.

37. The last item constitutes a dubious achievement for a wetlands conservation organization. However, in North Dakota, flood control is a major utilitarian value of potholes.

38. Institute for Conservation Leadership, Evaluation of the North Dakota Wetlands Trust 1994–1997, February 15, 1998, 1–4.

39. NDWT Strategic Plan 1997–2000, 4–5.

40. Dakota Water Resources Act of 1997, H.R. 3012, introduced November 9, 1997.

CHAPTER 8. GREAT LAKES FISHERY TRUST:
BLENDING GOVERNMENTS AND
NONGOVERNMENTAL ORGANIZATIONS

1. Two key documents resolve the dispute: a "state agreement" and a related FERC agreement. It is the state agreement specifically that sets up the trust. See *Kelly, et al. v Consumers Power Company and Detroit Edison Company*, No. 86-5705-CE (joined with No. 87-60020-CE), Consent Judgment, March 17, 1995. A memorandum from Stanley F. Pruss, Assistant Attorney General, Natural Resources Division, to Jack D. Davis, Great Lakes Fishery Trust Counsel, "RE: Declaration of Trust," November 26, 1996, provides a simplifying interpretive veneer for the fainthearted.

2. The Ludington Project is owned by Consumers Power Company (now Consumer's Energy) (51 percent) and by Detroit Edison Company (49 percent).

3. See memo from Pruss to Davis, 2.

4. The federal government's dedication to its fiduciary responsibilities to the tribes has been intermittent at best. See chapter 1. For a variation on those themes, see the discussion of the federal role in the native Hawaiian trust in chapter 6.

5. The Department of the Interior was not a party to the state agreement that

established the trust. As a federal agency, "it was unwilling to subject itself to the jurisdiction of the Michigan state courts" (memo from Pruss to Davis, 2).

6. Wisconsin and Canada, which border on Lake Michigan, did not participate in the litigation, and their interests were not discussed until the trust began to consider the nature of trust beneficiaries.

7. Discussed in memo from Pruss to Davis, 2.

8. Although the legislature approved the settlement, its concerns were not resolved. The Michigan legislature attempted to secure considerable funds from the GLFT for a program the state had historically funded. The trustees refused to supply the funds. In addition, the legislature has considered enacting legislation restricting the ability of the state to participate in the creation of a trust.

9. The legal team made two arguments in favor of the proposed settlement. The first was the practical response: The trust is an allocation mechanism, a way to settle the divergent interests. The parties have agreed to it, and it would be expensive and difficult to begin again. The second was a legal argument: The other parties had legally cognizable interests. State ownership of the resources is not clearly defined by law. The Native Americans and the Department of the Interior had clear rights, and the state must recognize that aquatic resources were not its sole domain.

10. GLFT Declaration of Trust, 1–2.

11. One participant argues that the language contemplating land acquisition was "inserted largely on the insistence of the tribal parties, so acquisition of real property by the Trust might be considered principally for their benefit." He argues that the trust lacks appropriate staff and liability insurance and should not contemplate holding land for any length of time. See memorandum, Douglas B. Jester, Michigan Department of Natural Resources, to Trustees, "RE: Considerations for the Great Lakes Fishery Trust Program Strategy," August 21, 1966, 12. Although land has been acquired with trust funds by local and tribal governments for fishing access, the trust itself has not acquired land.

12. Normal business is conducted with a two-thirds vote.

13. In its few years of existence, the GLFT has experienced modest turnover of trustees due to promotions, resignations, and deaths among the trustees appointed by the NWF and Michigan United Conservation Club.

14. Transactions involving properties offered to tribal governments are approved in the settlement agreement and do not require a vote of the trustees.

15. The trustees' power to amend the carefully negotiated settlement is the most constrained among the trusts we studied. They cannot make amendments that are contrary to the trust's 501(c)(3) status, which is normal. In addition, they cannot "substantially alter" the trust purposes, trustee composition, or decision-making requirements.

16. See, for example, Great Lakes Fishery Trust, Phase I: Strategic Planning, September 8–10, 1996, 3–4, noting that the GLFT must "soon address its administrative needs so that the DNR is not unduly burdened and subject to legislative criticism for the attention devoted to the Trust."

17. It is not possible to be more precise, as the settlement agreement intended that the annual payments would decline if mortality was reduced. Conversely, the value of the real estate escalated considerably between the settlement and the land sales.

18. The annual payment is capped at $2.5 million for the first three years. The early payments were $2.5 million. The first year, the damage was clearly in excess of the $2.5 million, but in 1998, improvements in the net's effectiveness reduced mortality among young fish. Monitoring demonstrated that the net was

keeping more alewife less than four inches out of the pumps than initially anticipated. Because the smaller fish were more numerous, better protection for them
reduced damages to just under $2.5 million. However, each year's payment is also
adjusted for inflation, which brought the damages in 1998 up to the $2.5 million
cap. It is estimated that future damages will fall somewhere between $2.25 mil-
lion and $2.5 million.

19. Due to increased real estate values, it is estimated that the trust realized,
on average, about 25 percent over the appraised value when it sold the properties. Forested land, which had been valued at $400 to $600 an acre at the time of
the settlement, sold for at least $1,000 per acre.

20. Many of the properties created management difficulties for the utilities.
The parcels were widely dispersed, often small, and subject to trespass. The utility companies had to maintain a management staff and pay liability insurance and
taxes on the properties. Disposing of the property would allow the utility companies to reduce their internal costs and assist their preparation for deregulation.

21. Memo from Jester to Trustees, 10–12. One of the reasons given for abstain-
ing from long-term holding of land was that the trust did not own and should not
have to buy appropriate landowner's liability insurance.

22. The Michigan attorney general identified a number of potentially problematic areas in the settlement's definition of SAT and trust responsibilities. Most
interesting is that under the settlement agreement, the SAT has a mission potentially at odds with the trust's interests. The SAT's "principal and foremost" objective is to reduce fish mortality arising from the pumping operations. That, however,
would have the paradoxical result of reducing the payments to the trust. This and
other SAT issues for the GLFT are discussed in memo from Pruss to Davis, 4–5.

23. Consent Order, 16–17.

24. A cynic might suggest that the power companies stayed out of the trust
with the intention of controlling its activities through the SAT.

25. The state had only a few months to do the assessments and had to assemble information from earlier surveys and aerial data. A key point was to evaluate potential contamination from, and possible liability for, prior land uses.

26. GLFT Declaration of Trust, 10. This provision is another one that responds
directly to the tribal plaintiffs' priorities. The tribe soon exercised this right and
has acquired a small parcel of land, its first since the federal government formally
recognized it as a tribe.

27. Settlement Agreement, 8.

28. The exception is an easement for wetlands protection. The property is
being farmed but was not being cultivated in the wetlands area. The easement
allows farming only in the area that was in cultivation at the time the easement
was created.

29. One observer notes that environmental advocates involved in the trust
were among those most insistent on spending the corpus down rather than attempting to establish a perpetual trust that would provide less mitigation in the
current generation. This contrasts with our portrayal of conservationists as consistently in favor of perpetuity.

PART IV. FAMILY, CHARITABLE, AND LAND TRUSTS

1. See, for example, Land Trust Alliance director Jean Hocker, "Patience,
Problem Solving, and Private Initiative: Local Groups Chart a New Course for Land

Conservation," in Henry L. Diamond and Patrick F. Noonan, eds., *Land Use in America* (1996), 248–49.

2. Changes in the tax code after 1965 have also been important in the development of the land trust field. For instance, the 1997 Taxpayer's Relief Act permitted landowners donating conservation easements to reduce their estate taxes by up to 40 percent of the land's remaining market value, increasing the potency of institutions organized to accept conservation easements. Conversely, the tax cuts proposed in 1999 that would significantly reduce estate taxes across the board might seriously limit the function of land trusts by diminishing the economic incentives for landowners to donate easements.

3. For more information, see Stephen J. Small, *Preserving Family Lands: Book II* (1997).

4. Frederico Cheever, "Environmental Law: Public Good and Private Magic in the Law of Land Trusts and Conservation Easements: A Happy Present and a Troubled Future," 73 *Denver University Law Review* 1077 (1996), discusses the statutory basis of conservation easements and some of the problems that may arise from downstream interpretation of state law. Other useful analyses include David Farrier, "Conserving Biodiversity on Private Land: Incentives for Management or Compensation for Lost Expectations," 19 *Harvard Environmental Law Review* 303 (winter 1995), and Gerald Korngold, "Privately Held Conservation Servitudes: A Policy Analysis in the Context of Gross Real Covenants and Easements," 63 *Texas Law Review* 433 (1984).

5. The major grit in the butter seems to be the issue of recreation access. In the San Francisco Bay Area, for example, less than 10 percent of the contemporary conservation easements provide for unrestricted public access. See Darla Guenzler, *Ensuring the Promise of Conservation Easements* (1999), 13. Many believe that public funds should not be spent to protect land from which recreationists are excluded. Others question whether agricultural land protection—which still allows farmers to engage in land conversions (rangelands to grape vineyards, for example) without constraining their option to use pesticides, fertilizers, and other chemical poisons—is a reasonable approach to habitat or even open space protection.

6. However, the discussion of federal acquisition authorities in the EVOS case in chapter 5 gives a rather surprising perspective on potential federal flexibility that ought to be factored into this general line of argument.

7. In *Preserving Family Lands: Book II*, Small argues that conservation easements actually extinguish development rights (24). He claims that what a land trust receives is not a development right but the right to *enforce* the recorded deed restrictions against any current or future owner of the property. Although this may seem to be a trivial distinction, it significantly redefines the negotiating position of a land trust accepting a conservation easement. A charitable organization imagined to "hold" development rights appears to gain a profitable resource from a landowner. An organization that gains only the right to perpetual enforcement responsibilities on a private deed restriction gains only accountability. Tax law seems to support this vision of land trust as enforcer. An organization truly holding development rights would be expected to pay taxes on those rights. Land trusts do not pay taxes on conservation easements, and most carry the value of easements on their books at zero. If a land trust enforces deed restrictions, it seems to provide a clear benefit both to the easement donor or seller, whose aspirations for the property are perpetuated, and to the public.

8. Janet Diehl and Thomas S. Barrett, *The Conservation Easement Handbook: Managing Land Conservation and Historic Preservation Easement* (1988).

9. The Mount Vernon Ladies Association, built by Ann Pamela Cunningham and her colleagues, began a national fund-raising and stewardship program that protected the property from both sides during the Civil War and continues to manage it. It has provided the model for many subsequent efforts at historic preservation. See Gerald W. Johnson, *Mount Vernon: The Story of a Shrine: An Account of the Rescue and Continuing Restoration of George Washington's Home by the Mount Vernon Ladies Association* (1991). It is perhaps useful to note that the Mount Vernon Ladies Association is not listed in the Land Trust Alliance directory.

10. For example, the Sempervirens Fund was started in 1900, and Save the Redwoods was established in 1920, both in California. In Massachusetts, the Trustees of Public Reservations was started in 1891.

11. Discussed in Cheever, "Environmental Law," 1092–93.

CHAPTER 9. STEPHEN PHILLIPS MEMORIAL PRESERVE TRUST: PEBBLES CAUSING RIPPLES

1. To put this area in perspective, it is similar in size to the more famous Acadia National Park. See Jeff Clark, "First Lady of the Lakes," *Down East: The Magazine of Maine* 41 (May 1955): 32.

2. Herbert P. Shirrefs, *The Richardson Lakes: Jewels in the Rangeley Chain* (1995), 17. Those inclined to think of Maine in terms of lobsters and the coast are not wrong, merely incomplete.

3. Shirrefs's volume is an engaging and informative source of praise for the region's beauty and a chatty recounting of its history. See especially chaps. 2, 10–14.

4. The history is taken from decisions in the key cases, which are *Cushing v Cohen*, 420 A.2d 919 (1980), and *Cushing v State of Maine*, 434 A.2d 486 (1981). Once state title was established and the awkward mix of ownerships adjusted to provide contiguous blocks of state land, a fight began over use of the new public lands. See Phyllis Austin, "Public Lands Debate Shifts to Parks, Timber Acreage," *Maine Times*, August 6, 1998.

5. See Ed Kfoury, "President's Comments," *Watersheds: The Newsletter of the Rangeley Lakes Heritage Trust* (spring/summer 1996): 1.

6. Stephen Phillips Memorial Preserve Trust, Book 983 Oxford Registry of Deeds, May 8, 1978, 113–22, 2–5. It is interesting to compare the prohibitions imposed by Mrs. Phillips and the SPNHF approach to easement restrictions discussed in chapter 10. One important element to weigh when drafting provisions is the future cost of monitoring and enforcement.

7. Scenic, Wildlife Habitat, and Public Recreation Conservation Easement on Northwest Rangeley Forest Land, Essex County, Massachusetts, December 20, 1991, 5–8.

8. Information for this section is drawn from discussion with Rangeley Lakes Heritage Trust personnel and from Andrew K. Weegar, "A 22-Year Quest," *Maine Times*, September 17, 1993, 4.

9. See, generally, Laura S. Beliveau, "The Forest Legacy Program: Using Conservation Easements to Preserve the Northern Forest," 20 *Boston College Environmental Affairs Law Review* 507 (1993).

10. 16 U.S.C., §2103c. Actually, the "farm bill" is the Food, Agriculture, Conservation and Trade Act of 1990, PL No. 101-624. See also Senate Report No. 101-357, Food, Agriculture, Conservation and Trade Act of 1990, July 6, 1990, and House Conference Report No. 101-916, October 22, 1990.

11. Dick Spencer, quoted in Weegar, "A 22-Year Quest," 4.

12. Because Mrs. Phillips was barred by the terms of her marital trust from putting those lands into the Phillips trust until her death, they were arguably somewhat unprotected. The easements provided protection for the marital trust lands both before and after they were included in the Phillips trust under the terms of her will.

13. See Scenic, Wildlife Habitat, and Public Recreation Conservation Easement on Northwest Rangeley Forest Land, 3.

14. See Andrew K. Weegar, "What Bessie Phillips Wanted to Save," *Maine Times*, September 17, 1993, 4.

15. See Scenic, Wildlife Habitat, and Public Recreation Conservation Easement on Northwest Rangeley Forest Land, 11. Of course, the RLHT will have to go to a lot of expense and trouble to monitor and enforce those provisions. For a significantly different approach to easement conditions, see the discussion in chapter 10.

16. Weegar, "What Bessie Phillips Wanted to Save," 4.

17. This was almost five years before the marital trust lands actually became part of the Phillips trust.

18. Rangeley Lakes Heritage Trust, "An Atlas of Protection," brochure, n.d., centerfold. See also, Weegar, "What Bessie Phillips Wanted to Save," 5.

19. Weegar, "What Bessie Phillips Wanted to Save," 4.

CHAPTER 10. SOCIETY FOR THE PROTECTION
OF NEW HAMPSHIRE FORESTS

1. This is a topic that demands feature-length treatment in a dissertation. Pending that, the best resources are Paul E. Bruns, *A New Hampshire Everlasting and Unfallen: An Illustrated History* (1969), and Evan Hill, *A Greener Earth* (1976). Both provide indispensable overviews of Society evolution, but both are celebratory rather than analytical. Also useful is *Forest Notes*, a Society publication begun in 1937.

2. The Society continues to be deeply concerned about the management of White Mountain National Forest. Having spent several decades deeply involved in the forest planning process, it is presently a major participant in a statewide effort to find an alternative management structure for the forest. It has strongly opposed efforts to foreclose economic use of the forest by turning it into a national park.

3. Acquisition of its first reserve, Lost River Gorge, began in 1912. The Society presently owns and manages 30,000 acres in 114 reserves.

4. Potential tree farmers are rated on a number of dimensions, including their forest management plans for long-term land protection, wildlife habitat enhancement, and recreational use of their properties. The Society continues to be a sponsor of the program, which currently includes 1,700 tree farmers and 1 million acres of New Hampshire forests. New tree farmers receive a free one-year membership in the Society. Another Tree Farm sponsor, the New Hampshire Timberland Owners Association, has offices at Society headquarters in Concord.

5. Discussed in Liz Lorvig, "Highest and Best Use: Current Use Has Helped New Hampshire Families Keep Their Farms and Forests Intact." *Forest Notes* 210 (summer 1996): 22–23.

6. Land Trust Alliance, *1998 Directory of Conservation Land Trusts*, 115–20. Rhode Island has thirty-four.

7. As intended, the Trust for New Hampshire Lands sunsetted in 1993, having protected more than 100,000 acres.

8. Which is not affiliated with a national organization of a similar name.

9. "Society News," *Forest Notes* 213 (spring 1997): 9.

10. Even if it is, the donor can change his or her mind about the recipient nonprofit at any time. And the dollar amount and timing of the donation are unknown until the donor dies.

11. On the FASB requirements, see Robert Turner et al., *Financial Reporting and Contributions: A Decision Making Guide to FASB Nos. 116 and 117* (Coopers & Lybrand, April 1994), from which the basic definitions are distilled and quoted.

12. 16 U.S.C. §2601 et seq.

13. We took this yarn from "Advocacy Update: Pontook Dam Update," *Forest Notes* 216 (winter 1997–98): 19, and supplemented it with comments from SPNHF staff members Paul Doscher and Charlie Niebling.

14. The material in this section is based on conversations with Rose Freeman and Edgar Brodeur, the first and second trustees of the Brodeur trust, and on trust records maintained by them, particularly, minutes of the meeting of the trust, May 10, 1989.

15. Edgar Brodeur described his trustee responsibilities largely in terms of removing old tires and construction waste illegally dumped on the property.

16. The trustee was surprised and not wholly pleased to receive points, during the Tree Farm rating process, for recreational use of the property in the form of snowmobiling. The family unsuccessfully sought to write the easement to proscribe snowmobiling in the wooded area of the property and confine it to an abandoned road running along one boundary. This was not possible. SPNHF easement monitoring is based on annual arial photographs and site visits. Ephemeral uses such as hunting, snowmobiling, and pesticide application are difficult to detect on an annual assessment and are not typically included in the enforceable conditions of an easement contract.

17. California law is similar, but the application is different, and the landowner worries anyway. If someone is hurt, the claim of negligence arises, so insurance is needed. The fees for defending against a claim are high, even if the landowner ultimately wins.

18. The organization began with an executive director but was unable to raise the money to support the position and dropped it. About a year ago, it hired a part-time office manager in charge of membership, newsletter mailing, and similar tasks. CCT information comes over e-mail from Chris Kane, immediate past chair of the CCT board.

19. In 1963, the state of New Hampshire enacted NS RSA 36-A:4, which authorized towns to form Conservation Commissions. Their powers are slight, and their required duties minimal. However, the commissions provide a focus for conservation education and diverse activities. The Jackson Conservation Commission began holding easements in the 1980s, and it received the second Burgess family donation in 1993. Not surprisingly, the SPNHF played a key role in securing the legislation that authorized the commissions, and the statewide Association of Conservation Commissions that supports and encourages their activities is located at the Society's office complex.

20. Meaning that fertility would be penalized, as beneficiaries with numerous siblings would hold a smaller portion of the trust than would those with few or none.

21. A family typically seeks legal and tax advice, the land trust involved acquires baseline data and conducts surveys of the conservation values of the property to assist in future monitoring of the easement, and sometimes a survey of the donated property is required. Finally, the land trust frequently requests a dona-

tion to a perpetual fund that supports monitoring and enforcement of the easement provisions. The SPNHF typically asks easement donors for $1,000 for its Easement Stewardship Fund when accepting an easement. See Sylvia Bates, "Donating a Conservation Easement: A Step-by-Step Guide to a Satisfying Process," Society handout reprinted from *Forest Notes* (autumn 1993).

CHAPTER 11. NAPA COUNTY LAND TRUST

1. Of the county's 508,000 acres, approximately 38,000 acres are planted to grapes, with about 250,000 acres used for cattle grazing. Conversion of rangeland to vineyards is a major issue in neighboring Sonoma County and for the land trusts operating there.

2. The annual value of the grape crop is presently in the area of $125 million, with the value of the wine produced approximately $900 million. Indirect economic benefits of wine industry tourism amount to an additional $390 million. See Agricultural Commissioner, *1998 Annual Crop Report for Napa County*. It is not clear to local planners, however, whether the wine or the biotech industry makes a greater contribution to the county economy.

3. This and many other interesting factoids, as well as a participant-observer's account of the Napa land use fights, can be found in Volker Eisele, "Twenty-five Years of Farmland Protection in Napa County," in Albert G. Medvitz et al., eds., *California Farmland and Urban Pressures: Statewide and Regional Perspectives* (1999), 103 ff.

4. Passed in 1965, the Williamson Act allows current use assessment of agricultural property if it has been included in an agricultural district established by the county.

5. Discussed in Eisele, "Twenty-five Years," 105–11.

6. For example, the NCLT has transferred lands that add to Robert Louis Stevenson State Park and county marshlands to the California State Fish and Game wildlife preserve in Napa County. It holds easements on two small undeveloped parcels in the city of St. Helena managed by the city government as a tiny downtown park. It is currently in the process of helping CALFED and the Army Corps of Engineers acquire floodplain lands along the Napa River. CALFED is a federal-state planning effort for the San Francisco Bay–Delta Estuary founded in 1994.

7. Once it was on its feet, even the relatively small NCLT helped establish the Quail Ridge Wilderness Conservancy, a tiny land trust committed to preserving as a research reserve the wild California oak woodland, savanna, and chaparral complex that covers the southern peninsula in Napa's Lake Berryessa. This is likely a result of personal preference rather than an NCLT commitment to creating new organizations, however.

8. Napa County Land Trust, *Board Member Policy Manual*, rev. ed. (March 1999), 36.

9. The amount of the donation is related to anticipated monitoring costs associated with the property. Size, location, and the type of rights reserved to the donor in the easement are among the factors considered.

10. A recent Land Trust Alliance study indicates that all 435 serious conservation easement violations were committed by post-transaction owners (Land Trust Alliance, "Easement Violations" [1999], www.lta.org).

11. Although this arrangement seems unusual, the pattern of putting one's own assets into a trust that one manages is common. For example, in estate plan-

ning, one might establish a revocable trust in order to avoid paying probate costs while bequeathing assets.

12. *Board Member Policy Manual,* 17; emphasis added.

13. Ibid., 15.

14. Ibid.

15. Ibid., 1.

16. The policy manual also includes specific steps that must be taken should the organization choose to accept an out-of-county easement. These include attempting to get the landowner to negotiate with local land trusts that are structured to accept lands in that region, requiring additional funds from the landowner to pay for the extra time and energy necessary to monitor an easement farther from the NCLT's offices, and notifying any local land trust. The manual also indicates that an out-of-county easement should not be undertaken unless the property is of particularly high priority in terms of conservation value or development threat.

17. *Board Member Policy Manual,* 1.

18. It is difficult to say what percentage of offered easements the NCLT turns down, because it is hard to identify at what point in a long talking process an easement is "offered." NCLT staff estimate that somewhere between 30 and 50 percent of the people who make inquiries about a donation drop out during initial conversations, and the NCLT discourages another 20 percent after an initial site visit. Of the "real" projects that survive these preliminary stages, some run into tax or similar problems, but few are rejected by the trust.

19. *Board Member Policy Manual,* 39.

20. This approach to the organization of nonprofits, in which dues-paying members do not vote, is presently the norm. The Society for the Protection of New Hampshire Forests represents an older style. Of its 9,200 members, approximately 200 to 400 attend the Society's annual meeting to vote for new trustees nominated by the board and from the floor. The board elects its own officers. Members also are responsible for adopting and revising the organization's bylaws.

21. Eisele notes that in 1992, "an extremely modest tax to finance the acquisition of open space by purchasing easements" was turned down three to one by county voters. Unfortunately for supporters of the initiative, the vote was taken during the severest economic slump in the state's history ("Twenty-five Years," 117).

22. *Board Member Policy Manual,* 23.

23. Regulatory easements are easements that a local government requires from a development project in order for the project to be permitted to go forward.

24. Eisele has argued that conservation easements have not been a major land protection tool in the county ("Twenty-five Years," 117).

CHAPTER 12. CONCLUSION

1. See Randal O'Toole, *Reforming the Forest Service* (1988).

2. As anyone involved in the debate surrounding below-cost sales of environmental goods and services on federal lands (below-cost sales of Forest Service timber, Bureau of Land Management grazing permits, or below-market leases for coal, recreational access, or ski developments) can attest, keeping track of the money is an important element of preventing subsidized destruction of public resources and is vital to public accountability.

3. Perhaps the most lucid discussion of the failures of the progressive model of public land management is Robert Nelson, *Public Lands and Private Rights* (1995).

Index

ML   12/02